The Possibility of America

The Possibility of America

How the Gospel Can Mend Our God-Blessed, God-Forsaken Land

DAVID DARK

WESTMINSTER
JOHN KNOX PRESS
LOUISVILLE • KENTUCKY

Revised and expanded edition of a previously published book by David Dark titled *The Gospel according to America: A Meditation on a God-Blessed, Christ-Haunted Idea* (Louisville, KY: Westminster John Knox Press, 2005).

Revised and expanded edition
Published by Westminster John Knox Press
Louisville, Kentucky

19 20 21 22 23 24 25 26 27 28—10 9 8 7 6 5 4 3 2 1

Book design by Sharon Adams
Cover design by Nita Ybarra

Library of Congress Cataloging-in-Publication Data
Names: Dark, David, 1969- author.
Title: The possibility of America : how the Gospel can mend our God-blessed, God-forsaken land / David Dark.
Description: First edition. | Louisville, Kentucky : Westminster John Knox Press, 2019. Revised and expanded edition of: The Gospel according to America. 2005. | Includes bibliographical references. |
Identifiers: LCCN 2018046256 (print) | LCCN 2019006923 (ebook) | ISBN 9781611649383 (ebk.) | ISBN 9780664264659 (pbk. : alk. paper)
Subjects: LCSH: Christianity—Influence. | United States—Church history. | Christianity and culture—United States. | Church and state—United States. | Dark, David, 1969- Gospel according to America.
Classification: LCC BR526 (ebook) | LCC BR526 .D36 2019 (print) | DDC 277.3/083—dc23
LC record available at https://lccn.loc.gov/2018046256

For Doris Dark

Contents

Acknowledgments

It is a major joy to have the opportunity to address the shortsightedness, the omissions, and the embarrassing deficiencies of my own work. I'd like to extend my deep gratitude to Bob Ratcliff, my editor, and David Dobson, longtime advocate of what I'm up to, for giving me another crack at this extended epistle of celebration and attempted admonition. All eloquence is borrowed, and family, friends, colleagues, and students will rightly discern their prompts and provocations throughout. There are also writers who've helped me form these thoughts in other contexts and challenged me, through direct encouragement and example, to say more succinctly what I see. I'm thinking of Jessica Hopper, Charles Marsh, John T. Edge, and Heather Havrilesky. I want to thank Todd Greene, Lee Smithey, and Trevor Henderson for conversations that gave rise to this book, and Dorothy, Sam, and Peter Dark for regarding me hopefully when I felt I'd reached a dead end. Joel Dark and Cary Gibson remain a constant but affectionate check on my proneness toward exaggeration as well as my tendency to err on the side of optimism, and Elizabeth Dark was kind enough to ask about my process with a curiosity that often spurred me on. And for constant insight, inspiration, and a relentlessly poetic intuition to which I hope I bear some form of faithful witness, I thank my mentor and partner, Sarah Masen Dark.

Introduction

Notes on the New Seriousness

Like many Americans, my father was haunted by the Bible, the very fact of it. Awash in the hypocrisies of self and others, figuring out what it said, what it all meant, and how to live a life somehow faithful to it was a lifelong obsession. The Bible was always in the back of his mind. Like a leather-bound black hole, it pulled on his thoughts, painted the matter-of-fact a different color, called into question whatever anybody nearby described as common sense, and uproariously unsettled the agreed-upon obvious of every scenario. For better or worse, it was the measure of authenticity for all talk, and speech that claimed to have its backing ("It's biblical," "According to the Bible," "God says . . .") was the most suspect of all, because the Bible was nobody's property. It had no final arbiter, because he believed it belonged to any and everyone. It had an untamable weirdness about it, this Word of God received, discerned, treasured, and cobbled together over time by a millennia-long caravan of asylum seekers.

This sometimes-centering, oft-times explosive, double-edged totem was so trickily up for grabs that trying to pull it into your own schemes of self-legitimation was one of the worst things a person could do. Mishandling it, we knew, drives people to despair, death in life, and genocide. Like absolute truth,

1

God's truth, it's definitely out there, but anyone who presumed—in word or deed—to own the copyright on such a thing was a danger to themselves and others.

With this vibe at work throughout my growing-up years, my father made it very difficult for anyone in our family to keep religion and politics in their assigned categories, because the Bible, as he read it, didn't go for that kind of thing. He understood as well as anyone that there is a hard-won arrangement at work in America whereby we're expected to keep our talk of the Lord, eternal salvation, and a certain coming kingdom to the side of discussions concerning allocation of resources, party platforms, and the ups and downs of markets. If we're going to be civil, nobody's imagined direct line to God gets to trump someone else's conscience, but the demands of genuinely candid, human exchange, with all the hilarity and illumination that frank discussion can yield, will challenge these boundaries. Why not look deeply into the mixed bag of our arrangements? What feats of candor and conscience might yet await people of goodwill in the messy alliance that is the American public?

In the deepest sense, he didn't think it polite or even friendly to pretend that certain elephants aren't in the room; that Jesus and the prophets have very little to say about a nation's talk of threats to its security, national anthems, and undocumented humanity; or that the demands of Allah or Yahweh upon humankind can be conveniently sequestered within the "spirituality" section of the global market. Unless we're willing to let one thing have to do with the other, the possibility of truthful conversation (a prerequisite for the formation of more perfect unions) is tragically diminished, and responsible speech that communicates what we're all actually thinking and believing and hoping for becomes a vanishing art.

In his lifelong enthusiasm for candor, fair play, and the well-chosen word, freewheeling Bible study as a space in which everything could be talked about (war, celebrity, R-rated films, a living wage) was among my father's favorite jams. Karl Barth's dictum concerning life lived with a Bible in one hand and the *New York Times* in the other was an imperative he took up with glee. He understood and made the most of the notion that "religion" is always "politics" under a different name (and vice versa), and as a conversation partner, he treated words with an amused affection and reverence, intensely conscious of the many ways we go about fooling ourselves and getting fooled. Needless to say, the Bible is a raging torrent of insight concerning this human drama of concealment. As a lawyer, he could appreciate the skill with which professional politicians could deftly accuse other professional politicians of playing politics, divert attention from their own misdeeds by hiding behind a flag, or successfully dispel recognition of a world of verifiable data with magical words like "bias," "partisan," and "agenda." He was hyperaware of all the methods whereby we can create or undo the impression of order and control through our use of language, and he never lost a sense of the tragic as he contemplated the evil we underwrite with our votes and tax dollars and all the ways that it doesn't have to go this way. He felt that absolute justice would leave hardly anyone completely justified, and he reverenced every form of observational candor, whatever its source: that earthbound, everyday honesty that mixes things up, disturbing the fixed scripts of the powerful.

By watching him, I saw that reverence and obsession are to one another near allied, and, for better or worse, I'm a child of his obsessions. I worry over words, whether they're pledges, oaths, promises, or insinuations. I sweat the details of who said what and how generalizing statements hide specific atrocities. Like many Americans, I wake up wanting to weigh in and am blessed (or cursed) with the technology to do so. I know the thrill of tweeting what seems to me just the right Bible verse, song lyric, or rhetorical question, and, if I'm not careful, that thrill can pull me away all day long from those I allegedly love. I am also that anxious person who can't stop wondering how it is that an electorate would allow a man to take the oath of office for president of the United States without verifying that he has read—or will ever consent to sit quietly and have read aloud to him—the Constitution of the United States of America.

THE COMMON GOOD OF
ATTEMPTED TRUTHFULNESS

This anxiety is rooted in my innate hope for a certain sacred space that is also, in one sense, the subject of my day job. At my best, I conjure it up like a table in the wilderness before myself and others, for a living. It is, wait for it, *the common good of attempted truthfulness*. I think of it as a rare but perpetually available resource in family, politics, friendship, religion, business, or whatever other abstraction we deploy as a placeholder for the living fact of relationship. Though we fall for such abstractions again and again, I think we all long for a space in which we might level with ourselves and others. Our longing for this common good is why we listen to podcasts, check Twitter, binge-watch television series, take in music, go to comedy clubs, turn on "the news," attend rallies, read books, and do our work in cafes where (fingers crossed) some interesting person might engage us unexpectedly. It's a space we want to access so badly that we'll pay money in the hope that it might suddenly appear in front of us. Without it, we're easy prey for those who accrue power for themselves by weaponizing, at every opportunity, our escalating estrangement from ourselves and others.

Making a space for the common good of attempted truthfulness is what I'm paid to do as someone who impersonates a teacher for a living. I put it this way to avoid shame and embarrassment. In what could be the most insanely presumptuous task undertaken by any member of our species, I actually attempt to help people with their own thinking. I sit in classrooms with women and men in prisons and on college campuses, and, together, we make assertions, put questions to one another, tell stories, read poems aloud, and wonder over our own words. The job, as I understand it, is to help people pay deep attention to their deepest selves in relationship with other selves. They write sentences. I write sentences next to their sentences. And we get a conversation going somehow. We attempt truthfulness together. For some students, I sometimes have the feeling that this might be the first time someone's calmly and respectfully urged them to think twice. I hope it isn't the last.

This biggest of deals is of course a little-by-little, everyday-do-over kind of process, but as I understand it, there is no fellowship, neighborliness, or common good available apart from the work of attempted truthfulness, of examining the fact of what we're going through together with others and figuring out how to organize our energy and resources in the direction of mutual thriving. And it is in this sense that I imagine attempted truthfulness to be at the core of anything we might rightly call patriotism. As a hoped-for extension of my teacher-impersonation vocation, this book is an effort in moral orientation, an attempt to make sense of our times, and, if you like, a project in anger management. It is also a call to confession and a primer in patriotism as I understand it. That's patriotism as a form of moral seriousness we practice or abdicate in everything we're up to; the new seriousness that is the old seriousness, the ancient work of owning up to ourselves with ourselves when we finally, as one saying has it, "come to Jesus." To practice it is to take it up anew every day as we take clearer stock of what we're doing, saying, and amplifying while keeping in mind that we can never entirely disavow the chaos we fund with our taxes, our presumed consent, and our negligence. It is alert to the casual dishonesty that corrodes our common life. The new seriousness is the habit of wanting to know what you don't want to know before it's too late, because sin, as I understand it, is active flight from a lived realization of available data.

To take seriously the fact of one's Americanness is to recognize that we get the dystopia we pay (and vote) for. Admittedly, this can feel like a real downer. But the new seriousness also invites us toward the realization that even though we're unendingly enmeshed, entangled, and responsible within and to our world, it need not be a cause of despair. It might actually hasten the breakthrough we're looking for.

In this spirit, the following is offered in the hope of inspiring and somehow reigniting here and there that fundamental ritual of a thriving democracy, the give-and-take of candid exchange. Like many Americans, I find myself frightened by my own anger level, a despair that can have me demonizing others all day long, and the fear that there isn't anything much anyone can do about it. With the help of remote, moneyed interests who appear hell-bent on persuading millions of Americans to vote against their own self-interest and that of their neighbors in every election, it's as if our government is destroying the possibility of human thriving for most Americans at every turn. I worry over the ways we've reduced our own bandwidth and the likelihood that future generations will be so emotionally stunted by the habits we've modeled that, true to our example, they'll be largely incapable of receiving the witness of anyone who challenges their read on reality. I don't want them to inherit a militant ignorance that confuses rage for power and the silencing of opposition with victory, a militant ignorance that appears to be winning elections all over the world.

As every sacred tradition assures us, anger alone will not generate righteousness (although it usually feels terribly exciting and effective in the moment), and, to the extent that many of us incessantly tune into our media feeds on our always-available screens, each day seems to yield more crisis data than we know what to do with, a broken fire-hydrant spray of audiovisual stimulation that seems to paralyze us even as it monetizes our anxiety. As we try to access breathing space and avoid panic attack, we're often further dispirited by the mere mention of "politics," triggered by the word "religion," and hungry for any reassuring distraction we might receive from entertainment networks that advertise themselves as news outlets while airbrushing and organizing the real world to suit whatever versions of America will keep ratings up and advertisers happy.

Amid this mix of high-tech haste and the soaring stocks of media conglomerates, we've come to intuit that "America" is up for grabs as a word that can be successfully incorporated into a brand (a red MAGA hat, for instance) that can be transmogrified to suit practically any perverse purpose. Chants of "USA!" can be effectively deployed to drown out honest questions, righteous dissent, and cries for help. When confronted with the fact that our government has tortured terrorist suspects, confiscated rosaries, or forcibly separated children from their asylum-seeking parents on our behalf, appeals to an earlier state of righteousness don't cut it. "This isn't who we are" or "We're better than this" might work as a late step in a season of repentance, but it fails on delivery in light of our history, a crime scene of carnage, captivity, and seizure consistently undertaken in the name of freedom and security and God.

In one sense, America is an extended argument about what human beings owe one another, but if we're to keep the back-and-forth possibility alive, we have to look hard and humbly at the data of the now lest the argument prove to have been more like a long con. Our history, as James Baldwin teaches us, can't be bracketed away any more than breathing can be put to the side of speech. We live in and by the fact of what happened: "History is not the past. It is the present. We carry our history with us. We are our history. If we pretend otherwise, we literally are criminals."[1] The work of remembering is the work of awakening to our own lives. To meaningfully *respond* to available data is to enter a state of *respons*ibility, the constant task of a responsible people. To know the felt joy of responsibility is to refuse at every turn the "protective sentimentality,"[2] Baldwin's phrase, that prefers a mythic American innocence over a clear-eyed index of violence perpetuated, suffered, and unmasked in our land's history. To challenge the script of protective sentimentality in an election season or an age of forever war can pose certain risks, but it's the very risk that makes democracy possible within and in spite of the fake empire that would otherwise render us a population of passive spectators each alone in our informational echo chambers. The new seriousness invites us to wake up to the history that *is* our present, to *say* what we see, and to ask what the hope of a more righteously ordered world might require of a people who mean to be free.

ONE HUMAN BARNYARD

How does one respond righteously to the possibility of true and undivided living within and in spite of the up-for-grabs poltergeist called America? I have an adage that will be helpful moving forward: Spirit knows no division. I refer not only to the false covenant implicit in any rhetoric that proposes a strict and final division between religion and politics; I also have in mind the suggestion that popular entertainment and foreign policy and literature and representative democracy and the wide world of sports and public education and the fashion industry can be meaningfully understood as separate lanes on humanity's highway. Stay in your lane, the saying goes. We need only slow the tape for a moment to resolutely recognize—perhaps with a degree of urgency—that it doesn't work this way. It never has. Spirit knows no division.

In our world, we've watched an oft-bankrupt millionaire with a history of alleged sexual assault stage what would prove to be a successful bid for the White House by partnering with a movement demanding a sitting president's birth certificate, all the while leveraging his brand as the host of *The Celebrity Apprentice*. Along the way, he body-slammed and shaved the head of World Wrestling Entertainment CEO Vince McMahon, presided over beauty pageants, hosted *Saturday Night Live*, and participated in a promotional video for an artist who would be among his most outspoken critics after he assumed power: Marshall Mathers, a.k.a. Eminem.

There are no lanes. We can draw lines and make laws. We can resolve that we, as a nation, will never allow on the presidential ballot a man no responsible adult would leave alone with a child. We can insist that a refusal to release one's tax returns or receive the counsel of a scientific adviser will be, from this day forward, a deal-breaker for anyone seeking elected office. But if we're to be a people capable of situational awareness in our radioactive days of everything all of the time, we need to be clear with ourselves and others about what we're cultivating or degrading with our commitments and our disassociations. We're never *not* cultivating in one way or another. Culture, it turns out, is nonoptional. One human barnyard, after all. Everything matters. It always did.

And as Vince Staples once observed unto Tyler, the Creator, "Art drives the culture forward."[3] What has been imagined about the meaning of America in and for the world, the good, the bad, and the horrific, is at the core of its legacy. The honesty America harbors, hosts, and sometimes punishes arises out of the cauldron of its betrayals and denials. Within the human barnyard, America proceeds, a beacon of hope as the fabled city on a hill from time to time and a global mechanism of vast carelessness, aggressively ignorant to the lived experience of the rest of the world every so often, a mobile army of symbol, legend, promise, paperwork, and unpredictability.

What I spy, cherish, and hope to magnify is an artfulness of a piece with the attempted truthfulness that is the new seriousness I seek to commemorate in this book. As a student of Scripture, I see prophetic consciousness around every corner. I am a collector of the poetic thinking that gives rise to poetic action, and I believe my primary vocation is bearing witness to it, this gospel among us, sharing it, and attempting it myself. My guide in this work is June Jordan, who teaches us that "poetry means taking control of the language of your life." In word and deed, it's a work of the imagination, first and foremost, but it's also a matter of what we choose to embody and broadcast. For Jordan, poetry is an "action undertaken for the sake of information, the faith, the exorcism, and the lyrical invention, that telling the truth makes possible." Most beautifully, poetry occasions and conjures "a revolution in which speaking and listening to somebody becomes the first and last purpose to every social encounter."[4]

How's that for art driving culture forward? What kind of America would that be? I would say it's an America we've had among us for some time, a seriousness we've had on offer in song, television, film, literature, letters, and even the occasional law throughout our history. It's a matter of sifting through, celebrating and lifting up, of gathering the things that remain. And it is, of course, also a contest of wills.

"THERE IS NO WORD TO BE HAD!"

On that note, I'd like to call attention to a concept that unites poetry with the unfulfilled promise of America's founding documents and what I take to be the good news of Jesus and other prophets: Beloved Community. For the women and men of what the Reverend James Lawson refers to as the Nonviolent Movement of America, a movement associated with but not confined to the civil rights era, Beloved Community signals the fact that everyone within earshot of nonviolent confrontation with white supremacist terror was (and is) invited to enter into the drama of lived righteousness. This of course includes law enforcement officers, elected officials, and bystanders who sometimes believe nonviolent demonstrators are stirring up unnecessary trouble. For those who mean to be participants in Beloved Community, there are always resources, inner and outer, to bring new seriousness to our every exchange, even when our attempts at seriousness are met with denial or even the threat of violence. There is often an artfulness we have yet to discern that might yet flip the script on the reigning dysfunction. Students of Beloved Community live by it.

As I search my mind for examples, I often draw strength from a scene recounted in Congressman John Lewis's *March* trilogy, when 500-plus activists preparing to march to demonstrate for the right to vote were confronted by Alabama state troopers on the Edmund Pettus Bridge in Selma on Bloody Sunday, March 7, 1965. As these pioneers of human seriousness prepared themselves for the tear gas and the beatings to come, an exchange occurred.

With state troopers under his command, Major John Cloud gave the order to disperse: "This is an unlawful assembly. Your march is not conducive to the public safety. You are ordered to disperse and go back to your church or to your homes."

Standing at the forefront of the marchers gathered on the bridge, the Reverend Hosea Williams wondered aloud if Major Cloud might be talked out of the state-sanctioned terror he was about to order: "May we have a word with the major?"

The response was definitive, "There is no word to be had."[5] The decree came at them with the seeming force of cosmic finality.

The brutality that followed, by being televised, changed history, but not to the advantage of white supremacy. There *was* a word to be had, the next day and the day after that and the decades to come down to our day, our days of manufactured crises, weaponized despair, and the erosion of our common public good. The poetic and prophetic actions undertaken in Selma, preceded and followed by countless others (famous and not so famous), are essential still to the meaning of human history, at the center of our cultural canon wherever Beloved Community is evoked, where there are *always* words to be had. No government, political party, or presidential administration can prevent such feats of thoughtfulness whether born of a moment, long strategizing, or mostly improvised. There is so much precedent for dealing with human madness, so much righteousness to which we might yet be true in new and surprising ways. So many avenues for dramatically conjuring up, for ourselves and our fellow humans, a serious vision of what's true and lovely and good. So many words yet to be had.

To the extent that we aspire to bear witness to Beloved Community, our hopes for America, its citizenry, and the rest of the world won't be dictated by any government or political party. Beloved Community is a call to embody a more comprehensive patriotism wherever we find ourselves. Like discipleship, the practice of democracy is a widening of our capacities for moral awareness and an expansion of our sphere of respect. If we have a steadily narrowing vision of people to whom we're willing to accord respect or if the company we keep is slowly diminishing to include only the folks who've learned to pretend to agree with us, we can be assured that we're in danger of developing around ourselves a kind of death cult, a frightened, trigger-happy defensiveness that is neither godly nor, in any righteous sense, American. Or as one of Ursula K. Le Guin's characters famously asked, "What is love of one's country; is it hate of one's uncountry?"[6] Might Beloved Community come to serve as a norm, the core ethic of what we mean when we speak of America as a hope?

In such dreams begin deep responsibilities, the lived demands of the new seriousness I mean to champion in these pages. Beloved Community is an enlarged sense of neighborliness that strives to maintain "neighbor" as an ever-widening category, even when the neighbor appears before us as a threat or an enemy. The injunction to love the neighbor in the minute particulars of speech and action has never been an easy one, but it might be the nearest and most immediate form of patriotism available to any of us. It is also the one vocation that, if neglected, will lead to the forfeiting of any and all soul.

The terminology of Beloved Community wasn't available to Henry David Thoreau when he published *Civil Disobedience* (1849) and *Walden* (1854), but his witness exists along a trajectory of prophetic artfulness that includes Jesus, Tolstoy, Gandhi, Dorothy Day, Fannie Lou Hamer, and that eventually takes us to Selma, athletes kneeling during the national anthem, and Bree Newsome reciting a psalm while climbing a pole in Columbia, South Carolina, to remove a Confederate flag. Thoreau argued that our responsibilities to ourselves and others include all the ways we're complicit in unrighteous norms. We aren't responsible only for our own ideas; we're responsible for the conflicts we avoid to more effectively get by, the lies we allow others to voice and propagate unchallenged in our presence. He worried over all the ways he played along and didn't raise a fuss in the face of the terrors his government enacted and aided and the subtle fashion in which his own behavior, by proving polite and acceptable, abided injustice: "The greater part of what my neighbors call good I believe in my soul to be bad, and if I repent of anything, it is very likely to be my good behavior. What demon possessed me that I behaved so well?"[7]

This is very much of a piece with what Congressman John Lewis refers to as "good trouble," that disruptive social newness we undertake when we recall that we need never resign our consciences to legislators, law enforcement, or the reigning status quo. Then and now, if we aren't agitated, we aren't paying attention, but the question is always this: What do we *do* with our agitation? It will require strength and courage and determined wit, but there are many words to be had, many examples and feats of artfulness to consider, to imitate, and to meet with our own. Others have been here before.

The work of trying to love self, law enforcement officer, legislator, and agitator alike in our climate of perpetual panic attack will take some doing. It is so easy to demonize when we don't know what to do with our despair, and there are industries calibrated to monetize our helplessness. In this regard, Dwight

D. Eisenhower knew the score. For all of his pragmatism as a war strategist and his famously laconic read on divinity ("Our form of government has no sense unless it is founded in a deeply felt religious faith, and I don't care what it is"), Eisenhower was also alive to the fact that a nation enamored by nothing other than its own superior firepower would eventually become one more fascist stronghold. In 1961, in his farewell address, he argued that America's historical significance would depend "not merely upon our unmatched material progress, riches and military strength, but on how we use our power in the interests of world peace and human betterment . . . to enhance liberty, dignity and integrity among people and among nations."[8] As he famously put it, "the military-industrial complex," ever expanding and operating according to its own methodical, self-manufacturing logic, is a clear and present danger as it comes to alter the very structure of society and view itself as "the miraculous solution to all current difficulties." Our unquestioning faith in our own rightness and effectiveness can make us incapable of seeing that there is no military solution to a particular problem until we've given it a costly and destructive try. Eisenhower worried about what would become of a culture so altered. Absolute faith in America's not-to-be-questioned, innate goodness can create a witlessness among the citizenry, desensitize our moral imagination, and make of democracy, in Eisenhower's words, "the insolvent phantom of tomorrow."

Given the developments we've witnessed in the buying up of local news sources by owners who demand uniform editorial allegiance to their preferred narratives, the decline of print journalism, and the attack—sometimes lethal——on the labor of investigative reporting as "fake news," I think it appropriate to expand Eisenhower's formulation. Now included in the dangers he described is an endlessly self-legitimating culture that seeks to mold the public's imagination in its own image of order, security, and retribution: the military-industrial-entertainment-incarceration complex.

This is what Martin Luther King Jr. saw as the emergence of "a thing-oriented" society that reduces people to "assets" in an international alliance of moneyed interests: "When machines and computers, profit motives and property rights, are considered more important than people, the giant triplets of racism, extreme materialism, and militarism are incapable of being conquered."[9] A moment's consideration of our popular news cycle suffices to see how prescient he was. Whether by way of manufactured crises, the million-dollar messaging of campaign funders and their politico pretend–public-servant proxies, or the endless impinging of one more text message, it's as if our ability to see and think clearly is constantly compromised by an endless diversion from the facts on the ground. As a serial tweeter myself, let it be known that this sermon comes self-administered. We find ourselves lost in feedback loops that seem to have been purposefully designed to make us feel endlessly inadequate. Whatever the platform, so much of the content we access is an endless flight from deep awareness, catered and calibrated to appeal to our fantasies even as they leave us drained, diminished, and largely alienated from the possibility of true, noncommercialized human interaction.

In this sense, carefully cultivating consciousness against prolonged mental rutting might be viewed as a homeland security issue. But this is no easy task when we're caught in the traffic of angry chatter, frazzled nerves, and one panic attack after another. In an effort to describe and be free of it, we call this phenomenon "politics," but we probably shouldn't surrender the word so easily. Politics is how we govern ourselves. It's the way we conduct our lives. To say, "I'm not a political person" is to claim an above-the-frayness that isn't possible for actual human beings. In the same way, we often say, "I'm not a religious person" to avoid being pigeonholed as a toxic conversation partner. But religion and politics are conjoined abstractions. And the mythology we've constructed to keep them separate in our descriptions of ourselves and others is dissolving before our eyes.

JESUS AND AMERICA TOO

The movement of Beloved Community is larger than whatever category we'd like to put it in, and it happens within history. It makes history. The tradition is a patchwork of hard-won, long-learned moral insights in human affairs. And its impact can't be calculated or cordoned off to suit the interests of states or multinational corporations. It's a relentlessly civilizing presence in human history, but it doesn't endorse nations or sanction the status quo. It's too big on its own, too cosmic in scope, to play chaplain to anyone's empire. Despite the desire to package, contain, or commercialize it, Beloved Community won't ultimately serve as anybody's "spiritual component" or "religious angle."

The question we have to bring to any appeal to its vision (whether in the citing of Bible verses, "spirituality," Rosa Parks, or any civil rights era icon) is to what extent these appeals are faithful to the continuums we can trace to the prophetic consciousness of sacred traditions. Is a political candidate's intoning of the word "Christ" or "God" or "biblical" even vaguely concurrent with the witness of the early church or that of any prophet in any sacred tradition, or is it a vague generalization that serves to reassure or distract a demographic easily moved by words that insinuate a basis in the Bible? With such questions in mind, this book is both a celebration of the uniquely American manifestations of the insight of Beloved Community and an examination of American culture in light of its witness. And while "no other gods before me" is surely the biblical imperative against overzealous dedication to any particular tribe or nation, I'm confident that it is possible and even appropriate, as Tom Petty assures us, to somehow love Jesus and America too.

The faith of Beloved Community, as I understand it, evades any and all manufactured publicity. But these questions of historical coherence should prove relevant to anyone living within the shadow of an empire whose leaders' electability depends on the appearance of some degree of lip service to the God of Abraham, Isaac, Jacob, and Jesus. The concept of "God" is constantly invoked in our public life, but prophetic consciousness is kept bracketed to the side lest it say more about affordable health care, drone strikes, enemy combatants, the death penalty, and the hoarding of resources by the wealthy few than we feel we can afford to insert into a party platform. Reference to "Christ" inspires respectful nods, and insistence on saying "Christmas" can motivate a voter base, but specific reference to Jesus seems to risk too close an association with what the peasant revolutionary actually taught. In this, our hypocrisy might know some boundaries. Jesus' instructions are ignored and implicitly derided even as many are eager, as the old song has it, to be somehow washed in his blood.

There is constant talk of Jesus' sacrifice among many Americans. "He died for me" is a moving phrase passed around like a code word that often seems to serve as a preemptive strike against the example of the life Jesus lived and the question of whether or not we dare to apply his witness to the way we imagine ourselves and others and respond to perceived threats. There's even a knee-jerk "he came to die" that avoids the specificity of Jesus' approach to enemies by suggesting that he simply said and did what he had to in order to hasten the process of getting killed for our sins. Imitating him in regard to enemy love is therefore unnecessary and maybe even naive and for many, it must be admitted, a sign of radicalism. By reducing Jesus to the one who atones for our sins, the ethical demands of the undocumented peasant the New Testament calls "Lord" can be kept to the side when it counts. Nevertheless, we're haunted by him and his stories of what the righteous future of God requires of those of us who hope to bear and carry forward a witness to it.

At our best, Americans keep constantly before ourselves the realization that we're still learning what civilization really consists of, that most of us have only begun to take on the work of Beloved Community. There's always further to go. In the meantime, America's vast cultural heritage, the long-haul struggle between human conscience and blind power, offers us a common nourishment, a reservoir of insight from which to draw courage and wit. If we look hard and humbly, we might find that, even in our anxiety, there's always still another good word to be had.

Chapter 1

The Moral Mercury of Life

An Exercise in Patriotism

> *There's no country in the world that loves "right now" like America does.*
> —Andy Warhol

> *I love America more than any other country in this world, and, exactly for this reason, I insist on the right to criticize her perpetually.*
> —James Baldwin

> *Have you ever ridden on a train, a mighty streamlined monster, bulleting its way over plain and mountain, and shrieking defiance to any obstacle which would hinder its progress? America is like that mighty train to me and the privilege to be a passenger on the greatest trip in all history is part of what America means to me.*
> —Graham Finney, "What America Means to Me"

The poet Layli Long Soldier gives us a phrase with which to contemplate the everyday arrangement whereby certain considerations of the meaning of the United States of America are dimmed or decreed ill-mannered in favor of others: "the American casual."[1] The context is *Whereas*, her lengthy poetic response to the congressional resolution of apology to Native Americans that was signed, but never read aloud to anyone, by Barack Obama. If I receive her meaning rightly, the American casual names both the space in which Long Soldier sat as she first heard tell of the apology and the alleged order—our country's reigning order—that thought it fitting and appropriate that the signing on December 19, 2009, occur without a single tribal leader or official representative of any of the more than 560 federally recognized tribes in our country present to witness or receive it. As a dual citizen of the Oglala Lakota Nation and the United

States of America, Long Soldier chronicles her own existence and that of the lives to whom she hopes to bear right witness ("I'm going to tell you what I know, but this is only one telling"[2]) in her art.

For our context, which I hope is somehow conjoined to Long Soldier's in the shared hope of Beloved Community, the American casual names an air of imperturbability—an unaccountability even—when it comes to thinking hard about what our government has undertaken on our alleged behalf and in our name. The American casual poses certain difficulties for anyone grasping for situational awareness under a government whose representatives sometimes rhetorically confuse our nation's perceived self-interest for the reign of God. It's almost as if the American casual insinuates that you can only love a country by lying about it, by downplaying or even hiding our history from ourselves at every turn.

I wouldn't presume to speak definitively on behalf of a dream, a spirit, a principality, or a poltergeist. But in the hope of being exceedingly aware, of expanding the sphere of sanity little by little, it's often necessary to pull out the hyperbole, question the metaphors, and name the voices that get our pulses pounding. Who are we? What are we doing? Whose interests does my anxiety serve? Examining our context (both geographical and historical) and seeing it clearly will involve a stretch of our powers of description and the occasional foray into the outlandish. And if we have a tendency to mistake our most cherished, insistent illusions for righteousness, integrity, or the spirit of God, there will be some states of euphoria that will only unhand us after much prayer and discernment. How else might one begin to question an image, a brand name, or a nation-state?

The apostle Paul understood the challenge. In his efforts to name the occupying forces in the bodies and minds of his community (whether their understanding of Mosaic law or the sometimes beneficial, sometimes murderous presence of a Pax Romana), he would heap words together to paint an all-purpose picture: weak and beggarly world powers, principalities, elemental forces, rulers of this age, and even angels. It's as if the new creation, the new way of being free made known in Jesus of Nazareth, has exposed whole new levels, doors within doors, of enslavement. Testing the spirits and making sense of things under the illumination of Jesus' good news (the gospel) will be an ongoing work of discernment, resistance, and faith-fulness. And the convoluted, maddeningly multifaceted nature of the challenge would assume strange new forms that the apostle could not have possibly foreseen.

What if the Gentile converts came to outnumber the Jewish believers in this fledgling community? And what if the Roman Empire decided to crown this Jewish messianic movement as its official religion, with an unbaptized emperor convening councils to decide issues of doctrine? And what would become of its gospel as it was co-opted by the very powers and principalities who had executed its founder, not knowing, as he had put it, what they were doing?

Do the authorities in what we consider the civilized world know what they're doing now? Do we?

It feels treacherous to speak too knowingly of the United States of America—the personality, the hope, or what George W. Bush once referred to as "the angel in the whirlwind." But given the claim of Donald Trump that "in America, we don't worship government—we worship God,"[3] and the suggestion early in this century (as stated government policy) that our government can and will, in the foreseeable future, "rid the world of evil,"[4] it might be an appropriate time to examine the good news of Jesus and its occasional reception within American culture.

SIR, WE HAVE A SITUATION HERE

In an interesting take on the meaning of patriotism, Karl Barth once suggested that true loyalty to one's land cannot be known apart from the example of Jesus. Apart from exemplifying a higher and more grounded Christology than most have thought to imagine, this suggestion is also an illuminating way of thinking about Jesus' own perceived vocation to the people of Israel and other people-groups living under Roman occupation.

The coming reign of God and the necessity of repenting in view of its arrival was the germ of his *euangelion*, his good-news campaign for which he lived and died. The term "evangelical," at least in America, might be so definitively thought to refer to a sleeper cell of the Republican Party and thereby to be tied to the ideology of white supremacy and climate denial that to say it aloud is to court misunderstanding. But I'd like to assert that considering its origin as an announcement that called forth a witnessing community (*ekklēsia*), a peasant artisan movement that shares resources, loves enemies, and forgives relentlessly, "Beloved Community" might be one helpful operative phrase with which to redeem it from its sectarian associations. The posture of this evangelical mindset is perpetual openness to those who hunger and thirst for righteousness. And if Jesus himself followed Jeremiah's call for Jewish diaspora to seek the welfare (the shalom) of whatever culture they find themselves sojourning in (Jer. 29:7), what might it mean to stand within his social movement (once termed "the Way") as dwellers within the land called America in these very odd times?

Jesus was born into a tribe that, from long before his birth and long after his death, struggled to maintain faithfulness to Yahweh despite constant persecution. If the fair and balanced scribes of Jesus' time had borrowed the language of twenty-first-century news media, they might have referred to their plight as one of "freedom under attack." He was a second-class citizen. In the jargon of "good vs. evil" he'd have had no trouble recognizing the "evil" ones, namely, Rome and its puppet governments, which, in his case, took the form of the house of Herod and his cronies. (The scholar N. T. Wright has suggested that

Herod the Great has a contemporary parallel in Saddam Hussein, except that Herod never broke away from his creators so boldly as to provoke their wrath.)

According to the Gospel of Matthew, Jesus was born under a death sentence. He would have heard of numerous insurrections performed on behalf of his people having been violently put down, often leading to numerous crucifixions, and of alleged insurgents being disappeared all the time. He could be struck across the face or made to carry a soldier's belongings at any time. His plight was similar to that of an Afghan farmer wary of death raining down at any moment in the name of someone else's security, or a Palestinian living a life of restricted mobility in an apartheid state. In an effort to evoke a context many of my students might find more sympathetic, I've suggested that Jesus lived in a situation similar to that of Mel Gibson's characters in both *Braveheart* (1995) and *The Patriot* (2000). The opportunities of what we think of as life and liberty available to Jesus were, in an even more severe way, limited.

It was in this context that Jesus announced his *euangelion*, his "good news," that summoned forth Beloved Community. Because this gospel begins with a call to repent, to live and think differently, we have to keep in mind that there is no gospel apart from politics. When some Americans refer to the gospel, they might be speaking of the idea that, if you believe a certain list of true propositions, you'll go to heaven when you die. Or they might be suggesting that if you accept Jesus as your "personal savior," you'll find it easier to overcome addiction, guilt won't be the problem that it used to be, and you'll be the bearer of a secret password ("Christ") that will keep you out of hell. From the point of view of the rapture theology popularized by the Left Behind series, the good news of the gospel can mean that when you give intellectual assent to the claim that Jesus is God, you become one of the people who'll disappear before the trouble starts. Billy Graham popularized the signing of a "decision card" as commemorating an hour of decision in which one suddenly joins the saved. And Franklin Graham arguably helped swing an election when he publicly avowed that Donald Trump had made the move by somehow indicating that he was among those who "gave their hearts to Christ" at his father's birthday celebration in 2013 just before flying to Moscow for a beauty pageant and other activities.[5]

While all of these reads on the gospel of Jesus gain ground throughout America and the rest of the world (perhaps even assuming the form of a uniquely "Americanized" Christianity), it's important to note that none of them would have made the slightest bit of sense to Jesus' hearers. They were under the foot of the latest oppressive regime, and Jesus' announcement meant, if it was deserving of the title of "good news," that things were about to turn around, that the kingdom (the rule) of God was at hand. They understood that he was inaugurating a movement that, for starters, was "good news to the poor" (Luke 4:18) and bad news for the powerful on their thrones and those who are proud in the thoughts of their hearts. When we read the prayers of Mary (the rich will be sent away empty, Luke 1:53) and Zechariah ("saved from our enemies and from the hand of all who hate us," Luke 1:71) in the first chapter of Luke's Gospel, it's hard to miss the call, echoed throughout the Hebrew Scriptures, for regime change soon and very soon.

Did this mean that Jesus was preparing to retaliate? It seems apparent that many of his followers thought so. Their way of life had been under attack as long as any of them could remember, and there were at least a few Zealots among them who, by definition, were set on armed revolution. He had to rebuke them for misunderstanding his movement when they expressed their desire to call down fire upon the opposition. And as Peter listened to Jesus' repeated insistence that he would be arrested, tortured, and killed, Peter made it clear that he would gladly kill and be killed to prevent such a fate from befalling such an innocent as Jesus. On hearing this, Jesus didn't turn to Peter and, with a somber bow, declare, "Praise and honor to you, great warrior, for offering to die on my behalf." On the contrary, we have the devastating "Get behind me, Satan," in which Jesus recognizes, in Peter's impulse to defend his lord with lethal means, another manifestation of the spirit of accusation, another Tempter in the wilderness.

The defining ethic of Jesus' movement (his gospel) was at least as difficult for his generation to accept as it is for ours: "Love your enemy"; "Bless those who curse you"; "Do good to those who hate you." The scandalous ineffectiveness of such commands, given the climate of fear and hatred, would have been met with the same hostility and disgust they're met with today. He might have been told that you can't fight evil with sensitivity, that you win through humiliation or you don't win at all. And doubtless, many would have suggested that Jesus was failing to live up to what was required of any decent, upstanding member of his tribe. They might have called him a self-hating Jew. But more than anything in the way of yet another fighting fire with more fire, he was inaugurating a new understanding of effectiveness, a truly revolutionary revolution, a renewed vision of the good passed down in the school of the prophets, a tribe to end all tribes, a new way to be human, a Beloved Community. And as news of his resurrection would attest, his way was the way everlasting, the path that would endure.

This newness isn't a by-product of the gospel. According to the New Testament witness, Jesus' way *is* the gospel, the good news for all nations, for every tribe, now and forever. And the body of Christ, that community that would try to take his life into its own, understood itself as nothing less than a new nation, a royal priesthood that seeks to embody the more excellent way.

As we've seen in Germany, South Africa, and the American context, this vision often gets lost especially—it has to be said—among white people whose allegiances, in this regard, are glaringly divided (if there's any lived allegiance to the teachings of Jesus at all). When the church is the blind, uncritical endorser or "spiritual" chaplain of whatever a nation decides to do, it has largely renounced its vocation as the body of Christ. It is neither the salt of the earth nor a light to the nations. And it has traded its commitment to the witness of a publicly executed Jewish revolutionary for one more constellation of idols.

To return to Jesus' historical context, it's admittedly difficult for many white Americans to sympathize. But we don't need to look far to ask questions of or live in more conscious relationship with those whose experience is closer to the position of a Jew in first-century Palestine—whose status was essentially that of a slave (Phil. 2:7). For many in the world, struggling to survive under tyrannical regimes with normal trade relations or most-favored-nation status with the United States or barely surviving under the less life-sustaining end of a global trade agreement, America is undoubtedly Rome. And for many people of color, the possibility of extrajudicial violence is as close as the nearest law enforcement officer. How do we follow the lead of this peasant-philosopher-storyteller and his countercultural movement, live along its continuum two thousand years later ("Whoever is not with me is against me"), and bear faithful witness to the future to which he invites us and for whose coming we are taught to pray? How do we go about participating in this story?

The book of Jeremiah offers an account of a maddening situation. Jeremiah is told that he was set apart in his mother's womb to declare God's words. He is also told that no one will listen to him and that he will be reviled. He is told to announce the destruction of Judah, which is the result of their social wickedness, the exchange of their glory for that which doesn't profit. Devastation will come, but he is also called to announce restoration, the forgiveness of sins, and hope for the hopeless. The book is a record of his struggle with a God who tells him to condemn his people, grieve for them, pray for them, plead with them, plead for them, and treasure them. When we note Jesus' similar vocation toward his own people, a vision (a beginning anyway) starts to develop concerning what it might look like to embody or practice the aforementioned movement within the world called America. How does one love it without lying about it?

WHAT IS AMERICA DOING?

"If we're honest now, we're going to save ourselves a lot of embarrassment," spake Jean Arthur earnestly unto her suitor, Jimmy Stewart, in Frank Capra's quintessential American classic, *You Can't Take It with You*. And we know she's right. America, like any relationship, is at its best when it isn't lying to itself about itself. But the rituals of honesty in the direction of public repentance that the governments of other nations have undertaken are toxic to many within our electorate. Given the mythic goodness we expect most candidates for public office to parrot against mounting evidence, it's as if our government is storing up for itself reserves of concentrated embarrassment we won't uncork until we absolutely have to. Denial, meanwhile, is the currency of power. In fact, elections can be won by depicting an opponent as one who shows weakness by apologizing (or seeming to apologize) for America and doubting, even for a moment, our innate goodness. It's as if interstate denial is the price we pay for the grandiloquence of our advertising, the promise of asylum for those huddled masses who can prove they love freedom the way we do. Is denial the price of admission? Is the observational candor of the biblical prophets allowed?

Something of the strangeness involved in America's relationship to the biblical witness is captured by G. K. Chesterton's observation that America often understands itself as a nation with the soul of a church. In Chesterton's view, this isn't to suggest that America is especially faithful to any particular creed, but it's probably the only nation in the world founded on one. And most uniquely, according to our documents as most Americans seem to understand them at least for now, no ethnicity, faith profession, family tie, or economic standing can make one citizen more American than the next. The creed won't allow it. It's self-evidently true that all are created equal, with equal access to justice. On paper anyway, Americanness is defined by this gospel. Chesterton notes that, taken to its logical extreme, this faith won't be held by pessimists or wealthy cynics and will necessarily extend its goodwill even beyond national boundaries to people outside its perceived self-interests (the foreigner, the enemy, the evildoer). He then suggests that Americans have committed themselves to something either entirely heroic or completely insane.

Stranger still, the declaration of the faith is steeped in metaphysics ("Laws of Nature and of Nature's God"), but the extension of equal rights to individuals (endowed to them, in fact, "by their Creator") doesn't require any statement of faith or doctrine on the part of the individual. Dignity is recognized within the infidel, the true believer, and the enemy combatant, God-given whether they like it or not. They don't even have to agree on the "God" part, and apparently the Founders didn't either.

Here, a good many of us might want to take a moment to thank God for deism and the room for creative interpretation left available by our alleged Founders and whoever it is they had in mind when they imagined their equally created white men and explicitly excluded, a few lines down, "merciless Indian savages." The extension of inalienable rights to the whole of humanity was, in this sense, denied from the start, but the serendipitous wording would lead to an ever-expanding definition of the "all" to whom the founding documents refer, blooming into a more righteous sense of self and others. James Madison would insist that an attempt to coerce correct belief is a sin against the God in whose image the not-yet-convinced neighbor is made. The Quaker economist Alice Paul was among those who conducted the final push to receive its meaning in such a way as to extend the right to vote to women. And Martin Luther King Jr. zoomed out so far that the Beloved Community of inalienable rights extended "beyond our nation's self-defined goals," past the sacred paperwork and even unto our nation's perceived enemies and its certain victims: "We are called to speak for the weak, for the voiceless, for the victims of our nation, and for those it calls 'enemy,' for no document in human hands can make these humans any less our brothers [and sisters]."[6]

As if by miracle or poetic acumen, we find a righteous elasticity to "all men are created equal" by which it can mean more than it meant, carrying us past the trivial and tribal into better convictions than our worship of domination and homeland might, for the moment, allow. Abraham Lincoln came to view it as a stumbling block to tyranny. And as the strength of America's military presence grows beyond that of any nation in history, there's something almost salvific in the fact that, according to the document going back to 1776, no elected official or citizen is supposed to believe that some lives are more equal than others. In an assertion that's almost painful to recall in light of our wars in Iraq and Afghanistan, George W. Bush took the matter further by announcing, in his inaugural speech of 2001, that no insignificant person has ever been born. If this is a kind of creed, then a phrase like "collateral damage" is probably a kind of heresy.

The righteous elasticity of the American ethos can yield, from time to time, an assertion like *there are no insignificant people*. Something like this is at the heart of that up-for-grabs faith of our civil religion. It's the dream of equal access, hard work, *right* making might, and welcome for huddled masses accompanied by many a sacrosanct accoutrement (flag, anthem, holidays).

And yet, it isn't exactly. Not yet anyway. Anyone seeking public office has to sing its songs in one way or another, but it's a contested lore often held back by the prerogatives of white fragility. The American creed is elastic enough to have brought us where we are, but it also gets stretched far enough in the other direction to accommodate white-supremacist dog whistles, the use of nuclear weapons, torture, and a refusal to truly reckon with our government's devastation of our continent's indigenous people and the seizure of their land. When we apply the standard of Beloved Community to our government's policies (which are ultimately the citizen's liturgies), the idea of America starts looking less like a mission accomplished and more like—at best—a long-haul experiment always under way.

WHAT HATH WASHINGTON
TO DO WITH JERUSALEM?

Needless to say, Beloved Community has the advantage of giving flesh to both the reign of God and American greatness in one handy vision. "Community" implies social relation and therefore politics. When we try to deny the political heft of God's gospel, we only ensure that our God talk becomes hopelessly enmeshed within and co-opted by the dominant order of whoever happens to be in power. Though the term is primarily associated with America's civil rights movement, we're free to trace a trajectory further back. If we were to draw a time line of source materials for Beloved Community—beginning with Moses telling the leader of his world, "Let my people go," moving through the March on Washington for Jobs and Freedom in August of 1963, and eventually arriving (but not stopping) at the day Beyoncé's *Lemonade* dropped—we would do well to include the words of the prophet Isaiah (in the tradition of Amos, Hosea, and Micah) and his vision of a peaceable kingdom; the Jewish apocalyptic of Daniel's imagining a greater government—an iconoclastic rock not cut by human hands—that exceeded the present understanding of Babylon; and Jesus' inaugural witness in Nazareth proclaiming good news to the poor, release to captives, and recovery of sight to the blind. And of special interest to students of human rights history would be Paul's letter to the churches of Galatia in Asia Minor.

Occasionally referred to as the Magna Carta of Christian liberty, the imperatives insisted upon within the letter would guarantee that the radical politics of Jesus (once considered simply one of many messianic sects) would go global. There are enslaving forces at work, false gods, that compel human beings to divide themselves and others according to ethnic, economic, and gender status, but in view of Jesus' now-accomplished servant-reign over all creation, these distinctions are relativized: "There is no longer Jew or Greek, there is no longer slave or free, there is no longer male and female; for all of you are one in Christ Jesus" (Gal. 3:28). To be sure, these distinctions haven't disappeared. They're alive and kicking in wage inequality, extrajudicial killing, and border detention facilities the world over. But their legal legitimacy and cultural credibility have been undone by Jesus, and the momentarily under-the-radar new world order—the new creation community to whom Paul addresses himself—has no business behaving otherwise. There is another kingdom under way, and their convivial communion is called to bear witness to it.

Similarly, a countercultural consciousness is present further back on the time line, as Moses repeatedly reminds his community of the context of the covenant: "Remember that you were a slave in the land of Egypt." The phrase appears throughout Deuteronomy, and, what is more, on setting aside the first fruits of the harvest, Israel is instructed to state aloud, "A wandering Aramean was my ancestor; he went down into Egypt and lived there as an alien" (Deut. 26:5). While not quite a wholesale affirmation of egalitarianism, a close identification with the easily exploited outsider and a renunciation of the profit-over-people ethic of Pharaoh are nevertheless nonnegotiable tenets of Israel's historical memory. We could paraphrase Exodus thusly: You must not oppress an undocumented person; you know well the heart of the undocumented, for you yourself are undocumented.

Along this same Beloved Community continuum we witness Jesus sacralizing the experience of "the least of these" and how the nations are ultimately judged by their reception of beleaguered individuals (Matt. 25:31–46). And closer to America's present, we might submit, as a corrective to any nativist delusions of the nonindigenous, a recitation for the historical memory of our nation of diasporas: "A wandering immigrant was my ancestor."

But to return to Paul's explanation of Jesus' new way of being human, it's easy to forget the social novelty at work in his letter and the quiet revolution that would come of it. Within a few decades of Paul's writing, the Christian communities of Asia Minor were sufficiently widespread to come to the attention of Pliny the Younger, governor of Bythinia. In letters to the Roman emperor Trajan, Pliny the Younger notes that the sect includes people of every class and observes, after torturing two unnamed slave women who were deaconesses within their community, "I found nothing but a degenerate sort of cult carried to extravagant lengths." He also complains, "They have a passion for liberty that is almost unconquerable, since they are convinced that God alone is their leader and master."[7]

This outsider account of the visible convictions of the early Christians should give us pause as we consider how easily many Americans speak of their faith as a private, personal matter somehow magically to the side of politics. Such a characterization of the movement wouldn't have made much sense to the early church, and Pliny certainly wasn't describing a group of people who simply held an unconventional opinion or two about the afterlife. Admittedly, he doesn't find them especially threatening. They aren't about to take up arms against their oppressors, but they are holistically and unswervingly invested in a revolution. They are not apolitical. Their allegiance is to a different polity that is uniquely and radically *for* all people, including those who would incarcerate, torture, and even kill them. What survives them will be among the primary starter kits for Beloved Community. In this sense, we might think of them as omnipartisan. They are not *of* this world's way of doing things, but their hope is still scandalously this-worldly. And the intensity of their passion for a socially disruptive, enduring freedom won't be diminished, divided, or conquered by the prerogatives of any government. When brought before the authorities and pushed to the point of confrontation, many manage to matter-of-factly refuse recognition of all other gods even unto death.

Their revolutionary tactic of overcoming evil with good and offering the possibility of fellowship across any and all communal boundaries is so inexplicably effective that the Roman historian Tacitus, offering a brief sketch of the development of this "deadly superstition," regretfully concedes that the execution of its founder was only "a temporary setback."[8] In time, the good news of this different kind of kinship would bubble up through history like a beleaguered yet enduring effervescence eventually viewed as the common possession of anyone with an ear to hear and an eye to see. But neither Paul nor Tacitus could have anticipated a day when the Holy Roman Empire would put to the sword any who refused baptism into this "deadly superstition," or foresee that the alleged second-in-command of American empire, Vice President Mike Pence, would verbally confess Christ at every opportunity and also schedule a Sunday afternoon flight to Indianapolis to publicly shun, on the taxpayers' dime, the Christian witness of Eric Reid, a San Francisco 49er whose devotion to Jesus of Nazareth compelled him to kneel during the national anthem and, like Colin Kaepernick before him, put his career in the National Football League in jeopardy.

THE GOSPEL AS DEMYTHOLOGIZING VIRUS

Before the emperor Constantine proclaimed toleration of worship of "whatever heavenly divinity exists" in the Edict of Milan (313 CE), the difference between the good news of the empire and the good news of Jesus and the prophets was reasonably clear for all interested parties. But this reversal of fortunes, accompanying Constantine's conviction that the Christian God was granting him military victories, would complicate the church's thinking on the subject of God's coming government and the governments of this world. Did this mean the prayer of "your kingdom come" had been answered? Are the principalities and powers no longer rebellious? Is Jesus' victory over death hereby accomplished?

Then and now, thinking historically (which is to say, faithfully) involves vigilance and a mindfulness that looks critically at the supposedly commonsensical notions (or the opinion polls) of the age. This work of communal discernment will be especially crucial if there are deluding spirits and enslaving forces (who by nature are not gods) looking to win battles over hearts and minds. In his letter to the churches of Galatia, Paul speaks of this state of affairs as if it's obvious to anyone who's paying attention (Gal. 4:8–11). And it is to our great loss if we assume the apostle was simply imagining fiery red, sharp-eared creatures with claws and winged babies.

Somehow, the crucified Christ has conquered death, and the powers of darkness and delusion are still at work in the world. They lived within the tension of a new kingdom that had yet to come in its fullness, and the kingdom was the property of nobody's nation. Neither the legalization of Christianity nor the strategic use of biblical phrases in televised speeches mean that God's preferred country is now on the rise. And while the polity that is the church can be pleased to reside within a culture that allows the freedom to gather and worship, the church mustn't confuse that freedom for "the glorious liberty of the children of God" (Rom. 8:21 KJV) or the freedom for which the Christ has set us free (Gal. 5:1), as if we have any government or political party to thank for either.

Properly understood, the good news of Jesus is a rogue element within history, a demythologizing virus that can't help but actively undermine the false gods of any culture that would presume to contain it. While all nations are perhaps prone to seek to absolutize themselves in the minds of their citizens/ subjects, American history serves as an example of how the gospel itself can instruct a nation in the ways of religious tolerance. What else should we expect from a vision of Beloved Community committed to infinite hospitality toward foreigner, stranger, and enemy alike?

But our understanding of this gospel is made peculiarly innocuous when its witness of socially disruptive newness (in whatever culture it finds itself) is underplayed or assigned the part of a "spiritual component" or a "religious role" in the human barnyard. To reduce the living culture of the peasant-artisan revolution of Jesus and other prophets to "a faith element," for instance, is to rob it of its social heft. When the Bible is viewed primarily as a collection of devotional thoughts, its status as the most devastating work of social criticism in history is forgotten. Once we've taken it off its pedestal long enough to actually read what it says, what does the principality called America really make of the prophetic imagination? In an age when many churchgoing Americans appear to view the purposes of the coming kingdom of God and the perceived self-interests of the United States as indistinguishable, as if the living Word of God can be made to sing a duet with the White House, what does faithful witness to Beloved Community look like?

The appropriation of biblical imagery within America's cultural consciousness is both a testimony to the tenacious inventiveness with which the prophetic consciousness takes hold and a stumbling block to the relentlessly penitent posture that prophetic consciousness demands of all nations and the cultures they harbor. Unless we're vigilant, we forget that "God bless America," while perfectly acceptable as a prayer, is a blasphemous boast. America may manifest, on occasion, as among the less wicked Babylons our world has experienced, but it's still a Babylon. There is no level of moral grandeur to which a nation can rise beyond which the critique of Jesus and the prophets will have nothing more to say. If it did, it would no longer be Babylon; it would be the New Jerusalem, the reign of God on earth as it already is in the heavens.

Like the Day of the Lord envisioned by the prophets, Jesus' announcement of a better kingdom puts any and every Babylon on notice, and woe unto any nation that would presume itself above the call to repentance, refusing to call into question its sacred symbols and assuming a posture of militant ignorance. Does the biblical witness disturb the mental furniture of the average American? If we only perceive wickedness afoot when one particular party is in power, I'd like to suggest we're doing it wrong. Do we have the ears to hear a prophetic word? When we pray, "Deliver us from evil," are we thinking mostly of other people from other countries or different party affiliations, or are we at least occasionally noting the axis of evil within our own hearts and at work in the lives of whomever we've come to think of as the right kind of people?

At our best, Americans are intensely awake to the contradictions we live and are determined to remain righteously troubled by them. Slow to repent, many of us are at least ironists. I refer here to a standard often held aloft by figures like Barack Obama, Jimmy Carter, and James Comey and made famous in the witness of Reinhold Niebuhr, who articulated this vision of tragic enmeshment in *The Irony of American History*. Our idealism, he noted, can leave us "too blind to the curious compounds of good and evil" at work in every human undertaking. As ironic realists, we get to own up, again and again, to the short-sightedness with which we, almost of necessity in Niebuhr's view, play with other people's lives while looking hard and humbly at "the ironic tendency of virtues to turn into vices when too complacently relied upon."[9] The constellations of power that comprise our culture are perhaps unavoidable, but whether we conduct ourselves with awareness or complacency is up to us. Niebuhr invites us to take responsibility for the unintended consequences that follow our alleged "use" of strategic violence.

Needless to say, George W. Bush's famous "Mistakes were made," that eerie disavowal of the consequences of his own complicity as the self-described "Decider" at the command console of empire, does not reach the level of Niebuhr's realism. The same can be said of Donald Rumsfeld's musings on behalf of the Pentagon in the face of civilian deaths in our wars in Afghanistan and Iraq: "Freedom's untidy." Both embody the very complacency Niebuhr warns us against. Our moral recklessness equals someone else's death. In the case of the US government's response to the attacks on September 11, 2001, that would be myriad someones.

Because again, irony only appears to work well for those who can afford it. And those who have the power of office and other platforms, presiding over what they take to be the good of others, are slow to repent for fear of losing the power they believe they have. Niebuhr would commend the likes of Gandhi and King for the gift "religious imagination" offers "political life" in the witness of nonviolent resistance, but there was still a divide here in which a strictly "spiritual" insight seems reduced to a means to another end. As I understand it, the gospel of Beloved Community overcomes this division, even demythologizing our sense of critical detachment and evoking a higher realism than irony allows with the long-haul labor of insistent love, one human exchange at a time.

Whatever the mythologies we use to explain ourselves to ourselves—in business decisions, ethical lapses, legal wranglings, or military interventions—there persists the deeper awareness of soul, of interrelation, of kinship in the cultural insight housed in Beloved Community that recognizes the corruption that comes with the illusion of self-sufficiency, total power, and the suggestion—rarely spoken aloud, but often implied—that America itself (or whichever party holds power) somehow owns the copyright on human meaning.

Whenever the tradition of Beloved Community begins to take root in any meaningful way, interpenetrating the imagination of a people who often speak their country's name as if they were praying to it, the psychological power of nationalism is lessened or at least checked by an ancient wisdom reminding us that a nation might gain a strong economy, everyday low prices, and all the homeland security in the world and still forfeit its soul.

THE SALVIFIC POWER OF NOT LYING

"The penalty of deception is to become a deception, with all sense of moral discrimination vitiated. A man who lies habitually becomes a lie, and it is increasingly impossible for him to know when he is lying and when he is not. In other words, the moral mercury of life is reduced to zero."[10] These words come to us out of the wise witness of the mystic Howard Thurman, who hailed from Daytona Beach, traveled widely, and eventually landed at Boston University. They were published in 1949 in his most widely read work, *Jesus and the Disinherited*, which functions as something of a sacred text for many students of Beloved Community, most notably Martin Luther King Jr., who is said to have often carried it on his person and drawn on its counsel constantly.

One can really tell. For Thurman, there are worse things than dying a violent death. There's the danger of becoming so far gone in one's patterns of defensiveness and self-legitimation that one becomes a living deception, something other than a completely present person, a being which, while breathing, plays host to a kind of death in life. If "anima" is the current of conviviality most English New Testaments translate as *soul*, I believe Thurman is giving us an illuminating phrase for what we risk forfeiting when we start speaking and thinking according to the generalizations of those obsessed with power and influence. "The moral mercury of life" slowly dissipates when our imaginations are relentlessly captivated by the drive for control and more control. One can almost feel it vanishing sometimes when claims to deal-making, impact, and administration predominate in boardrooms and social gatherings across the world.

Beloved Community, of course, is also interested in control, but not the kind that humiliates people, shuts down dissent, or tries to force-feed a realization. Thurman understands that when we're resistant to the space in which we might honestly voice what matters to us in our exchanges with others, we carry around—and even conjure—a kind of hell in which the moral mercury of life is not welcome and is even viewed as a threat to the deception we've become.

This hell operates in every sphere of life throughout the human barnyard. It's the hell of social deception that only wants to hear about sexual assault charges leveled at people we aren't aligned with and didn't vote for, a selective outrage that worships at the altar of optics. On the national level, it occurs when the inalienable rights of indigenous people come into conflict with the fossil fuel industry and those whose financial investments depend upon its pipelines; or when the epidemic of soldier suicides conflicts with the story the nation seems to want to tell itself about itself. When it comes to our myths, can we incorporate the fact that George Washington's mouth contained the teeth of terrorized and enslaved people of color endowed by their creator with certain inalienable rights?

Our souls, it turns out, are in play. It's hard to want to know what we don't want to know, but to really love a neighbor or a culture is to go to that place of not lying, of wanting to know what's true more than we want to feel safe and assured. Or as the poet Fanny Howe observes, "There is a point when you realize you are spending more time covering the traces of your dishonesty than you spend plotting it."[11] Denial is a heavy yoke. It can wear a body out.

If the moral mercury of life is to remain within us, we have to be at least occasionally receptive to the notion that we ourselves might prove to be the prospering wicked of whom the Hebrew prophets speak. If we're not, we only appropriate biblical phrases (usually taken out of context) to somehow christen our already-made-up minds and surround ourselves (and our listeners) with a biblical-sounding aura.

There is a tale, possibly apocryphal, of a bemused Elvis Presley sitting in front of his televisions reading the Bible while taking in a Robert Goulet performance and feeling so lonely he could die. With the Bible open to First Corinthians 13, it is reported that Elvis had a moment of clarity, reached for a gun, and opened fire on the bright electronic images making their way into his home. There's something very compelling about this scene. It's as if the man whom many would call King stepped past all that had been and would be made of his personality and all the dark stratagems of Colonel Tom Parker in order to render a decision. Though it has a sadness and frailty to it, the seemingly powerless gesture nevertheless delivers a bold, authoritative judgment, not without a certain dignity. With the apostle Paul's witness to everlasting love on his mind, Elvis compares the love that has overcome death to the brain ray that is television and all the mass hypnosis of the entertainment industry it represents (inseparable as it is from the phenomenon called Elvis) and finds it wanting, deserving of, in fact, immediate execution. The King has spoken.

Or consider Abraham Lincoln, who, like Jimmy Carter, stands out among American presidents as a lifelong student of the Bible. Among his letters is a fragment titled "Meditation on the Divine Will," written in 1862.[12] There's something that anticipates Niebuhr (and draws on Paul) in his identification of "human instrumentalities" that somehow unwittingly carry out God's inscrutable will by "working just as they do." There's no sense of triumphalism or strong leadership or might-as-right, no particular confidence in his own decision making at the helm of one of these instrumentalities. He sees no cause for pride in being a caesar, a pharaoh, or a president if the nations, in God's hands, are just a drop in the bucket. He just strikes a note of grim confidence that, somehow, the Lord's judgments will prevail and, whatever may befall, they are true and right altogether.

He would say as much in his second inaugural address.[13] It functions as what might be viewed as a kind of uniquely American antirhetoric. It certainly doesn't inspire consumer confidence or a resolute aggression toward the enemy to imply ominously that the War between the States has been given to both North and South as the woe due the offense of slavery. Lest any "human instrumentality" insist it's on the side of civilization in the war against chaos and unreason, Lincoln waves that posture aside by declaring, "The Almighty has His own purposes."

"Malice toward none. . . . charity for all. . . . firmness in the right as God gives us to see the right." There's a modesty here that, drawing on First Corinthians, we might view as the Through-A-Glass-Darkly clause (or Through-A-Mirror-Dimly, as some translations have it). There is no moral mercury of life left if we take our own limited standpoint for the whole of reality at every turn. We are learners, not possessors, of truth. We proceed and make decisions based on our convictions of what's right as we understand it. We *mean well*, according to our understanding of meaning and wellness. But our understanding is not, we get to remind ourselves and others repeatedly, a God's-eye view. In Lincoln, we have an elected official who calls on the public to know that it doesn't know by seeing ourselves as immersed in mystery; to stay the course, certainly, but to maintain the modesty that won't presume to take the will of the people (any people) for the will of God. Pursue the right, as we dimly perceive it, with an ongoing, lively awareness of our fallibility (which is to say, our humanness) and with the humility that accompanies such awareness. Follow your sense of right (what else can a human do?), but don't mistake your will for the right and true judgments of the living God. And if you see a vain delusion on the road (or on a screen), slay it. Right away.

Without making of Lincoln or Elvis or anyone a Brahman somehow above the fray of the rest of us, those of us who aspire toward Beloved Community can treasure these moments of insight as essential to the practice of eternal vigilance against the deceptions and denials that yield, with humiliating exactness, the breakdown of social coherence and the systematizing of injustice. A moment's review is sufficient to see that every moral reform within American history has involved a refusal to be bound by the norms of unjust laws written and enforced to maintain the power structures of the morally complacent. Keeping one's head safe for the possibility of democracy (or avoiding the worship of false gods) will require a diligent questioning of what's been placed before us as the way things have to be. We will have to look especially hard at the forces that shape our discourse and the various high-powered attempts, new every morning, to invent public reality.

DISCERN THE SPIRITS

Our attachments to the cultures into which we happen to be born are some-times so powerful that we find it hard to view the crowd or coalition with which we identify most strongly as but one human instrumentality among oth-ers ("USA! USA!"). Beloved Community relativizes every claim on our identity and invites us into a deeper history and a higher realism, confronting us with a demystifying, holy continuum that our divisions of church or state, sacred or secular, and religion or politics conceal to the detriment of any hope of thinking historically. If we consult our time line again, the account of Moses' engagement of Pharaoh on behalf of the God who hears the cry of every mixed multitude under oppression begins to look a lot like an early refutation of what would eventually be called the divine right of kings. And Jesus' witness before Pontius Pilate to a kingdom not of this world undoes the boasts of any king-dom that would claim superiority or unquestionable merit worthy of global dominance. That would include the decree of a man in a red tie before the Republican National Convention that nominated him as their candidate for president: "I alone can fix it."

It has long been the habit of potentates to claim as much, and no consign-ing of religion to the private sphere protects a citizenry from the mad euphoria that demands a worshipful allegiance to the proclaimed interests of the cult of state. But a culture that allows itself to be demystified by the prophetic witness of Beloved Community will learn to doubt its own euphoria; be haunted by the prophetic imagery of arrogant, oppressive nations at whom the Lord in heaven laughs; and note that humans stoked into a frenzy of what they take to be righteous indignation (whether by waves of resentment, white supremacy, or nationalism) often have an unfortunate habit of disappearing people. So long as people of good conscience take up this prophetic witness, gathering up the good that remains and attempting truthfulness one human exchange at a time, I spy hope. Such gestures are not, after all, without precedent.

Alongside the report of Presley's lucid moment and Lincoln subordinating all human instrumentalities (most notably his own) to what he took to be the prerogatives of providence, we do well to consider a confession (affirmed by some Christian denominations in North America) that was composed as an appeal to Christian congregations in Germany in May of 1934. Repudiating the claim that any power apart from Christ should be considered a source of divine revelation (whether an elected official, the triumph of any national will, or Führer Principle), the Barmen Declaration called on German churches to "try the spirits whether they are of God" and to reject all "alien princi-ples" or "figures and truths" that would presume to place themselves alongside (or above) the lordship of Christ. Written primarily by Karl Barth and Hans Asmussen, the document rejects the false doctrine of "other lords" and checks the totalitarian impulse of the state when it presumes absolutely or coercively to define life, liberty, and order for the human community.[14]

Many Americans are often already so immersed in what they take to be biblical language that distinguishing between the sayings of Benjamin Franklin and the wisdom of the book of Proverbs is sometimes a difficult task. Similarly, we are often prone to confuse the reign of God with our sense of patriotism and forget—again and again—that the two are not synonymous. To carefully examine what we find ourselves falling for and weirdly mobilized by—holding it up to careful scrutiny with a determined awareness of our own tendency to confuse matters—is neither an unpatriotic act nor an intellectualization of what ought to be straightforward and simple. Instead, it might be better viewed as a response to the apostle Paul's admonition to "test the spirits" (as echoed in the Barmen Declaration) and the costly, patriotic practice of eternal vigilance against our tendency to hypnotize ourselves into unawareness.

Whether they assume the forms of marketeering, electioneering, or simply achieving and balancing the desired optics within our military-industrial-entertainment-incarceration complex, the words and images that come our way are fraught with meaning. Joan Didion has noted that elections are won with "a series of fables about American experience"[15] carefully calibrated to smooth over whatever revelations might impede its momentum. Civil religion, in this sense, is a rolling enterprise. We in the viewing audience are prone to measure content by how it makes us feel instead of examining exactly what's happening to us, whether or not the information we're receiving is demonstrably true. This is the discipline of Beloved Community. If we exercise no circumspection in regard to the language to which we pay heed and then find ourselves deploying, we run the risk of being swayed by whatever false doctrines prove most emotionally intoxicating from one day to the next and whatever interpretation of current events achieves the highest ratings.

A few days following the inauguration of Donald Trump as president of the United States, the Council of Bishops of the African Methodist Episcopal Church issued a statement that, if we have ears to hear, is as essential to our own time as the Barmen Declaration. Citing the campaign promises that were quickly becoming the pursuit of policies (the 1,900-mile wall, the Muslim ban, and the assault on the possibility of affordable health care for all Americans), the statement invites "people who are committed to justice and righteousness, equality and truth" to join members of the African Methodist Episcopal Church in the effort "to thwart what are clearly demonic acts."[16]

From what I could tell, this communal gesture was not widely publicized by any major news organization and was amplified on hardly anyone's social media feed, but for the record, it quietly but resolutely vindicates a tradition, Christianity specifically, as a living possibility to be taken up by people of conscience at any time, and Beloved Community as a general work available to everyone despite what happens in national elections. The discernment of some acts as visibly and plainly demonic and others as based in commonsense righteousness (the general welfare of most people) is a discipline that is always there and never quite complete.

WONDER-WORKING POWER

As Karl Barth noted, applying the gospel of Jesus and the prophets to our vision of the world unfolding before us will involve a yes and a no. Yes to the hope of a new day coming and the watchfulness required to see it. No to the suggestion, sometimes only dimly hinted at even to ourselves, that our own good intentions or pure hearts will hasten its coming or that we are knowers (rather than learners) of the good purposes of God. In the interest of such watchfulness, let us consider the concluding words of President George W. Bush's remarks delivered on Ellis Island on the first anniversary of the attacks of September 11: "Be confident. Our country is strong. And our cause is even larger than our country. Ours is the cause of human dignity; freedom guided by conscience and guarded by peace. This ideal of America is the hope of all mankind. That hope drew millions to this harbor. That hope still lights our way. And the light shines in the darkness. And the darkness will not overcome it."[17]

Like the language of the Declaration of Independence, the stated vocation of the country ("the cause of human dignity") can be interpreted to include the have-nots within America and without. Thus interpreted, the enormity of the challenge (a challenge, incidentally, that would probably be recognized as foundational to America's civil religion, Amnesty International, the American Red Cross, the witness of the Roman Catholic Church, and the United Nations) will be impossible to overestimate. With the stakes this high, it's always important, in the interest of vigilance, spirit testing, and an aliveness to our capacity for self-deception in Beloved Community, to have in mind a confession or acknowledgment of the occasional moral lapse, on the part of the US government, in living up to this vocation.

This isn't to say that any president, commemorating a day of national tragedy, should be expected to use the opportunity to confess the nation's shortcomings. But the discerning viewer will want to keep in mind the need for confession and historical mindfulness (an obligation of citizenship) even in mourning. Admittedly, focus groups are likely to suggest that public officials can't get elected or remain in office without maintaining an air of insouciance regarding the less righteous moments in America's history, and career politicians have long learned how beautiful on television is the face of the one who brings good news, announcing peace and proclaiming news of happiness.

But most of us aren't running for office and need not have our consciences dictated by someone else's talking points. Keeping matters clear in our own minds and noting the possibility that some honest hearers of these words about

America's ideals might think of global warming, tortured detainees, or drone-strike victims, we can affirm these phrases for their worth without getting carried away. Yes to the cause as stated. No to the suggestion that anyone not yet convinced that we're living up to it is somehow against us.

Unless we hold unwaveringly to the yes and the no of a righteous witness like Beloved Community in our listening and watching, we fall prey to a kind of confidence game that is believed to be, for better or worse, a key part of maintaining consumer confidence and holding on to power. This is where the pragmatic purposes of realpolitik, when successfully achieved, inevitably appeal to what are usually described as religious sensibilities. The cause (human dignity) is described as America's "ideal," which, in turn, is "the hope of all mankind." "That hope still lights our way," asserts George W. Bush. We hope that human dignity is a priority in the lives of most Americans, and yet some, viewing our culture industry, trade policies, and unilateral actions, might be forgiven for thinking otherwise. And then there is the biblical reference: "The light shines in the darkness. And the darkness did not overcome it" (John 1:5).

Many Americans were likely pleased to hear the Bible quoted at all. For the demographic who would come to feel somehow vindicated whenever "Merry Christmas" trumps "Happy Holidays," they might also be happy to hear, in President Bush's 2003 State of the Union address, an altered recitation of a popular hymn: "There's power, wonder-working power, in the goodness and idealism and faith of the American people." But language that connects American motivations with the divine Logos or Americans' presumed goodness with the blood of the Lamb who was slain should probably give us pause. We have to examine ourselves closely whenever we try to claim (or imply) continuity with the early Christian community. What do we mean? Are we thinking, speaking, and acting faithfully? We have to ask. Not, I hasten to add, in order to go around policing theological correctness, but to attempt to embody a vigilance that is, in one sense, deeply Christian and, I tend to think, essential in discerning and preventing demonic acts undertaken with an implied association with Christ. Generalization, we might say, is the antichrist's air supply. Specificity cuts it off.

AMERICA AS SALES FORCE

Being slow to applaud a generalization or wary of a conflation of a figure like Jesus with a particular people-group is not a diversion from promoting the general welfare. In fact, a steadfast refusal to settle for the status quo, especially in regard to whatever unfreedom we've given our allegiance to, is at the root, in the most positive sense, of our historical identity (think Anne Hutchinson, Thomas Paine, Sojourner Truth, and Black Elk). As we look closer at various voices within America's literature, popular music, science fiction, and film, we will note an ongoing resistance to being entirely at ease with wherever we are, a perpetual movement forward, and a determination to speak truthfully to power, perhaps especially when that power assumes the form of an intoxicatingly unself-critical and arrogant voice inordinately amplified.

Umberto Eco once described the moment in 1943 when he realized, as a young man, that the Fascists weren't the only political party in Italy. He suddenly began to observe how Mussolini, in power since 1922, had seemed to control the thinking of his surrounding culture at every moment and in all aspects of life, with complete power, it seemed, over everyone's imagination. Having felt tremendous pride in his Fascist uniform, winning a writing competition for young Italian Fascists at the age of ten, and only occasionally noting another way of looking at the world via Radio London and an odd relative or two, it was quite the apocalypse to hear on the radio that Mussolini had been imprisoned by the king. As Eco tells it, "Like a butterfly from a chrysalis, step by step I understood everything. . . . It was inconceivable that this man, who since my birth had been a god, had been kicked out; I was astonished, amazed, amused." And in one mad moment, "I discovered the meaning of plurality, democracy and freedom."[18]

Astonished, amazed, and amused. If I might be allowed the pleasure of having it both ways, I'd like to suggest that America, mythologically speaking and thanks to the beleaguered and loving people at the receiving end of its violence, might be helpfully viewed as both the most self-consciously anti-Babylonian world power in history and, given its current status as a world power withdrawing from the Paris Climate Agreement and constantly positioning itself beyond the bounds of international accountability, a power most at risk of being completely deaf to the prophetic witness against our inner Babylon. Our elected officials and their enablers are prone to search the Scriptures and quote them self-servingly, so certain that the Bible speaks for us (and we for it) that we become contrition proof. And yet we also have a heritage (Christ-haunted, if you like) that is astonished at how absolute power so subtly corrupts absolutely, amazed at the self-justifying logic that accompanies our moral ruin, and amused over how thinly our self-congratulatory rhetoric conceals an impenetrable ignorance. In a strange but consistent cycle, too noisy an assertion of America's moral grandeur and superiority occasionally betrays a nagging doubt or two, and we awaken again for a time. Captured in films, novels, songs, and television series, it's the cycle of doubt and overconfidence concerning our own loudest and brightest publicity that might keep the rest of the world looking hopefully on our broadcasts.

As a younger man, I once had an astonishing, amazing, and amusing moment of my own in a Belfast pub after watching Clint Eastwood's *Unforgiven* (1992). I'd been working with the YMCA in Northern Ireland for a few months, and for the first time in my life I'd experienced my Americanness as a distinguishing feature. It was strange to be referred to as an American (by way of description), occasionally unsettling even, but also extremely gratifying. It disturbed an ease that I hadn't known was there. The folks with whom I'd gone to the cinema were an international gathering, and all agreed that this was Eastwood's finest work yet, a western to end all westerns. (The Kid: "He had it coming." Eastwood: "We all have it coming, kid."[19]) Something of Niebuhr's tragic irony seemed to be in play in a Cormac McCarthy kind of way.

Only a couple of years away from having lived on a steady diet of Rush Limbaugh, I did have a slight qualm concerning one of the final scenes. Eastwood's protagonist, having wreaked vengeance on all parties involved in the murder of Morgan Freeman's character, cries out, like a mad cowboy Lear, that he will hunt down and slay all evildoers and their wives and their children in his battle against injustice. I thought it a bit much to have an American flag flying in the background during the speech. It's not as if America is the only country guilty of falling prey to the myth of redemptive violence, I pointed out defensively, and while I believed that Eastwood's direction was, otherwise, completely brilliant, this struck me as overkill, a slight misstep in the direction of the dogmatic.

An Ulsterman, slightly older than me, laughed at my fastidiousness. "But that flag's everybody's," he protested. "It's shorthand for human nature. It's redemptive violence and freedom and pride and all that. Clint's all of us. The flag too." The rest of the world, he presumed I understood as well as anyone, had been made to drink the wine of the wrath of America's fornication for many years now. It's everybody's. Didn't I know it? And with this, I began to suspect, probably for the first time, that I'd lived and breathed and grown up in the thick of a cosmic metaphor, a citizen of what, for much of the world, is a very big idea that obviously isn't always true—mind-numbingly hypocritical, in fact—when it comes to its big, bad, brave and bold claims of freedom and justice for all.

It's a great big human experiment in democracy always on the verge of collapse. What's the big deal in acknowledging as much? Nobody's perfect, right? We all want to win. We all get carried away. We're all only human. It began to dawn on me that I'd come from the land where drama happens, where most of the big-budget action films and popular sitcoms take place, and I felt like I'd just been stopped short in the middle of a sales pitch. Not long after that, I eagerly attempted to explain the concept of Manifest Destiny to an inquisitive Frenchman. He nodded knowingly as I struggled to be a good commercial on behalf of my country, but I eventually realized that I misunderstood his question. He wanted to talk rock 'n' roll. He'd asked me to describe Memphis, Tennessee.

Around this time, it began to occur to me that being properly introspective and self-critical concerning America and less anxious when someone doubts its publicity was probably a positive step toward emotional maturity. Trying to explain America outside of America, and finding that, for better or worse,

America had been on most people's minds already for some time, was a deeply disconcerting experience. It was as if I'd emerged from an alternative reality (à la *The Truman Show*).

More recently, I was with my students at a hotel in Arusha eating dinner with my Tanzanian friend, Jimmy, when a Kenny Rogers song came on the speakers. I wondered if someone had put the music on for my group's benefit or if it was commonplace. Jimmy's eyes widened and he shook his head with a sense of awe: "Kenny Rogers is the best. 'The Gambler'? 'Coward of the County'? I love those songs."

I mentioned that the songwriting culture I've grown accustomed to as a native Nashvillian can leave me weirdly underappreciative of how remarkable it is that such songs travel and enter people's lives, but yes, these songs are amazing. As a point of interest, I noted that I'd seen Don Schlitz, who wrote "The Gambler," perform at a benefit or two around town and that, as the saying goes, the royalties are so significant that he probably doesn't have to work anymore.

Jimmy gave me a serious look and observed, without a trace of irony, "He shouldn't have to work anymore. He wrote 'The Gambler.'"

I felt more than a little bit chastened. In my eagerness to disassociate from certain cultural artifacts that sometimes strike me as trivial or somehow beneath my interest, I'd missed a sense of my own context and a universal lyricism Jimmy spied and treasured in an American pop song. Jimmy speaks four languages and would risk imprisonment if he were overheard criticizing the president of Tanzania in front of the wrong people. What else am I missing in America's cultural output? Have I overlooked the moral mercury of life? What else do I have yet to treasure properly?

Chapter 2

For Mine Own Good
All Causes Shall Give Way

When I asked her who killed the man and why, she said, "An Evil Spirit killed him. You gotta be a good girl or it will kill you too." So since I was seven, I had lived in fear of that "Evil Spirit." It took me eight years to learn what that spirit was.
—Anne Moody, *Coming of Age in Mississippi*

So come out of those ugly molds and remember good is better than evil because it's nicer to have around you. It's just as simple as that.
—William S. Burroughs, *The Ticket That Exploded*

This train is known as the Black Diamond Express to Hell. Sin is the engineer, Pleasure is the headlight, and the Devil is the conductor.
—Rev. A. W. Nix, "Black Diamond Express To Hell," part 1

Any lengthy consideration about what telecommunication has done to the American mind can draw some incredibly helpful wisdom from onetime president of CBS News Fred Friendly. Played by George Clooney in *Good Night, and Good Luck* (2005), he's often referred to as the other half of Edward R. Murrow. Friendly was an indefatigable journalist who believed that his vocation (and that of any organization that aims to report what can rightly be called "news") was to provide individuals with information on which they can actually act. What is more, he believed that journalists have a moral responsibility to resist the pressure to reduce news to best-selling "news product" that simply confirms the prejudices of a targeted audience and should strive instead to tell it like it is in such a way that the viewer is drawn into the agony of having to make a decision. According to Friendly, the journalist's job is to create a pain in the audience's mind so intense that it can be relieved only by thinking. Given this conviction concerning the role of the press in a functioning democracy, he felt compelled to resign his position in 1966, when network executives canceled live broadcasts of testimony on the subject of Vietnam before the Senate Foreign Relations Committee, opting instead to air sitcom reruns.

Like Rod Serling, Friendly believed that television was an almost unimaginably powerful tool for positive social change, but it also had the potential to become nothing more than a high-tech totem pole of mass hypnosis that serves the ends of multinational corporations and the governments that serve them. Noting the pattern whereby content is driven by ratings, which drives the advertising that funds the operation ("Promotional consideration provided by . . ."), Friendly eventually observed that "television makes so much at its worst that it can't afford to do its best."[1] He would later pine for the days when news programs would regularly feature people lost in thought or ready to admit that a particular issue would require more thinking before a comment would be prudent. In Friendly's ideal future, television might have often featured the rare happening of people actually changing their minds or conceding a point in a conversation. But it wasn't to be. So much for Socratic dialogue beaming its way into a nation's living spaces.

Trying to imagine what Friendly would have made of the social media to come can have me wanting to throw my cell phone through the window, but the habits of mind he worried over and the challenges of sustained attention, of slowing the tape, and of responding thoughtfully instead of reacting impulsively to the media content placed before us are probably merely intensified by the technologies that populate our lives. Social media amplifies, for better or worse, our passions. If the practices that make for toxicity (degradation, humiliation, and accusation) are our primary moves, these tools can serve as a quick delivery system for that dubious skill set. But we can play the healing game of thoughtfulness and right remembrance too. What follows is an attempt to chart the latter path of leveling carefully with ourselves and others and exercising the joys of responsibility befitting Beloved Community in a culture that often mistakes heat for light and projection for fact.

TO SPIN IS HUMAN

Advocates of civil discourse as an indispensable aspect of a stable democracy will want to affirm the legacy of Fred Friendly. But this is an especially difficult affirmation to keep a grip on in a mass-media age of everything all of the time. Friendly hoped to amplify, perpetuate, and expand the space of the "talkaboutable," literacy as a party to which everyone is invited. Keeping our hearts and minds safe for democracy involves a widespread moral imagination, a people who enjoy the thrill of a well-articulated argument and are capable of distinguishing between information and accusation.

Needless to say, we've found ourselves in a cultural climate that appears increasingly incapable of teaching or even valuing the skills required to think coherently about ourselves or to properly converse with each other. Ours is a sound-bite culture that often resents complexity and lacks the patience to listen to (or read) any account of people, places, or events that doesn't somehow confirm what we already thought. One pitfall of this situation is that it eventually becomes a sort of feedback loop playing over in our heads even when we aren't tuned into our screens. Our minds become populated with the slogans, sayings, and memes that made us feel strong, vindicated, and in control when we first took them in. It's hard to part with anything that seems to fend off chaos.

Sooner or later, we avoid the company of people who don't nod knowingly when we say what's what or respond favorably to what we post on our feeds, and we unknowingly define our community by the people who seem to agree with us or who have at least learned to dutifully avoid particular topics in our company. Tragically, it can become what we mean when we think of friendship. We become our own issue silo (or death cult), and the algorithms are there to keep us rutting within it. We are easy prey, we know too well, for automated disinformation campaigns.

Ancient wisdom tells us that it's the insane person who can't change his mind and won't change the subject. If the light that is in you is darkness, Jesus warns, how great is that darkness. Consider the investigative insight of this aphorism. People can become so inured to what doesn't fit their own conception of self that they mistake an ever-thickening darkness for light and seal themselves up in an active mind-set of militant ignorance, improvising a defense against any moral realization. "Bias" comes to function as a magic word that can be made to shut down incoming data. With a word like "bias," I can rationalize away every fact, every honest word attempted in my presence, the lived experience of millions.

If, as Islamic tradition teaches us, the true jihad is the inner jihad (the true struggle is the inner struggle), to be human is to be biased. To be human is to be situated within a particular context within which we might yet struggle more righteously. Impartial judgment is a noble and hopeful pursuit, rather than a boast, for those of us who try to live with the awareness that we only see through a glass darkly. Like humility, it probably isn't the kind of attribute someone can possess knowingly. We spin, whether beautifully or toxically, whenever we speak. If we claim to be without spin, we lie to ourselves and the truth is not in us. We might just as well claim we have conquered anger or selfishness or finiteness. But advertising language (which, by definition, misleads) is not accountable to confessions of mortality and can decree itself fair and balanced with an audiovisual blitzkreig. It can present itself as being without spin and is more than able to cast the first stone. With the backing of a media conglomerate, pundits can vouchsafe a sense of false community and sound mindedness on anyone who gives the Amen to their view of the cosmos. The listener gratefully reciprocates the passing of the peace of mind (I think what you think), a commodity that sells itself.

If we take Lincoln's meditations on divinity (your pounding pulse is not the Holy Spirit) and Presley's cryptic triumph over television as exemplary moments in Americans' struggles to more accurately perceive ourselves and our place in the world, we might say we're at our best when we're at our most bewildered, when we're eager to have our made-up minds undone by new and better testimonies, when we want truth spoken to our own power, and when we're afraid of our own anxious tendency to dismiss information that might make us think twice about ourselves. Self-congratulatory paranoia might sell and, to some minds, popular witlessness might even strengthen the economy, but a nation of sociopaths isn't in a position to project democratic values on the world. America as a commodity becomes less appealing to the global village when America presents itself as a creature that listens only to itself. It's hard to appreciate a service provider that denies all negative feedback in advance of hearing it.

With this in mind, our ability to feel disaffected with the self-referential stories we've clung to, discovering (blessedly) that we don't know the half of it, might be the nearest available avenue toward Beloved Community. We can turn around at any time. And given the ease with which the alleged representatives of the American people consistently downgrade America's brand identity, undertaking this work right in conscious relationship with the other 96 percent of the world's population is not unrelated to the popular abstraction of national security.

I BELIEVE IN MY HEART

The hours we spend tuned in as a captive audience to the princes of the power of the airwaves and the ease with which we can convince ourselves we've scored a point in a debate with a keyboard or a click of the mouse have left many Americans in a lonely bind. Tragically, our yearning for community makes us especially vulnerable as host bodies for whatever force might hold a megaphone closest to our ears, and the hype that gets hold of us won't generally make us more loving in our responses to friends and family. We're free-floating, unnerved, and easily susceptible to multimillion-dollar, manufactured versions of reality.

On top of this, we have that much-touted notion of American individualism that, in one sense, is inseparable from the trajectory (from Moses to

Beyoncé) we're celebrating. The American creed (no insignificant person was ever born) exalts the human being as the infinitely valuable bearer of God's image and eventually deems every person as so endowed with dignity that all are to be accorded, with all deliberate speed, rights. But this insight, divorced from its historical moorings and lived awareness of the generations who struggled against the brutalizing of humans as fodder for the gods, can make people rather nasty, brutish, and blissfully egotistical, with little understanding of the hard-won humanism they've inherited at great cost. Spirit, like Beloved Community, knows no division. When we lose a sense of all the words to be had and all the pain endured and soul sustained to get us here, we're prone to forget that human rights weren't discovered by statesmen or scientists. In polite American company (as of this writing), humans are deemed worthy of food, shelter, education, and trial by jury, but it's the creative yield of Beloved Community (Marguerite Porete, Fannie Lou Hamer, Pauli Murray) that instructs the powerful, over time, to believe as much.

But the exaltation of one's own gut feeling can cut both ways, especially when it exalts as somehow sacrosanct the isolated delusions of men with power over others. In practice, this leads to a hopeless privileging of personal fantasy, over observable fact, as the definitive and binding take on reality. Mistaking the still, small voice in our heads for absolute truth isn't a uniquely American heresy, but combined with the deifying of whatever it is we might mean when we talk about the ineffable virtue of following our hearts, one prevalent understanding of personal strength becomes an insane sense of personal infallibility. Being true to oneself, in the most vapid sense, might simply be a matter of being true to one's endlessly self-justifying ego.

In our age of "hurry up and matter!" the practice of pause, of consistently slowing the tape of the story and spin we intake, can feel like a career liability, a privilege the upwardly mobile and aspiringly "impactful" people can't afford. This pattern can make all of us professional politicians and the victims of our own self-publicity and that of famous others. It can feel as if there's no escaping it.

At the risk of homing in on the example of a considerably famous person to the exclusion of the rest of us, I'd like to consider the case of Ronald Reagan. Like anyone whose presumed power depends upon believing (or pretending to believe) whatever it appears expedient to believe from one moment to the next, he lived much of his life in a psychic pickle. The question of expedience is always with us, but devoting too much of our lives to it can deplete the conscience considerably. Our hold on reality can prove disturbingly—even perversely—malleable. When forced by the 1987 Tower Commission Report to consider again his public denial of involvement in the Iran-Contra affair, Reagan offered his viewers at home an odd statement that illustrates the phenomena I have in mind: "I told the American people I did not trade arms for hostages. My heart and my best intentions still tell me that's true, but the facts and the evidence tell me it is not."[2]

For Americans, an elected official's pattern of evasion often mimics, by design, that of the culture over which that office presides. In some phantasmagoric bid, the job isn't just to conjure but to somehow *be* the product of enough gerrymandered voters' preferred imaginings. I hasten to add that this brand of egotism isn't the sole property of any particular political party, economic class, or group. "I believe in my heart" is a stunningly effective phrase in the perception of the American public, if the polls are to be believed, and presidents can refer to their "heart of hearts" and talk about the unique truth of what's deep down in their hearts as if feeling something deeply is an argument in itself. G. K. Chesterton famously observed that the highest concentrations of people who most intensely believe in themselves aren't to be left on their own recognizance, but, taking a page out of Joseph Goebbels's notes, we can be assured that unquestioning self-confidence still somehow feelingly persuades.

In *Habits of the Heart*, Robert Bellah and his colleagues document one particular form of American self-worship and identify it as "Sheilaism," the professed, private faith of a young nurse named Sheila Larson (a pseudonym) who named her most consistent religious conviction after herself. She's quick to point out that she believes in God, but she isn't religious: "My faith has carried me a long way. It's Sheilaism. Just my own small voice."[3] Self-love and being gentle with herself concerning possible shortcomings are her primary creeds. The authors don't question that Sheila has had experiences with a living God, but it does seem clear that God, viewed exclusively through the lens of rampant Sheilaism, can become nothing more than "the self magnified."[4]

Given the mental fight one has to undertake to hear oneself above the din of other people's projections, sales pitches, and empty promises, I don't begrudge Sheila her hard-won discernment of her own small voice for a second. There are so many ways we're taught to doubt and grow estranged from our own best intuition, the lively genius many within Beloved Community believe lies buried in every living person, even when we're reading teleprompted words we've been told we have to say aloud to avoid impeachment proceedings.

But there's more than one way to believe your own heart. My preferred text for undertaking this life's work rightly is Toni Cade Bambara's *The Salt Eaters*, a movable feast of healing, discernment, despair unto death, and communal exorcism. In a revolving cast of characters whose wise utterances speak to one another's psychic dramas sometimes purposefully and sometimes accidentally, one of them, Sophie Heywood, insists that "every event is preceded by a sign." Who has the authority to interpret them? That would be everyone who's ever lived: "We're all clairvoyant if we'd only know it."[5]

Try that. Know your own clairvoyance together with others. There is no other way.

THE CHRIST CODE

Like other Americans, our presidents often appear to embrace a variation of the Quaker doctrine of the inner light of Christ, but with the absence of anything in the way of communal discernment or accountability that might call into question the confidence with which a person heeds the voice in one's heart. "Personal religious experience" seems to strike an acceptable note in many a voter's minds, even as too visible a lived accountability to any visible community of faith (present or past) is viewed as a liability. Amid his own bid for the presidency, Barack Obama had to publicly disassociate from the Reverend Jeremiah Wright, who'd performed his wedding, once YouTube footage surfaced in which he made the same distinctions between God's kingdom and the United States that Martin Luther King Jr. dramatized constantly. Mike Pence and John Kerry can claim affiliation with the Roman Catholic Church while assuring the people that no church teaching or papal decree will have any actual effect on their decision making. And in what we need not assume was a calculated move, then Texas governor George W. Bush won the approval of millions in a primary debate by citing "Christ" as his favorite political philosopher. Needless to say, no moderator invited him to offer specifics on how his foreign policy or his position on capital punishment would line up with the Sermon on the Mount (political philosophy, after all), but this is well in keeping with what we've come to expect of the mass-market version of American Christianity. The actual politics of Jesus aren't on the table. How is it, then, that Jesus influences? "Because he changed my heart." When his interlocutor hinted that the American people might desire a little more elaboration, Bush smiled and observed, "If they don't know, it's going to be hard to explain."[6]

And . . . this generalization worked like a charm. It's what millions of people are referring to when they say that they know Christ as their savior. I don't mean to imply disingenuousness on the part of anyone when I suggest that this way of characterizing one's connection to Jesus is a heresy at best and a sign of the spirit of antichrist at worst. Harold Bloom has suggested that "knowing" Christ, believing yourself to have a one-on-one relationship with him (unmediated by tradition; "in the garden alone"; impossible to explain to anyone who doesn't know him like you do), is hardly more than a couple of centuries old and unique to the American experience.[7] Minus the obligation to aspire toward continuity with a historic, visible, practicing community (based in some recognizable fashion on what Jesus of Nazareth said and did), we're left alone with what we believe in our hearts our personalized Christ is telling us. The nonpolitical, fully spiritualized Christ asset opens doors in America.

As a cautionary measure against our tendency to tell ourselves the Christ in our heart of hearts is telling us to do whatever we've already decided to do, providentially blessing the presidential administration of an unrepentant sexual assailant, or that the Bible somehow buttresses whatever we feel is right, Beloved Community affords us the opportunity to recognize ourselves as fallible discerners of whatever it is the Holy Spirit is saying to the churches who are nevertheless invited to partake of communal clairvoyance. Trying to be faithful to this spirit, perceiving it with fear and trembling, is what Beloved Community does. The word "Christ" (a title, and not Jesus' last name) can't simply be inarguable shorthand for a personal sense of rightness, as if there's nothing to talk about and nothing to be explained. In some circles, it almost seems to function as a code word for white nationalism disguised as Christianity. To genuinely confess Jesus as the Messiah is to insist that his politics—his way of being in the world—goes, that his teachings are to be pursued as normative. It mustn't just be a secret handshake for those who are "in the know" concerning the importance of a certain kind of "spiritual component" that will have little or nothing to say on the subject of the disenfranchised, the incarcerated, or the devastation of the natural world. When someone claims to know him (or that someone else doesn't) is it a reference to the Beloved Community of Jesus and the prophets, or is it prayer coverage for the military-industrial-entertainment-incarceration complex?

YOU HAVE TO BE WHOLE TO SEE WHOLE

Within American popular discourse, the reigning standard that protects the latter from the former seems as natural as the air we breathe. It's the culture of endless war that's sacrosanct, and woe to anyone who'd dare to even imply that "religion" can be brought to bear upon it. We have chaplains for that. This is the move whereby George W. Bush can brand-associate with Christ as his preferred political philosopher in one context and intone the following when asked how an alleged man of prayer can order preemptive war:

> I don't bring God into my life to be a political person. I ask God for strength and guidance. I ask God to help me be a better person. But the decision about war and peace was a decision I made based upon what I thought were the best interests of the American people. I was able to step back from religion, because I have a job to do. And I, on bended knee to the good Lord, asked Him to help me to do my job in a way that's wise.[8]

As a testimonial, this is a powerful portrait of popular conception of, as the saying goes, "the role of religion," and it should be familiar to all of us. There is a pathos at work, and it's reflected in the way a person balances career with other commitments, designating some areas of life (business, worship, recreation) and dividing them up from one another. Many Americans feel obliged to put our faith to the side when we're buying and selling, the way we go about being realistic. Bush is relating a tale concerning the struggle of vocation, of faithfulness to a job with certain demands that might not coincide with the language usually associated with religion, of a human heart in conflict with itself. This view of God as a nonpolitical being that we can bring in for wisdom and comfort and keep respectfully separate from our business, our "job to do," is a view held by Americans across party lines, and it will often be hard to remember that it bears no resemblance to anything any sacred tradition has ever considered orthodox. Nevertheless, it's standard procedure.

And in a faithful reflection of these designations, we hold prophetic consciousness at a distance while simultaneously giving lip service to the sacrosanct status of everybody's private, personal faith. Getting the job done, living in the real world, and being effective, it is believed, require keeping one thing separate from another if we're to overcome these conflicts of interests. We're back to the question of expedience and the divisions it demands.

But spirit knows no division, and the kingdom of God won't relinquish its righteous prerogatives so easily. There is no stepping back from the fact of relationship. To try to step back from Beloved Community is to step into estrangement from self and others. Needless to say, no one whose first allegiance is to the reign of God and God's righteousness can ultimately settle for the title of "spiritual adviser" or a position as chaplain for a corporation or an ostensibly sovereign nation-state. A witness to it can't merely serve as someone's "theological underpinnings" or "religious influence." Beloved Community is committed to twenty-four-hour coverage, an unending appeal to hearts, minds, and bodies, and the biblical witness assures us that God wants it all—the earth and everything in it, all authority, because the Spirit that knows no division is being poured out on all flesh, and the knowledge of the Lord will cover the earth as the waters cover the sea.

As it summons us to recognize our every entanglement and lean into the fact of our kinship with one another at every turn, it could be that Beloved Community is ultimately an invitation to an utterly unmarketable freedom, an unquantifiable goodness, and a wisdom that won't fit any sound bites, sales pitches, conferrals of sovereignty, or anyone's system. In American history, this culture has most often been associated, in some way, with people whose interpretation of the Bible challenged the status quo readings of their times, and its fruits are discernible in lending libraries, the abolitionist movement, women's suffrage, child labor laws, the rights of indigenous people, and affordable health care. It is its own mode of living and thinking, unendingly open to the worlds it encounters, but in lively tension as it resides within various, never completely accommodating settings.

To be a learner of the larger freedom of Beloved Community requires a long unlearning of habitual defensiveness and self-justification at all costs and an adoption of the easier yoke and lighter burden of vulnerability and even confession. It isn't subject to our monetizing impulse, and it is on the side of life and liberty in more ways than we can ask for or imagine. You "have to be whole to see whole," Bambara's Sophie Heywood counsels, "There is a world to be redeemed, and it'll take the cooperation of all righteous folks."[9]

ALL LOVELINESS IS ANGUISH TO ME

Meanwhile, there is so much to be confused over in our own heady days as we try to think and see clearly amid the static and the noise. Beloved Community urges us to recognize how prone we already are to distort reality to suit our sense of self, and our electronic devices will often assist us in accelerating this process. By cutting ourselves off from conscious participation in the life that surrounds us, we become less capable of perceiving our own context, and Fred Friendly's worst-case scenarios are ever before us.

To my mind, Friendly is an especially helpful guide in curbing the contagion. He wouldn't mistake technology itself for content, but he would always ask if our media consumption is making us more or less capable of distinguishing between usable information and distracting nonissues that only serve to keep us glued, agitated, and addicted. With this kind of methodology, we're able to think more rigorously as members of Beloved Community and interact more meaningfully with platforms designed, it sometimes seems, to make Gollums of us all.

It might seem odd to bring someone like Nathaniel Hawthorne of *Scarlet Letter* fame into these musings, but a brief character sketch of a guilt-ridden man in one of his short stories ("Roger Malvin's Burial") resonates peculiarly well with a character type perhaps made more isolated by the pseudointimacy of remote interactions on social media platforms: "Reuben's secret thoughts and insulated emotions had gradually made him a selfish man, and he could no longer love deeply except where he saw or imagined some reflection or likeness of his own mind."[10]

I'm sure I'm projecting more than a little, but this sounds like a mid-1800s forecast of an Internet troll. It's as if the process has been accelerated as it's becoming increasingly difficult for many Americans to consider history, information, or even everyday gossip apart from who appears momentarily to benefit the most from the disclosure. There's a sealing off of self from insight and affection that looks to be an epidemic.

Twitter, for instance, magnifies our passions, for better and worse. It can't be blamed for the content we broadcast through it. If toxicity—degradation, humiliation, accusation—is our primary game, we're able to deliver it remotely and quicker. And yet, we can broadcast thoughtfulness too, with an ease that might have amazed and encouraged Fred Friendly. I don't know if, in the long run, Twitter will prove to have been a net gain for the cause of righteousness in the land of the living, but I know we're responsible for what we make of it. Out of the depths of the heart, the social media feed speaks.

The anxious pressure we feel in our desire to hear (and then repeat to our families, friends, and coworkers) a sound-bite-worthy solution to what's wrong with the world or a masterful judgment that will fend off all paradox is hostile to everything the biblical witness recognizes as wisdom. Jesus' admonition to "Judge not, lest ye be judged" and to call no person an idiot or a fool while carefully examining ourselves before attempting a word of discernment is binding upon our media input and output as people who, in a very real sense, are never not broadcasting. Fred Friendly anticipated the power we each have to either model the virtues of delayed judgment in the direction of better social practice or to join the rage by inciting ourselves and others toward defensive, endlessly self-justifying postures. Although the open hand is clearly more representative of Beloved Community than the clenched fist, both express the natural desire to keep chaos at bay. But the former recognizes the possibility of madness and crimes against humanity within oneself while the latter rejects, with passionate intensity, the suggestion that we might have a log or two in our own eyes.

The other half of that teaching that is often forgotten is the idea that seeing clearly and genuinely helping is the goal: "Then you will see clearly to take the speck out of your neighbor's eye" (Luke 6:39–42). And the goal is a means to the end of actually being present to the life of one's neighbor. But no clear vision is possible for those who boast of (or worse, really believe in) their own logless vision, a vision without spin. We might also recall the folk wisdom offered in Beck's observation that death has a way of creeping in slowly till we feel safe in its arms. Boiling point is only approached in not-quite-discernible stages, and the frog in the beaker won't know what's happening until it's too late.

While evildoers don't self-consciously or publicly recognize themselves as such while fighting to put down other evildoers, literature will often afford us language whereby violent souls actually talk about what they're doing while they're doing it. As Shakespeare always seems to offer an illuminating word for any and all issues that beset us, we now turn to a deeply troubled Macbeth. With his wife's help, he's already talked himself into murdering his king and the one friend who dared to question his career ambitions. As most of us do when we get to scrolling our feeds, he's now looking for a destiny forecast (the witches whose broadcast set him down this path in the first place will do). Wondering how he might best capitalize on events to make sure everything's going his way, he offers the following on how he might best go for the gold:

> For mine own good,
> All causes shall give way: I am in blood
> Stepp'd in so far that, should I wade no more,
> Returning were as tedious as go o'er:
> Strange things I have in head, that will to hand;
> Which must be acted ere they may be scann'd.[11]

Until recently, I couldn't imagine this brand of bluster being spoken aloud except in sleep, under hypnosis, and by characters in Shakespeare's plays. As a teacher, I collect the cosmic plainspeak that gives voice to our inner dramas, and I'm always trying to apply the words of regicides and other poor players to something a little closer to home. For anyone thinking through personal finances, the hopefully existent consciences of elected officials, and how we got here, there are some lines here that might strike a chord for those of us who saw Donald Trump decree, after winning his party's nomination for president: "It is so nice that the shackles have been taken off me and I can now fight for America the way I want to."[12]

With no vision beyond the inner logic of improvised explanations, Macbeth proclaims, "For mine own good, / All causes shall give way." We're human; therefore we angle and improvise, but if the first thought in our minds when we hear news is, "Does this make my team look good or bad?" or "What does this say about my brand image?" or "What are the optics?" then something might be going awry in our ability to see clearly. What we anxiously perceive as a boon for our own perceived fortunes is often bad news for friends, family, and foreign nations. Macbeth's dismissal of the possibility of regret or repentance (it's too tedious to step back through the blood he's left on the tracks) bears a disturbing resemblance to the false strength of denial, evasion, and blame that is an ever-present temptation within American culture. The pretense of omnipotence might play well in prime time, but it flies in the face of received wisdom from the Bible to Shakespeare to Tolkien.

For a more precise word of challenge against the darker impulses of an often-unacknowledged American mythology, we have an American prophet in Herman Melville. Borrowing heavily from the Bible and Shakespeare, Melville expresses ongoing skepticism about optimism concerning human intuition (Emersonian or otherwise) and seems to think that this might be where the uniquely American trouble starts. The crew of the Pequod are beginning to realize that their captain, Ahab, is tragically fixated on gaining vengeance over an animal blissfully unaware of Ahab's existence. When I behold a friend, neighbor, or family member rant against a politician, whom they've never met and with whom they will never exchange a word, and the tone and demeanor of the talk takes a turn for the apoplectic, I want to adapt Starbuck's words to whale-mad Ahab and cry, "Madness! To be enraged with a face on television seems blasphemous. What profit will thy anger yield thee? Go have a cup of coffee with thy partner or telephone thy child or dine ye with a homeless person."[13] I should add that Starbuck's words come to me self-administered. The allure of issue-driven newspeak has an alarming way of distracting me from the more needful and local concerns that could do with my attention. All too often, the siren song of electronic soul molesters (Baptist minister Will Campbell's term, which I find it helpful to apply to smartphones) draws me away from the company of actual living people.

But what makes Starbuck's rebuke especially tragic is that he hasn't told Ahab anything Ahab doesn't know. Like Macbeth, Ahab is a diligent student of his own downward spiral, and, like many Americans, he knows all is not well in his angry and weary soul. "All loveliness is anguish to me," he confesses, because, like Milton's Satan, he is damned most subtly and malignantly in the midst of paradise. And like Gollum, he can only read the world through the lens of his own covetousness: "I'm demoniac, I am madness maddened! That wild madness that's only calm to comprehend itself." If anyone feels compelled to accept my advice concerning a twenty-four-hour fast from the highly charged, hot-button words (liberal, conservative, bias, agenda) that keep us from thinking clearly, I'd also like to recommend (alongside Old and New Testament readings) chapter 37 of *Moby-Dick*, from which these phrases are drawn. Ahab feels his brain beating against what seems like the solid metal of a steel skull and imagines the path of his fixed purpose to be laid with iron rails, whereon his soul is grooved to run. Long before anyone knew what an Internet was or what the near-omnipresent sensory assault of multinational corporations on the human mind felt like, Melville penned this soliloquy concerning an iron necessity of self-seeking soul destruction, but I suspect there's a timeliness to it that strikes closer to our national psyche than we'd like to admit: "Over unsounded gorges, through the rifled hearts of mountains, under torrents' beds, unerringly I rush! Naught's an obstacle, naught's an angle to the iron way!"[14]

I CONTAIN MULTITUDES

Starting from weirded-out Nashville, where I was born, I was taught (like Ahab, Starbuck, and perhaps every American president) to view myself in some sense as an eternal soul. Haunted by the thought of what this might mean and alarmed at how cavalier most of my comrades were on the subject of eternity, I mostly associated this preoccupation with church services and that black Bible I figured I'd better read all the way through before it was too late. I don't regret my early childhood preoccupation with eternity in any way, but I know I was often tempted to view any and all life that didn't line up with my thoughts of eternity as tragically irrelevant to everything that really mattered, because all that mattered (wasn't it obvious?) was eternity.

To the extent that I began to view my passion for eternity as somehow nearer to the appropriate level of intensity than the passion levels of my peers, I suppose I fit the description of what is often termed a fundamentalist. But I don't think this habit of mind and imagination is limited to those who consider themselves religious, since demonizing the opposition appears to be what many of us fall into whenever we don't know what to do with our despair. To my thinking, it was with the presumed backing of the eternal that I passed reluctant judgment on all the interesting worldly things that, as far as I could tell, had no inheritance in the infinite. My enjoyment of the not eternally significant day-to-day was made only a little bit guilty by my suspicion that it was all going to burn. I had yet to view the Lord's Prayer as a calling of God's kingdom "on earth," and I probably viewed heaven as a little more like a netherworld or a phantom zone. This sad doctrine of unincarnate faith (mostly constructed in my own mind) began to be challenged in a high school English class when I turned in my literature book to a section called "Transcendentalism" and thought, "That's more like it."

What a word: transcendentalist. And what a thing to be. The whole thing seemed remarkably and scandalously grounded. Could I really have it both ways? Heaven and earth? Walt Whitman seemed to think so: "The SOUL: Forever and forever—longer than soil is brown and solid—longer than water ebbs and flows." And even better: "I say the whole earth, and all the stars in the sky, are for Religion's sake."[15]

Here was a poetry of new potentialities and an affirmation of what I'd begun to glimpse in the paintings of Howard Finster, what I'd already seen in particular episodes of *The Twilight Zone*, and what I thought I was hearing in the music of Suzanne Vega, Lone Justice, and R.E.M., a uniquely American mysticism I was tempted to call country music—comprehensive and curious but confident at nobody's expense. What does this have to do with the national psyche?

For one thing, it points in the direction of an alternative to the death-dealing dichotomies that drive so much best-selling, most-viewed deliberation on America, the rest of the world, and the future; an alternative to the Ahab curse that hastens America's nervous breakdown. Just as Allen Ginsberg's "Howl" will insist that all things human are somehow scandalously holy, Whitman submits, as a to-be-agreed-on basis for all speech and conversation and politics, the creed that all matter is charged with the grandeur of God; that the spiritual resides within all material (no nonspiritual, secular, or nonsouled human beings). We won't see clearly until we look humbly: "Bring all the art and science of the world, and baffle and humble it with one spear of grass."[16] As Macbeth and Ahab look upon creation, they feel mocked and anxious that life won't deliver on their mad desires or that they'll lose the ground they've insanely concluded is their own and no one else's. The affection that should have gone into treasuring the life around us, the people nearby, gets drained by our contempt for whoever's on the wrong side of our beloved issues. The beauty and complexity of the created world becomes irrelevant to our fixations. Against the blind and unreasoning rush, Whitman describes a single blade of grass as the journey-work of the stars.

I can hardly think of Whitman's insistent hopefulness without imagining the witness of Studs Terkel, whose hope for America (like Whitman's) always includes the notion of outgoing love as a moral imperative. Specifically, I recall a moment on television when Terkel was shown a copy of Nick Ut's 1972

Pulitzer Prize–winning photo of nine-year-old Kim Phuc, naked and on fire, fleeing a napalm attack. When asked what the image brought to his mind, Terkel quickly responded that this is our child, everybody's child, a moment of anguish for all people, an occasion for grief and urgent communal embrace. Our child. Not someone else's. Ours. Us. Terkel casually makes an appeal to the conservatively communal sensibility that insists on a reverencing of children, the ancient folk wisdom that says you should never walk past or look upon a child without speaking a word of blessing. And with an unmistakable degree of authority as an experienced connoisseur of American culture, Terkel seems to suggest that the meaning of America resides in our ability to say, without qualification, "Our child."

For many Americans, life is so full of persecution complex, fears of being tricked or made to feel guilty, and anxious anticipation of spin that we've come close to losing our ability to listen and look without defensiveness. We risk becoming unable to look at or speak to the world without assuming an adversarial posture, so in love with our abstractions that we can't look at human beings properly. We can hardly think of suffering children without feeling manipulated by an interest group. It doesn't have to be this way. And if we're going to engage the world without losing our souls, we won't let it be. Or as Sly and the Family Stone remind us, we're going to have to adjust our sense of self and untopple the tyranny of mad individualism, because we have to live together. We don't have to hold ourselves aloof from the troubled everybody who people our everyday. We are they. We're everyday people, and everybody is a star.

Long after I discovered Whitman in my high school years, it was pointed out to me that the Lord's Prayer isn't a call to be transported from the wicked world into unearthly, disembodied bliss but a call for God's abundance, God's shalom. It is a call to be fully manifested on earth as it already is in the heavens, a cry for regime change within a largely rebellious world that does not acknowledge its Maker in the way it treats people or regards itself. And all language, whether broadcast by entertainment conglomerates, news networks, or radio talk-show hosts and their avid listeners, is unavoidably, if unconsciously, religious. We can't speak of people or politics without speaking of the eternal. I began to remember what Fannie Lou Hamer and Dorothy Day never forgot: It's all religion, whether we like it or not. In Whitman's invocation of American ensemble (always looking to bring in all nations, "I'd sow a seed for thee of endless nationality"), a note of eschatological hope is struck.

I have no mockings or arguments, I witness and wait.[17]

Roaming in thought over the Universe, I saw the little that is Good steadily
    hastening towards immortality,
And the vast all that is call'd Evil I saw hastening to merge itself and become
    lost and dead.[18]

As the American creed of liberty and justice for all humanity takes on new and unexpected forms beyond the limitations of whatever we've settled for in the way of unequal justice and license mistaken for liberty, a vigilance against our Ahab-like mind-sets will be crucial. Religion is practice. Politics is practice. Religion is politics is what we do and how we speak and the way we think about other human beings. And America's cultural heritage is blessedly fraught with voices that won't let us forget it. Whitman's musings and Terkel's casual remark concerning the image of a child that many Americans once imagined to be an enemy of freedom are touchstones. As touchstones of Beloved Community, they can reactivate our moral imagination against our darker trends of world-as-vampire, midnight vultures, and big-fish-eat-little-one, which often portray themselves as homeland security issues, free trade, and, tragically, the American way. Fred Friendly believed there was more room for more rich conversation than we've even begun to guess and that there are myriad wise voices not yet amplified within our national life. The voices bear ample witness against the myopic moralism that falls so short of our more comprehensive, compassionate best. Do we have the ears to hear? Do we want to?

Chapter 3

Everybody Hurts

There is no time for despair, no place for self-pity, no need for silence, no room for fear. We speak, we write, we do language. That is how civilizations heal.

—Toni Morrison

They all hate and they never stop. They never get tired of it.

—Carrie White in Stephen King's *Carrie*

A little too much anger, too often or at the wrong time, can destroy more than you would ever imagine.

—Jonathan Ames in Marilynne Robinson's *Gilead*

In her memoir, *Why Be Happy When You Could Be Normal?*, Jeanette Winterson describes the asylum she found, as a traumatized child, in books. Her pantheon of elders came to be a collective of literary figures turned peers turned people who had been through it all, deep divers who offered words for what she was going through, words next to which she was more than free to place her own: "A tough life needs a tough language—and that is what poetry is. That is what literature offers—a language powerful enough to say how it is. It isn't a hiding place. It is a finding place."[1]

Like all the voices I mean to amplify in these pages, the wordsmiths we'll consider in this chapter come to me as a kind of miracle of finding, of coming out of hiding, of investigative heft. If the classic text is the text that never stops saying what it has to say, everything that follows, to my mind, qualifies. They come to our aid in our heady present, tough resources for tough times, rivers, it seems to me, of living water for anyone who hopes to try their hand at lived consciousness.

On the subject of the new day dawning all around him, Ralph Waldo Emerson noted the presence of something strange in the neighborhood when he observed, "It is said to be the age of the first person singular."[2] The "Our Father" would become "My Father"; a turn inward was becoming possible for more and more people; and a once rare dogma (political? religious?) was gaining ground, what Emerson called "the infinitude of the private man."[3] Emerson didn't invent American individualism any more than Martin Luther founded the notion of church reform. But just as Luther expressed regret over how calling into question the teachings of one particular pope sent shock waves that left many a man on many a dunghill in Germany fancying himself his own pope, I can imagine Emerson scratching his head over where we landed with the evasions we've come to credit and how they've yielded, with alarming exactness, a white-supremacist president addressing NATO on our behalf by assuring the world of his own "very stable genius." We, the people, have reaped the whirlwind of this psychic breakdown. We know the mental health hazards of sitting alone in front of a television trying to believe in yourself, and the trite language with which many Americans attempt to explain their moral deficiencies: "I'm so sorry you feel that way," "I regret that you misunderstood me," "I apologize if you were offended," and "I'm sorry that people seeing those pictures didn't understand the true nature and heart of America."

Strange days when requests for forgiveness are substituted with statements of regret over wrong impressions. I think of the mogul of all matter on *The Simpsons*, Montgomery C. Burns, and his determination to own all media outlets for the sake of self-image: "Well, I'm going to change this town's accurate impression of me."[4] If all we really regret is someone's ability to deduce who we are, is there any soul left to forfeit?

The language of confession in the drama of self, of actually repenting of one's sins of spin and misperception, is replaced by the strange concept of expressing regret that someone failed in his or her attempt to understand your true nature, your true heart, and how your words and actions bear no relation to your pristine, true, only-selfless-intentioned and pure self ("Mistakes were made"). Sorry about that and only that. Admittedly, Emerson didn't create this phenomenon or a mass-media culture that recognizes the above instances of self-abusing language as "formal apologies." I bring Emerson into the proceedings only to suggest that these trends have been with us for some time and that the madness of the moment has been prepared for. One can look askance at Emerson's belief that the sincere and simple man who worships God somehow becomes God (the tyranny of sincerity?) without losing Toni Cade Bambara's suspicion that we're all clairvoyants deep down, though occasionally suffering a delusion or two on account of our estrangement from our own intuition.

In F. O. Matthiessen's magisterial study *American Renaissance*, we're told that Emerson, Hawthorne, Thoreau, Whitman, and Melville self-consciously composed literature for democracy and hoped to help build "a culture commensurate with America's political opportunity."[5] Pretty fly for a monolithic tradition of five white guys. But as is always the case with whatever we come to call tradition, we're free to complicate, reckon with, and recognize the always-already-there complexity of what's been handed down, alive to what's been lost and cut off, namely, in Toni Morrison's phrase, "the breath of the disremembered and unaccounted for."[6]

Taking on the crucial work of complexifying our perceived continuums, W. E. B. DuBois once struck a note concerning the comprehensive souls he heard speaking to him across the construct of the color line; voices, let the record show, that are *with him* (or shall be made to be with him) on whatever subject arises: "I sit with Shakespeare and he winces not. Across the color line I move arm in arm with Balzac and Dumas, where smiling men and women glide in gilded halls. . . . I summon Aristotle and Aurelius and what soul I will, and they come all graciously with no scorn or condescension."[7] In what was then considered, from a white-supremacist angle, a scandalously inappropriate move, DuBois here offers his own work as an essential and equal part of an extended hurray of what came before in a lineage of ostensibly white bearers of wisdom and grace. We get to choose our forebears and locate our own voice among them in whatever way we please.

We are each perfectly free to access and celebrate the clairvoyance of others (obscured or open air) wherever we find it and to make of it what we will, voices to whom we feel compelled to remain repeatedly and repentantly attuned. I was once given a way of naming this assemblage of thoughtfulness by a mentor, Rahim Buford, as we read Wendell Berry together. Feeling peculiarly schooled by one of Berry's insights, Rahim exclaimed that Berry had just now entered his consciousness with a new pride of place: "He's up there with Tupac Shakur and Ursula K. Le Guin now, in my *pantheon of elders.*"

By conceiving our thinking, speaking, and acting in this way, our own media consumption can take the form of fellowship with a great cloud of witnesses, an ever-growing sense of, you guessed it, Beloved Community. We can spy, share, and draw upon literature that equips democratic culture against the clear and present danger of a culture of deception, voices that might serve as a sanity-restoring, soul-saving supplement to the average American's media diet; some forgotten transmissions that might tell better stories of adultery, severe domestic dysfunction, and demon possession than what we've grown accustomed to calling entertainment. The works that marketeers classify as "literary classics" sometimes feel like a harder pill than popular music, movies, and television series, but they await us as records of someone else's acts of conscience. We need them badly. We need content that will help our words (freedom, love, terror, mercy, evil, forgiveness, democracy) regain their heft. When they lose their heft, we're tools for whatever contagion best suits the stratagems of the prospering wicked. We lose the ability to question someone else's abstractions, and we're left with little means to learn or understand better stories than whatever seems to suit our anxious projections of ourselves. But a pantheon of elders is there for each of us if we're looking hard enough. And it is there in spades.

UNCLOSE YOUR EYES

A more knowing consideration of our own pantheon of elders (everybody has one) and a willingness to add, remove, or bring them into better conversations with one another can break us out of self-absorption and the tyranny of toxic voices by which we're otherwise unduly swayed. There is all manner of mental work to be done, and, as a master of the warping thought, Nathaniel Hawthorne creates the impression that he would worry less if he thought we were worrying enough over what we make of ourselves and others in our teeming brains. He helped forge an American literature that treads firmly on the ground, but he did so by portraying the way we're prone to project, painting pictures of ourselves and others that we conjure and then mistake for realities. His characters have a difficult time reaching past their images of each other to communicate or achieve anything in the way of intimacy. They have to remind themselves that life is infinitely larger than all their well-meant formulations and tightly held suspicions. They're all spooked in one way or another, and it seems clear that Hawthorne told these stories in an effort to, in some fashion, unspook himself.

There is a sealed-off, endlessly defensive sense of self that can easily become a habit of mind (to be resisted daily) and, in turn, a morbid vanity that makes of our reactive thinking, to borrow a military term, an antipersonnel weapon. Sensitive souls estranged from most forms of community can come to project their own chaos on any and everyone. As is the case for many American writers, getting this process down on paper appears to be one way Hawthorne devised of raging against the dying of the light.

In *Twice-Told Tales*, Hawthorne manages to prognosticate in the direction of the mad mind-set (Macbeth, Ahab, Trump) discussed in the previous chapter. In a strange meditation called "The Haunted Mind," he describes the sensation of being "wide awake in a realm of illusions . . . an intermediate space, where the business of life does not intrude."[8] And in an odd premonition of the sensation of taking in (or being taken in by) a popular news feed, he imagines a state in which "the mind has a passive sensibility, but no active strength: when the imagination is a mirror, imparting vividness to all ideas, without the power of selecting or controlling them."[9] The mind is left with no active strength to select, control, or properly discern the increasingly vivid ideas that come to it. And as "things of the mind become dim spectres to the eye,"[10] we're left to search desperately for whatever might remind us of the living world and whatever version of events might make our existence feel meaningful again.

Most maddening of all, we tend to mistake these dim spectres for true sight and our emotional intensity for weighty truths. This is where Hawthorne offers both a reforming word to the less admirable habits of thought among his Puritan forebears and a corrective to our contemporary confusing of blissed-out moments of emotional intensity for stairways to heaven. When we say "God," "truth," "America," or "liberty," we do well to remain open to people who might ask us to elaborate. Otherwise, we burn witches, wage war, or allow Vladimir Putin's mind-control app to tell us how to feel about people of color confronting state violence in Ferguson. Discerning between what's true and our momentary, multiplying delusions will involve no easy shortcuts.

As we can see, Hawthorne shared with Melville a contempt for easy abstractions. Words had to put on flesh. In a letter to Hawthorne, Melville remarked, "As soon as you say Me, a God, a Nature, so soon you jump off from your stool and hang from the beam. Yes, that word is the hangman. Take God out of the dictionary, and you would have Him in the street."[11] Wisdom will involve knowing that our signifiers do not equal the eternal absolute, and holding on to the blessed dirty and watery earth (amid the images, slogans, and dim spectres) will require the ongoing recognition that we're strangely drawn to easy untruth much of the time. The danger of taking one's blind fervor for divine illumination was inextricably bound to the ancestry of these men, and faithfulness would require moving forward, praying for improved DNA. In a letter to Melville, Hawthorne writes, "Let us thank God for having given us such ancestors; and let each successive generation thank Him, not less fervently, for being one step further from them in the march of ages."[12]

We should note the remarkably prescient understanding of history and human grasp of the divine as Hawthorne expresses the hope that future generations will thank God for their distance from the grim delusions of his own. Like Bambara and Flannery O'Connor, Hawthorne and Melville were troubled by haunted minds that deemed themselves unhaunted and by the belief that truth is easily accessible to any reasoning person's assent in an unembodied, unincarnate sphere of theological theory (Puritan or transcendentalist). As students of the Bible, Hawthorne and Melville understood that goodness and decency are stranger matters than most admit, and a culture of the people, for the people, and by the people would require looking at people and their actions as more paradoxical than grandiloquent generalizations and deadly abstractions allow. Telling it like it is and not how our vanity would like it to be (what Melville called "the usable truth") can open eyes to God in the street, the neighbor next door, and the never-uninteresting everybody. Within Beloved Community, we're all potential learners of our own clairvoyance, and fiction can tease us back into this tension. Melville observed, "It is with fiction as with religion; it should present another world, and yet one to which we feel the tie."[13] Understanding and trying to do good within one's present will be to partake in a muddy mystery.

Fiction reminds us that we don't know what we're doing. In an echo of Lincoln's thoughts on God's will and human passions, Hawthorne noted, "His instruments have no consciousness of His purpose; if they imagine they have, it is a pretty sure token they are not His instruments."[14]

LET THE BLACK FLOWER BLOSSOM

Hawthorne's world is awash in histories, resentments, misunderstandings, obsessions, and hopes through (and in spite of) which God is somehow allegedly at work. This is the atmosphere of phantasmagoric forms in which Hawthorne's characters live out their existence. He understands that disengaging ourselves from our worst imaginings—the theater of envy that makes real truthfulness, genuine generosity, and actual community next to impossible—will be a journey down a narrow path. Hawthorne worked in the days before mass media and the broadband that leads to destruction. But it might be appropriate to apply the wisdom of Hawthorne's tale of adultery and unforgiveness, *The Scarlet Letter*, to our own strange days.

The ideas that fester within aggrieved husband Roger Chillingworth aren't exactly thoughts or arguments, but they are definitely passions, and his raging, vengeful pride can possess him utterly while also, Hawthorne wryly notes, passing for a kind of calmness. He can be filled top to toe with direst cruelty, with writhing horror twisting across his features, dead without knowing it, but remarkably in control. His smiles of "dark and self-relying intelligence"[15] will come off as the most professional, upright expressions of a man in possession of himself while Hester Prynne, his estranged, legal wife, will correctly spy within him a man committed to the formal ruin, consecutive and slow, of his own soul.

Somehow, as the possessor of that ignominious brand, the scarlet *A*, Hester has developed a talent, not for seeing dead people, but for feeling the glance of every self-deceived, downward-spiral-bound, closet degenerate in view, namely, everyone around her at one time or another. She is blessed or cursed with a strange sympathy, because if truth were made fully known, the scarlet letter would blaze on many a bosom. Freed from the perfunctory practice of putting on the appearance of righteousness, Hester can see and feel everything, and, for all of her suffering, it is the most awful and loathsome aspect of her existence. When in the company of the community's supposed moral pillars, whom her society views as "mortal man in fellowship with angels," Hester is moved to ask herself, "What evil thing is at hand?" (61). She knows that the electricity is all wrong.

Against the airtight mythology of respectability and moral superiority that often seizes white-supremacist communities, Hawthorne's vision of a pre-1776 America is like a jeremiad, within which Hester sees in every face a sociopath. But unlike Hawthorne's Young Goodman Brown, for whom all humans in view will now undergo a witch trial in his deranged head (contemporary popular discourse in America?), Hester will work tremblingly toward moral enlightenment and a vocation as an especially sympathetic sister of mercy: "This badge hath taught me,—it daily teaches me,—it is teaching me at this moment" (76). She comes to understand that nobody is in a position to cast the first stone, and she's liberated by the insight.

Like many a preacher, priest, or politician whose livelihood involves portraying oneself as a professional good and decent person, Arthur Dimmesdale, the secret father of Hester's child, longs to cry out to his parishioners, "I, your pastor, whom you so reverence and trust, am utterly a pollution and a lie!" (99). But apart from the obligatory "humble, unworthy sinner" talk of a modest man (what Hawthorne calls "a remorseful hypocrite") and his standing on the scaffold in the middle of the night, hands joined with Hester and their child, Pearl, Dimmesdale's role as "a professional teacher of truth" repeatedly compels him to defer a public focus on his family till judgment day. Noting his unwillingness to live up to his convictions, Pearl laughs at him, informing him, as if he needed reminding, that he is neither bold nor true.

Today Dimmesdale might be shown (via video camera) waiting while a daytime television host opens an envelope to reveal Pearl's lineage to a studio audience as Hester weeps and Chillingworth rages. We have here a stressful scenario that we couldn't call too terribly uncommon. Chillingworth's vulnerability to certain madness is exactly proportional to his willingness to occupy the role of the accuser in the seat of judgment in a spiral of shame and sadness. Hawthorne says of Chillingworth, "A striking evidence of man's faculty of transforming himself into a devil, if he will only, for a reasonable space of time, undertake a devil's office" (116). When Hester urges him to leave off his harassment of Dimmesdale, he speaks as a bitter spectator determined to see his own rot and ruin spread like a contagion: "Let the black flower blossom as it may." (144).

The two men are thereby locked in a cycle of escalating hypocrisy that won't release them unless they own up to themselves. Dimmesdale's thought life is a "constant introspection wherewith he tortured, but could not purify himself" (100). Hester Prynne, meanwhile, is submitted as an apostle of coming revelation (fit for democracy) bearing witness within a hostile, uncomprehending, bewitched community. A moral that saves but might seem risky when it comes to optics and platforms: "Be true! Be true! Be true! Show freely to the world, if not your worst, yet some trait whereby the worst may be inferred" (175). Timely words for a culture with the occasional puritanical tendency and an unfortunate habit of prizing projection and accusation as the primary skill set of pastors, pundits, and elected officials. *The Scarlet Letter* admonishes us toward a costly transparency and humility of mind required for any community that wants to avoid destroying itself from within.

THAT MULTIFORM PILGRIM SPECIES, MAN

In his praise of Hawthorne (to whom he dedicated *Moby-Dick*), Melville counted him among "those writers who breathe that unshackled, democratic spirit of Christianity in all things."[16] Returning for a moment to the imagery of time lines and continuums, I can't help but think of Melville as the figure who most forcefully brings the imaginations of Shakespeare and William Blake to bear on the Declaration of Independence, claiming them on behalf of his understanding of liberty for all. Melville presumes that Christianity, properly understood, is unfailingly pro-human. Dissecting human freedom how he may, Melville knows he only goes skin-deep, and the awe he feels toward his predecessors' ways with words only invigorates further his sense of the possibilities of freer and truer expression. All eloquence is borrowed, after all: "All that has been said but multiplies the avenues to what remains to be said."[17]

Just as Hawthorne ran counter to the dominant impulses of his age by making an adulteress the voice of prophetic witness, Melville takes boundless sympathy toward all human forms to be a biblical (and democratic) imperative. Beginning *Moby-Dick* by way of a bold self-identification with a Muslim prophet and patriarch many in his audience would presume to be eternally cast off from the covenant ("Call me Ishmael"), our narrator begins with a more magnanimous eye than his readers would be prepared for. He is called to see God's image in the face of the tattooed cannibal, the meanest of mariners and castaways, and whatever passes for "the least of these." The goodness of God toward each of God's far-flung children founds democracy by decreeing God's image in any and every human dress:

> This august divinity I treat of, is not the dignity of kings and robes, but that abounding dignity which has no robed investiture. Thou shalt see it shining in the arm that wields a pick or drives a spike; that democratic dignity which, on all hands, radiates without end from God; Himself! the great God absolute! The centre and circumference of all democracy! His omnipresence, our divine equality.[18]

God illumined "the swart convict, Bunyan" and lifted "the stumped and paupered arm of Cervantes," and now Melville (call him Ishmael) prays that the same bardic grace will surround his sympathetic portrayals of his disreputable cast: "Bear me out in it, thou great democratic God!" (104). As John Milton invoked the heavenly muse that once inspired Moses to show him how to justify the ways of God to men, Ishmael wants to make the world safer for democracy by witnessing God's comprehensive purposes (more mysterious than we can know) as he explores strange new worlds and seeks out new life forms and new civilizations. The unknown is neither strange nor new for Melville's democratic God ("the magnanimous God of heaven and earth—pagans and all included" [57]), and if this is so, perhaps we need not be so squeamish or xenophobic nor so quick to assume ourselves somehow already sufficiently converted to the ways of the Almighty. Perhaps the dignity that radiates without end from God extends to those we've heretofore deemed beneath our interest.

With an everlasting itch for things remote and the belief that "ignorance is the parent of fear" (34), Ishmael dismisses as most demonic of all the fastidiousness that would make of the stranger a demon and the cry of "Heathen!" a satanic obstruction to the only salvation anyone can know: the lifelong extension of neighbor love. Concerning the cannibal Queequeg he says, "The man's a human being just as I am: he has just as much reason to fear me, as I have to be afraid of him" (36). What a profoundly righteous sensibility. Gold, heredity, nationalism, and pride of place are the instrumentalities Hawthorne would refer to as "the big, heavy, solid unrealities"[19] that keep us from thinking properly of one another as children of God and fellow world citizens. These are idols to which Ishmael will not bow down. And between Queequeg and Ahab we can note myriad ways that one can go about worshiping that which, by nature, is not a god.

As a sailor, Ishmael will dutifully follow his orders, but with a mind toward a great reversal that, now and later, can put present anxieties in perspective: "What does that indignity amount to, I mean, in the scales of the New Testament?" He trusts that bosses won't be bosses forever. And given the biblical word on the last and the first and the manner in which the unrealities jerk a person about like a mixed-up marionette, Ishmael rhetorically asks, "Who ain't a slave?"[20]

The questions of freedom, savagery, civilization, authority, and reading reality rightly haunt Ishmael at every turn. Ahab moves his arm up and down and wonders aloud if it is he or omnipotent God who wills it. And in another Lincolnian turn, Ishmael hears a sermon before the voyage begins as a certain Father Mapple expounds upon the story of Jonah with the qualifier "I have read ye by what murky light may be mine," as he calls upon his congregation to stand against "the proud gods and commodores of the earth" (53, 54).

Warned against the idolatries that delude human thinking, Ishmael begins to have notions that would scandalize the commonplaces of his day when, for instance, he looks upon the face of a sleeping Queequeg and is oddly reminded of the popular busts of George Washington's head. Ishmael assures us that he was raised as a normal, self-respecting Presbyterian, but his constructs are slightly undone by the likes of Queequeg, who seems to possess "a nature in which there lurked no civilized hypocrisies and bland deceits." Daring to sense God's affection for an infidel who suddenly strikes him as somehow quintessentially American, he feels as if a burning coal has made new his unclean lips:

"I felt a melting in me. No more my splintered heart and maddened hand were turned against the wolfish world. This soothing savage had redeemed it" (56).

At the risk of digression, somewhere between Ishmael's renunciation of the militant ignorance of white supremacy and Studs Terkel's affirmation of "our child," I'd like to recall a moment on 1950s-era American television when Steve Allen asked Jack Kerouac for a definition of the term "Beat." Almost before he'd finished the question, Kerouac responded, "Sympathetic." If I read it rightly, the posture of the Beat moment is one of mutual beatenness before the world, and to feel worn down, tempted toward melancholy but not despairing, to be heartbroken in the direction of increased sympathy for all creation groaning and awaiting redemption. And if the alternative to this brand of beatitude is unsympathetic posture, uncompassionate and not prone to solidarity, then the venom with which a Kerouac, in his context, says a word like "Square" seems pretty well justified. Right up there with "hypocrites," "blind guides," "fascist," and "brood of vipers."

Ishmael, meanwhile, looks upon Queequeg and is seized by the revelation that he's just like everyone else. Ishmael speaks forth an acknowledgment of democratic dignity, perceiving an individual conscience equal to his own. Really believing as much is to come upon an antidote to the tyranny of our maddened hands. The clichéd quality of the insight risks becoming so commonplace that we lose the sense of the costly moral epiphany it was and is to suggest such a thing. Like the beleaguered heart of Dimmesdale, this insight concerning the mystical unity of human being comes to us from a couple of centuries ago. Are we ready to receive it today?

They're like us. Beloved Community sees the neighbor in every face. From Queequeg to Vietnam to Baghdad, do we see ourselves in these images? Does it slow us down? Is our royal "we" larger than our political party or our national borders? Do we sense solidarity out there? Do we really want democratic revolution, or are we preparing to pull up the drawbridge? Are we squares or are we Americans? I believe this moment in *Moby-Dick* exists along a trajectory with Bambara's vision of mutual clairvoyance, DuBois seeing himself next to Shakespeare, Terkel in kinship with a child in a photograph, and the daily epiphanies whereby people see themselves in others. We can sense here the immense responsibility of being and knowing oneself to be a human being among other human beings over and over again.

Ishmael is quick to recognize his own "maddened hand" assuming a destructively adversarial posture in "the wolfish world." There is a distempered spirit, easily discerned in Ahab and in so much discourse in our own day. The mind so possessed will not see, because it does not feel. This is the opposite of the disposition (Beat, sympathetic, slow to judgment) that Ishmael assumes in the telling of his story. He'd prayed that God would bear him out in his storytelling concerning the august divinity of humankind, and in *Moby-Dick*, Melville's unprecedentedly American and radically magnanimous voice would gain an audience and gradual vindication as it played progenitor to various humane sensibilities we now take for granted. We still haven't gotten to the bottom of it.

ALIKE IN IGNORANCE

What will not do, for this strand of Beloved Community's truth telling under the gaze of a God who radiates dignity without end, is to hold oneself aloof from the only-seeing-in-part communion of the all-having-sinned-and-fallen-short sainthood. This is not a problem for Ishmael. He looks at people (from Queequeg to Ahab) and creation itself as not-to-be-conquered mysteries, and he has no problem with the we-only-know-in-part part of the biblical witness. In continuity with the pantheon of elders I have in mind, he proclaims, "Heaven have mercy on us all—Presbyterians and Pagans alike—for we are all somehow dreadfully cracked about the head, and sadly need mending" (79). His is a most comprehensive soul, and when Captain Bildad (part owner of the Pequod with Captain Peleg) seems inclined to deny Queequeg employment on account of his failure to be a member of a Christian church, Ishmael explains that, on the contrary, Queequeg's a practicing member of the First Congregational Church. What church is this? Ishmael explains:

> I mean, sir, the same ancient Catholic Church to which you and I, and Captain Peleg there, and Queequeg here, and all of us, and every mother's son and soul of us belong; the great and everlasting First Congregation of this whole worshipping world; we all belong to that; only some of us cherish some queer crotchets noways touching the grand belief; in that we all join hands. (98)

Bildad catches his drift: "I never heard a better sermon." We all worship in one way or another (as the apostle Paul observed in conversation with the Athenians in Acts), and in our efforts to worship well, we all hold a screwy doctrine or two that will burn away like chaff when the real thing comes. In this variously dissembling silliness we can all join hands in strict solidarity, a creed worthy of Beloved Community's *koinonia*, a "heaven have mercy on us all" with which we're perfectly free to color all our speech.

Ishmael's improvised justification for a more hospitable reception for the outsider is characteristic of the vocation Melville will ply for the sake of a healthier democracy and a less self-deluding religiosity. Ishmael's speech is frank and free and exemplary as an idiom counter to the Ahab-like megalomania that loudly offers itself from time to time as the real America, tarnishing our better broadcasts throughout history. We need the idiom like we need a more tragic orientation in our talk of truth and victory and guarantees, an idiom better suited to a patchwork nation built by captives, asylum seekers, and indigenous people still waiting to be afforded the opportunity to welcome outsiders—a nation at its best when pressing forward to better ways of being human in a land of and for the free.

Alike in ignorance, whether thinking too little or too much, the humanity aboard the Pequod exhibits the dark wisdom and rude brilliance that Ishmael sees in every human face. But the biblical witness that mocks any and all supposed human grandeur profoundly informs Ishmael's study of man and beast: "There is no folly of the beasts of the earth which is not infinitely outdone by the madness of men" (300). A troubled and conscientious awareness of human folly is a prerequisite for truthful speech and sane imaginings, and in this regard, Jesus, the Man of Sorrows, is, by Ishmael's lights, the truest of all men. Immersed in the Beatitudes, Ishmael aspires toward the blessedness of downward mobility while viewing its opposite as a sickness unto death: "All men tragically great are made so through a certain morbidness. Be sure of this, O young ambition, all mortal greatness is but disease" (74).

Presuming that oneself possesses an absolutely clear head or is an anointed knower of good and evil is a genuine threat to democracy and the surest means of being used for wrong and becoming useless for right. This is the self-enclosed imagination of Ahab, mistaking his impulsiveness for integrity, staying the course toward self-destruction:

> The white whale swam before him as the monomaniac incarnation of all those malicious agencies which some deep men feel eating in them, till they are left living on with half a heart and half a lung.
> . . . All that most maddens and torments; all that stirs up the lees of things; all truth with malice in it; all that cracks the sinews and cakes the brain; all the subtle demonisms of life and thought; all evil, to crazy Ahab, were visibly personified, and made practically assailable in Moby-Dick. (156)

There's a mad simplicity in Ahab's war on terror. It's the evil originating, as all evil does, in the determination to eliminate evil. It would be straightforward enough if all human malice could be conveniently contained in one man, one nation, one terrorist network, or one white whale forever personified outside the self. But "the face of evil," for all its best-selling simplicity, doesn't actually work that way, and neither evil nor terror are "practically assailable." As an obsessive student of the Bible and Shakespeare, Melville could not imagine otherwise. And like Hawthorne, he understood that hardly anything is more dangerous than a closed and self-satisfied understanding of the Almighty, freedom, good, or evil. To suggest for the cameras or for one's sense of self or for the sake of consumer confidence that evil is out there, before us in plain view, unrelated to our own history, waiting to be eradicated, is to indulge the speech of the plainly deranged. To evade, in any way, the mendacity that often appears to be the native language of humanity will require awareness of this fevered ignorance that inspires our fearful talk and electrifies, here and there, a voter base.

I'LL TICKLE YOUR CATASTROPHE

Following the commercial disaster of *Moby-Dick* and the even poorer sales of *Pierre*, Melville delivered an elaborate allegory on the various species of insanity that vie for the position of status quo in American culture. Increasingly estranged from the popular reception that might make writing for a living a possibility, Melville let it all fly in *The Confidence Man*, which features Satan in St. Louis boarding the steamboat *Fidele* (Faithful) bound for New Orleans on April Fools' Day. While the Prince of Darkness plays the confidence man (con man) most aptly, his masquerade only serves to expose the variations of American faith as lesser forms of confidence selling. As a shape-shifter, he changes identity and engages passengers in conversation while representing (or referring to) American optimism, transcendentalism, professional salesmen of Christian faith (do you know Him?), and Indian-haters. Reading the novel can be a deeply disconcerting experience, because it becomes difficult to remember with whom Satan last spoke while trying to keep hold of which of the conversation partners (changing from chapter to chapter) is the devil. Somehow this seems strangely appropriate.

Within an egocentric and vulnerable American culture, inspiring confidence (or faith in one's faith) is slowly unmasked as the devil's primary weapon of mass destruction. The faith that is its own justification leads to the violence that believes itself to be liberation and righteousness and always in the service of virtue. Melville dedicates the work "to victims of Auto da Fe,"[21] and the reader will come to understand that confidence (or faith) that is its own referent is inevitably demonic, as victims of mob fury, inquisition, or the scapegoat mechanism will understand all too well. This confidence sucks young blood and worships nothing so much as its own appetite, an appetite that all too often will be directed by the highest-bidding media presentation, rarely going broke by appealing to the herd instinct and never wavering from the carefully scripted logic of a long con.

The complexity of the prose is such that you can't help but wonder if Melville has already given up hoping that America will receive his prophetic word. To be genuinely faithful to the biblical witness, America will have to temper its egoism with a tragic sensibility and a vigilance against self-delusion lest evil thrive, as evil will, unrecognized. Melville anticipated the catastrophes to come and the ways in which an uncritical and unironic sense of our own motivations can engender a deceptive and destructive self-righteousness. He warns against the storytellers' temptation to somehow tidy up complex realities to tickle the readers' (or viewers') ears. Image consultants beware.

When Melville, the narrator, steps out from behind the curtain in *The Confidence Man*, he reminds us that reality is hardly done justice by tidying efforts and that a story too tidy is probably, if we haven't already guessed, good news for Satan's kingdom: "That fiction, where every character can, by reason of its consistency, be comprehended at a glance, either exhibits but sections of character, making them appear for wholes, or else is very untrue to reality."[22] Just in case we need reminding, being untrue to reality and the complexity of actual life is what propaganda is for—lest we think Melville is simply praising his own incoherence. He is a lover of wisdom who demonstrates that love by knocking down any talk of truth as less than altogether unfathomable, even if this will require making a moral of the devil himself. Telling it like it is concerning God and humans will include descriptions of the deeply paradoxical and troubling: "No writer has produced such inconsistent characters as nature herself has."[23]

Television is impatient. The camera lies. And the sound bite, like the headline and the folk ballad, develops in response to the market's demand for information in a particular, digestible form. But the great novelist, like the prophet, reminds us that something is rotten with our abstractions and that a God whose wholeness is presumably grasped by a pamphlet, a formula, a commercial, or a pop song is a false god. And when a human being (the bearer of infinite mystery according to the biblical tradition) is summed up by a photo, a bad moment, or a phrase, the essential life of said individual has been slain. To remind us of the meaning of the psalmist's phrase "fearfully and wonderfully made" (Ps. 139:14), Melville brings in the example of the duck-billed beaver (a stumbling block to naturalists of his time) and reminds us that the waters of human nature can be readily seen through things that aren't human at all:

> Upon the whole, it might rather be thought, that he, who, in view of its inconsistencies, says of human nature the same that, in view of its contrasts, is said of the divine nature, that it is past finding out, thereby evinces a better appreciation of it than he who, by always representing it in a clear light, leaves it to be inferred that he clearly knows all about it.[24]

Of God and humanity we must not, according to Melville, present ourselves as (or worse, believe ourselves to be) authorities. And to return to Chesterton's observation of America's possibly insane creed, deluding ourselves in this regard, buying the propaganda of collateral damage, "with us or against us," or whatever reductionism serves to justify dehumanization, is unbiblical, unpatriotic, and unworthy of the American creed. Mad Melville felt compelled to compose a stranger fiction than his contemporaries wanted, but in our day we can receive his testimony on deluding devils, demon possession, and the moral necessity of admitting our bewilderment as an arsenal for democracy. Where there is no bewilderment, we might say, there is no humility, and without humility there can be no understanding, no empathy, and neither liberty nor justice for any.

DUST AND DESIRE

When asked what book (if any) he wished he'd written, William Faulkner didn't hesitate to name *Moby-Dick*. Faulkner understood that any literature of the human heart in conflict with itself will be revelatory and, therefore, strange. His work will appear willfully incoherent and odd to minds increasingly unaccustomed to the pleasure of listening to lengthy stories, explanations, arguments, or poetry and increasingly drawn to angry people on television and radio who are paid to wave away complexity in whatever tidying-up manner will keep the most people watching and listening. But the tidying-up impulse can prove toxic, and being true to Beloved Community will require familiarizing ourselves anew (or even for the first time) with the ancient wisdom regularly preempted by the sound and fury of the present. As an aspiring resource or vessel for such wisdom, providing a counterwitness to the present age, Faulkner hoped to, in his words, "scratch the face of the supreme Obliteration and leave a decipherable scar of some sort."[25]

Repeatedly, the wisdom that illuminates Faulkner's haunted American South is the wisdom of America's displaced people. In his appendix to *The Sound and the Fury*, tracing the fortunes of the Compson family into the twentieth century, he begins with Ikkemotubbe ("A dispossessed American king") whom he describes as possessing cleverness and self-awareness in equal parts."[26] A determined, unsparing mindfulness toward one's own intentions, justifications, and troubled inheritance is more than most of Faulkner's characters seem willing to muster, but even those who do, like Ike McCaslin (the protagonist of *Go Down, Moses*, who comes to view Sam Fathers, Ikkemotubbe's descendant, as his mentor), also understand that such mindfulness is rarely articulate: "The heart don't always have time to bother with thinking up words that fit together."[27]

Halfway through *Absalom, Absalom*, Quentin Compson of Mississippi recalls (in his head) the demands of his Harvard roommate, Shreve McCannon: "*Tell about the South. What's it like there. What do they do there. Why do they live there. Why do they live at all.*"[28] It is here in the middle that the novel, reading already like an immersion in thick, muddy mystery, almost absentmindedly recognizes itself as, among other things, one answer to a specific request in the room of a dormitory. Faulkner tells of Compson's hearing tell of Yoknapatawphan legend Thomas Sutpen, but as it proceeds, Compson is doing the telling, and the listening ear moves between Massachusetts and Mississippi in such a hypnotic way that, as one narrator observes, "you cannot know yet whether what you see is what you are looking at or what you are believing."[29] As Faulkner puts down this sort of thing on nearly every page, we have to remind ourselves that he isn't looking to dispense Zen koans or take a turn for the deliberately obscure. He's being descriptive. He's telling about the South and the difficulties of telling and remembering well. And like Shakespeare, his descriptions will often anticipate more than psychology, media studies, and market research have dreamt of in their philosophies.

Faulkner's narrators are free to philosophize over their misperceptions, skewed motivations, and the continuities of consciousness they've inherited from other people's stories, explanations, and professions. Nobody gets to get over anybody else, and they're at their worst and most hopeless when they honestly think they can. They're too haunted by one another ever to be free of one another's sayings, mottos, and biblical interpretations. Rearranging our mental furniture to improve our pasts, bettering posterity, and honoring ancestors by simultaneously pushing past their mistaken notions can be a tragically complicated business, but Faulkner's characters are doomed to try anyway. And if his account of our psychological plight is trustworthy, it's made all the more complicated as we appear to be, all of us, fixated on a white whale or two and shamefully self-conscious much of the time. Sizing up the people we've known and loved or hated might be an inevitable habit of the heart, but sitting in the seat of judgment while trying to make sense of ourselves can prove to be a damnation all its own. Our minds can't bear the strain. As Cash Bundren of *As I Lay Dying* remarks, "I ain't so sho that ere a man has the right to say what is crazy and what ain't. It's like there was a fellow in every man that's done apast the sanity or the insanity, that watches the sane and the insane doings of man with the same horror and the same astonishment."[30] Not a bad summation of the clairvoyance Bambara imagines is common to us all.

In this, Faulkner is a master of what we've come to call the internal monologue, but we have to remind ourselves that the teeming brain was and is *witnessed*, not invented, by our great wordsmiths. We may have little or no love for Patti Smith, Virginia Woolf, or *Notes from Underground*, but we probably protest too much if we dismiss it all as irrelevant or utterly unlike anything going on in our own heads. We're all stream of consciousness now. And given our proneness to judgment, we could do with the occasional vision or descriptive word on how we arrive at what we make of ourselves and each other. As Faulkner writes in *Light in August*, "man knows so little about his fellows. In his eyes all men or women act upon what he believes would motivate him if he were mad enough to do what that other man or woman is doing."[31] In a better world, we might have Faulkner's truisms scrolling along the bottom of our screens or inscribed on plaques inside the Pentagon. In the meantime, I'd like to offer Faulkner as an American sage who can assist us in the difficult but essential task of *thinking about our thinking*.

As Melville and Hawthorne demonstrate amply, our projections take on lives of their own apart from the facts on the ground (whether foreign or domestic), and our feverish desires build their own rationale into fixed explanatory grids that are difficult to overcome or imagine our way out of. In Faulkner's fiction, words from the ancient and recent pasts construct these fortresses of solitude in his characters' minds, but they can also liberate, bodying forth lamentation and longing otherwise left unarticulated. In Beloved Community, looking hard at our speech and the actions it effects is an ongoing work of moral discernment never unrelated to stories we tell ourselves. In *As I Lay Dying*, Addie Bundren thinks back on the words that marked and preceded the turns and twists of her life and, in a mesmerized fashion, notes, "I would think how words go straight up in a thin line, quick and harmless, and how terribly doing goes along the earth, clinging to it."[32] Melodramatic words and rhetoric are almost inevitably made flesh, in some form or fashion, and Faulkner's talk about talk is a national treasure for the moral development that only comes with a humble determination to watch our language.

EACH IN ITS ORDERED PLACE

As Faulkner understands, our desire for a quick fix, a to-do list, or an easy explanation of who we're supposed to love and who's most deserving of our wrath is born of a natural need for meaning and order. We want answers and resolution, and we'll pledge allegiance to whatever personality or principality can give it to us the quickest. But when the desire is accelerated or made hasty by the anxiety and fear that electronic media often appear especially designed to provoke, we grow impatient with history and the wisdom it affords by way of its "once upon a time . . ." When we're no longer willing (or able) to sustain the bandwidth required to hear, read, or listen to any version of history that can't be contained in a sound bite or a put-down, our capacity for right worship and right listening for a functioning democracy is compromised. To practice either, we have to have the skills to understand and locate ourselves not by way of mantras, sayings, and glowing clichés that come to constitute our character, but within a story that's faithful to history. If we're deaf to the oratory of careful, comprehensive storytelling (or even hostile to it), are we still capable of wanting to be truthful?

For instance, a photograph of Donald Rumsfeld shaking hands with Saddam Hussein in 1983 might unsettle a position or provoke an emotional state, but it isn't, all by itself, an argument for or against anyone. It isn't a "bashing." It's simply a record of a historical event, and history isn't a problem for "once upon a time." Such records invite opinions and positions to explain themselves in the larger context of a history in which tyrants, of course, never spring up out of nowhere as unstoried creatures, and America's relationship with the rest of the world is inevitably more complicated than the daily news has time to let on. It invites us to expand the stories we tell ourselves to include all that comes to our attention as history, not to fight it off as if some rogue element is conspiring to bring down our peace of mind. To recall the fact of an audio recording of Donald Trump describing his own act of sexual assault ("When you're a star, they let you do it") isn't to mount an attack or engage in slander. It's a consideration of available evidence. Or as comedian Lenny Bruce never tired of explaining to his fellow citizens, "The truth is what is." Will we believe it?

Almost inevitably, this expansion process will feel painful, because a challenged opinion will often seem like an assault on meaning itself, an assault on meaning by meaninglessness, on order by chaos, on truth by relativism. But it's really just history. More material for the blessed orator. For the mind that strives to order itself according to the biblical witness, turning one's mind around regularly (repentance, *metanoia*) is the way that leads to everlasting life. While adjusting your imagination to fit the facts on the ground doesn't always inspire confidence or suit the mad self-confidence that tries to pass itself off as respectability, refusing it as miserable weakness or wishy-washiness is to invite the thought police into your own head—to deny, in advance of hearing it, any facts to the contrary of your frantically held paradigm. Orwell called it Reality Control, and I often wonder if it might be related somehow to blasphemy against the Holy Spirit. We do it to ourselves.

Late one evening in 1928, around the time Faulkner's publisher Ben Wasson had finished working on *Sartoris*, Faulkner dropped off a momentously large envelope. Wasson removed the manuscript and read the title: *The Sound and the Fury*. "This one's the greatest I'll ever write. Just read it."[33] Declaring it his highest achievement, Faulkner abruptly left. Perhaps as much as any one work of American literature, this tale of a crumbling household contains multitudes. It is with this work that Faulkner, according to his own testimony, learned to approach words with the alert respect required when handling dynamite. And if Marshall McLuhan was right to define art as anything you can get away with, Faulkner would find that there are some things that simply have to be called Art. There is a blessed and tragic unmanageability at work in the world of which our artless managing of impulses needs reminding.

As a kind of portal into the mental anguish that comes with the failure of life to order itself according to our passionate expectations, the testimonies of the Brothers Compson demonstrate all the ways our faulty pictures hold us captive. They can't quiet down their mad minds, and their opinions, from the outset, seem to matter less and less while their imaginations (Faulkner takes us inside them) begin to feel like pancake batter. But in spite of their fixations, the lived witness of Dilsey, the Compsons' maid, holds together any hope of well-being within the family while also towering over its madness with the promise of a more lasting, humane reality than the Compsons, in their present state of degeneracy, can know or understand.

Long before the advent of either "reality TV" or the soap opera, Faulkner gave us Quentin Compson, who can't stop thinking about his sister Caddy's lost virginity. His obsession with violated honor, injustice, and all that is therefore wrong with the entire world accompanies him to Harvard, where he will brood over eternal punishment, the apparent absence of redemption evident in all things, and the option of suicide. He destroys his grandfather's watch that his father bequeathed him, despairing of the hope with which it was given him, terming it a tomb of all human desire (48).

And the voice of southern stoicism he inherited from his father is a cold comfort as he loses faith in a meaningful future: Half in love with easeful death, he will join the ancient preacher in declaring the pointlessness of all human endeavor and his own life a stalemate of inertia and wanting (Eccl. 1:1).

Committed to little more than personal acquisition, the gratification afforded him by his visits to prostitutes, and the secret hoarding of money sent long-distance from Caddy for the care and subsistence of a daughter she's only allowed to see with his assistance, Jason Compson is a machine. His mind is a constant rehearsal of who's done him wrong and how everything would fall into place if he was put more officially in charge of all things. Needless to say, he can only feel his own pain, and all he perceives in the sweet old world is the denial of his well-deserved freedom and the assertion of someone else's control. His narration is peppered with rationalizations, an endless insistence on his own consistency, and the constant refrain that he's the only person he has to thank for anything at all. Like a good many of us, his head is often filled with all the things he might have said (or might yet say) in various theoretical conversations that end with him victoriously proving his point. There's no telling what he might have done with a Twitter account. His miserly reduction of all of life to his own needs is never without justification as he keeps a strict mental account of who owes what to whom. He prides himself on his impenetrability to guilt and the cauterization of his own conscience (143). As is often the case with personalities who boast of their determination to be "realistic," he will notice nothing out of the ordinary as his supposed pragmatism becomes sadistic, and he becomes progressively perplexed and frightened by the power and endurance of Dilsey.

After Caddy's departure, it is Dilsey and Dilsey alone who esteems the mentally disabled brother Benjy worthy of attentiveness. He's moved mostly by the sight of firelight and the pasture (now a golf course) that was sold to pay for his sister's wedding and his brother Quentin's year at Harvard, land where he now listens anxiously to golfers yelling what he takes to be his sister's name. His obsessions are more easily judged and scrutinized by the watching world than those of his brothers, but Faulkner's portrayal of all three can lead the reader to ask whose vision is truly deficient.

The anxiety for order on our own terms, when the facts won't give themselves up so easily to any human mind, is the downfall for each of the novel's male protagonists. And we shouldn't let Faulkner's unconventional way of telling their story obstruct our ability to see ourselves. Something's gone a little funny if we think Faulkner or Melville inaccessibly weird while we feel boundless affection for outraged media pundits. For all its jarringness, *The Sound and the Fury* will show us ourselves if we let it.

UNVANQUISHED

Dilsey presides as a voice of grace and judgment in her long-suffering sojourn among the Compsons in a manner that I can't help but compare to Irma P. Hall's performance of Marva Munson in the Coens' version of *The Ladykillers*. Against the economy of meaning that would elevate Jason for his shrewd business sense and marginalize Benjy as an inconvenience, she takes Benjy to her Sunday morning meetings in spite of the local consensus, who mumble against the routine as inappropriate and scandalous. By her estimation, God makes no distinction between Benjy and everyone else, and anyone who says otherwise is only disgracing themselves (181).

In a conversation with Caddy over Benjy's changed name (he was initially named after his uncle Maury until his limited mental development was realized), Dilsey expresses her disapproval over their decision, insisting that they're buying into the world's wicked ways by thinking him unworthy as a namesake. She notes her own confidence that her name will outlive the confusion of the oppressive and insane present. Her name, Dilsey insists, preceded her own awareness of it and will persist when her contemporaries have forgotten her. How? "It'll be in the Book. . .Writ Out" On the Day of God's righteous reign, she won't even have to read it: "They'll read it for me. All I got to do is say Ise here" (37–38). Thomas Merton once remarked that this is one of the best statements, in all of literature, on the morally subversive vocation of Christian identity. The Jason Compsons of the world will correctly view it as a threat to almost everything they hold dear.

Her procession to the Sunday gathering, with Benjy in tow, is one weekly, palpable manifestation of a life that says, "Ise here." Hers is an embodied witness that derives from and partakes in the relentlessly embodied witness of Beloved Community. The gathering is one of comfort and unburdening and commission to stay the course in expectation of a coming day (that is and was and will be). The visiting reverend from St. Louis plays host to a voice that sinks into the hearts of the congregation as it broadcasts itself upon the listeners with "the recollection and the Blood of the Lamb" (183).

As the sermon concludes, Benjy sits transfixed while Dilsey weeps. As she exits the building with tears streaming down her face, her daughter complains over her lost composure, but Dilsey insists that she's beheld the beginning and the ending of all things once again (185).

Like Bayard Sartoris of *The Unvanquished*, who towers over every honor code and overcomes his cultural legacy of an eye for an eye by breaking it down with the offering of his own life, redefining honor in the process, and Ike McCaslin (*Go Down, Moses*) who demonstrates that the earth is the Lord's and everything in it by refusing the land that is his legal inheritance, offering it instead to his heretofore unacknowledged relatives of mixed race, Dilsey endures. There is a power and a glory beyond the decomposing civilization she finds herself in, and she will bear witness to it by seeking the welfare of her dysfunctional employers while living in watchfulness toward a day that was and is and is to come, a day in which all manner of things will be made well.

As visions of enduring, earthbound liberty (and without them, the people perish), these narratives offer powerful possibilities for the American imagination, and if they're taken to heart, Faulkner might well have left a decipherable scar or two on the face of Obliteration. He deconstructs peculiarly death-dealing, decrepit notions of honor and glory by telling better tales, redeeming the old dispensations by challenging our sense of ignorant ease. Literature does that.

IT'S NOT EVIL, JUST SAD

The conceptions of honor and glory that underwrite the torture and terrorizing of human beings are among the primary subjects of Toni Morrison's lyrical witness. She believes that Faulkner's project succeeds because he grasps so precisely how insanely America "holds whiteness as the unifying force" that gives life meaning as he chronicles the "collapse of dignity" among frightened white people who even now expend their spirits "in service to an evil cause."[34] Following Bambara's lead concerning the sometimes accidental clairvoyance that inhabits our speech, she praises something similar in Abraham Lincoln's Gettysburg Address for its refusal "to monumentalize" the casualties of race war and for the way "his words signal deference to the uncapturability of the life it mourns," and bear the "recognition that language can never live up to life once and for all." True speech communicates a deep awareness of its own incapacity, and Morrison insists that "Language can never 'pin down' slavery, genocide, war. Nor should it yearn for the arrogance to be able to do so. Its force, its felicity is in its reach toward the ineffable."[35]

With *Beloved*, that reach takes the form of an extended midrash on the apostle Paul's citing of the prophet Hosea in a letter to his sisters and brothers in Rome: "I will call them my people, which were not my people; and her beloved, which was not beloved" (Rom. 9:25 KJV). The passage serves as the epigraph to the novel, which is itself, by my lights, an essential prophetic text for Beloved Community. Without presuming or even trying to somehow pin down the lived experience of the white-supremacist terror imposed on millions, it nevertheless seizes on Paul's appropriation of Hosea in the very manner people of color in America have flipped the script on the slaveholder's alleged faith for centuries, making it illumine human endurance in a fashion whiteness won't know or understand or ultimately overcome. This is Morrison's stated method: "I like to dust off these clichés, dust off the language, make them mean whatever they may have meant originally." Her hope is "to restore the language that black people spoke to its original power" and to generate "peasant literature for my people."[36]

You can't force-feed a recognition or download a memory or hand over a realization, but you can lift up a song and proffer a witness. Morrison manages this feat of attentiveness repeatedly, lending coherence to an otherwise despairing and debilitating chaos, the history that is the present. *Beloved* takes inspiration from the true story of Margaret Garner, who escaped slavery with her husband and children by crossing the frozen Ohio River in 1856 and, when confronted by U.S. marshals trying to seize them according to the Fugitive Slave Act, killed her own daughter to spare her the terror to come. At her trial, the abolitionist Lucy Stone famously rebuked the compulsion to remotely judge, condemn, or demand punishment for the action: "If in her deep maternal love she felt the impulse to send her child back to God, to save it from coming woe, who shall say she had no right not to do so?"[37]

Like *The Salt Eaters*, *Beloved* is a work of remembrance that traces a lineage of terror and trauma coupled with a season of unbidden séance and long-haul exorcism. At its center is Sethe, a woman who tries to sustain a haunted household in Ohio after escaping a Kentucky slavery plantation called Sweet Home. Though some details differ, she shares with Margaret Garner a moment of decisive, tragic, and lethal decision out of which she tries to reassemble a life around, and in spite of, the repressed yet reverberating memory of a mortal wounding.

As a life of psychic negotiation, her existence is in sync with practically every other character in the novel insofar as protecting the present and the possibility of a future is a constant challenge.[38] Each of them have known and continue to know the danger in loving too much, in treasuring other people too extravagantly, and in remembering any pleasure too specifically. If everyday love is clung to too tightly, it will undo them, because carefree love is never as safe as it feels in the moment. There is a risk in treasuring for too long a newborn baby's hands or feet in view of the likelihood that the infant in whom you delight will soon be stolen and sold. Despite these precautions, Sethe's mother-in-law, Baby Suggs, reminisces over her lost sons and daughters, the question of what their permanent teeth came to look like and how they carried themselves into adulthood (139).

Living alone with her daughter, Denver, in a home constantly disturbed by the ghost of her slain child, Sethe continually struggles with her own buried memories, striving to let most of her own life go as unremembered as she can manage (6). But her success in this work is challenged by the arrival of her old friend Paul D, a beautiful man, long escaped from Sweet Home, whose inquisitive and kind nature invites, almost haplessly, a transparency among people in his presence. Buried feelings arose unbidden when he turned his gaze upon you and reality was made manifest (39).

Paul D has yet to hear tell of what occurred when "schoolteacher," the overseer at Sweet Home, caught up with Sethe and her children, but he senses an ominous presence just before he crosses her threshold. In reply to Paul's question about what lies beyond the door, Sethe replies that it is sadness, rather than evil, that he perceives (8). To begin to receive the witness of *Beloved* is to linger over exchanges like these—they're on every page—and consider the felicitous force with which they invite us to consider a community of people trying to figure out together what to do with their pain and their fear. It's certainly a ghost story, but for Morrison, fantasy is a form of scrutiny, of examining and lifting up a culture of wit and endurance and long-suffering love, of humans engaged together in the long work of not being driven out of their minds by what they've seen and heard and experienced. If a toxic personality is a traumatized personality, their work is to act and imagine their way out of this grim cycle. The book moves back and forth through time between Kentucky and Georgia and even ancestors drowned in the Atlantic, but it also comes down to Sethe and Paul D and what love might remain possible between them. It's one long probing between two souls who know that to love a person is to love a process.

It will take the length of the book for Paul D to know and hear from Sethe what became of her daughter, but what precedes that turn is a series of exchanges in which they take each other's measure with love, frustration, and, sometimes, escalating despair. She tries to tell Paul D everything is fine. "What about inside?" he asks. When Sethe replies that the journey inward is one she can't bring herself to take, he offers to hold her ankles to make sure that she comes back intact (45–46).

At one point, having long ago witnessed at Sweet Home the times men like Paul D were forced to go for days with an iron bit in their mouths, Sethe carefully broaches the topic in the hope that, now that they're together in free Ohio, he might be able to free up something within himself by saying what it was like. He explains that he's never tried to talk about it. It could be that he's sung about it, but he's never spoken of it to any soul (71).

Pressed to the limit of what can be said or sung, to even try to recall aloud their lives under schoolteacher is to risk a creeping feeling of stupefaction from within. We're given windows into all the ways the power he sought to wield over them was also the power of delineation, of decreeing, at every turn, what life itself meant. For instance, schoolteacher once accused their friend Sixo of stealing and eating a young pig. Confronted with evidence, Sixo denies the charge of theft but, upon interrogation, readily admits to taking and preparing and eating the pig. If this isn't theft, what is it? By Sixo's lights, it's the improving of schoolteacher's own property. More work will now be drawn from Sixo thanks to the nourishing of his own body. Such feats of observational candor, however, were denied upon impact. "Clever," one could concede, but "schoolteacher beat him anyway to show that definitions belonged to the definers— not the defined" (190). And because the past is never past, the sacrosanct delineations of free Ohio only go so far. Any white person had the prerogative of destroying any black person for whatever reason occurred to them. This is the inheritance of horror in which Sethe and Paul D try to see and imagine and love one another well, one embattled soul reaching for the other. Paul D wants to place his story next to Sethe's, but this possibility gives rise to hard questions: Are they allowed to feel? Is trusting each other a risk worth taking? (38).

THE CLEARING

Through it all, we have the witness of Baby Suggs, who, years before the novel's action begins, left Sweet Home and eventually secured the house in which Sethe and Denver reside. This was made possible years before schoolteacher became Sweet Home's overseer when her son, Halle, arranged to work extra days to gradually earn the money that would buy her freedom. By the time he'd worked off the agreed-upon amount and it was clear it would be seen through, she was well into her sixties and was faced with the difficult decision of whether to leave everything she knew and everyone she loved for an existence she could barely conceive. In the end, she accepted in the hope of making Halle less sorrowful. She couldn't see the point of a slavewoman over sixty entering a free life, but she could at least fulfill his wish (141).

In her new life in Ohio, she came to notice for the first time—and had to work to not be frightened by—her own heartbeat. When she acquires a house, she also stumbles into a vocation of relentless hospitality to anyone in need and an honorific that comes to follow her name: holy. Within her walls those in need found meat, drink, encouragement, and rebuke, each in its proper measure (86–87). As a healer and storyteller, she conjures, inhabits, and invites her hearers into a space beyond all pervasive psychic and physical degradation that treats black people as resources to be broken, trafficked, and tortured. As a free woman in Ohio, she serves as a herald and host of Beloved Community with no title, credential, or pulpit beyond the space of holiness she conjures with word, gesture, and expenditure of body and spirit.

In a wooded area that came to be called the Clearing, Baby Suggs, holy, leads a gathered throng in song and dance and revisioning of their own lives and the lives of others. The limits of recovery, redemption, and restoration, she tells them, are the limits of their imaginations. The grace they can access is the grace they're willing to try to imagine. Their task as a coming-to-be-free people is to *re*member that which has been *dis*membered, and it is a bold, new-every-morning work that is never quite done. The work of loving your own flesh in a world that despises it is God's work. Loving and dancing and touching one another are matters of soul survival. These practices are salvific imperatives that comprise a deep call to long-haul righteousness in the face of terror remembered and guaranteed to be visited upon kin again and even now. If sanity consists of loving and having compassion for your own body, that step that has to precede loving your neighbor in like manner, this is a liturgy that instructs a traumatized people in reversing the process which, left unacknowledged and unvoiced, settles within as a toxic sense of self. Not evil, Sethe assured Paul concerning the spirit inhabiting her home, just sad. And here in the Clearing, Baby Suggs, holy, invites all hearers to slow the tape and contemplate, with industrial-strength compassion, all the ways that mad is ever a form of sad, that rage is born of fear, and that love might yet be extended to our own beating hearts.

Literature is a call to consider again, with humility and humor and hope, our own creatureliness. *Beloved* itself undertakes the restorative work in our world that Baby Suggs, holy, conjures and facilitates in her own and extends this communal labor of mourning and esteeming and loving what remains: Put a hand on it, grace it, stroke it, and hold it up. If the grace we have is the grace we can imagine, holding ourselves and others dear begins as a heart-mind work, a question of what we're carrying and laying down and picking up again. Toni Cade Bambara offers a delineation of the order: "The dream is one piece, the correct picturing of impressions another. Then interpretation, then action."[39]

No word in the above formulation is disposable. This is how the work of Beloved Community gets done. As Morrison shows us, the question of how we imagine ourselves is at the core of our lives, how we relate (there is no escaping relationship), the way we dwell in the world. If we each dwell, as Martin Luther King Jr. most famously assures us we do, in an inescapable network of mutuality, *we dwell* and will continue to dwell no matter what. What shall we do in light of what we know?

KEEP COOL, BUT CARE

Thomas Pynchon's attentiveness to history and the details of the contemporary American scene (a hyperawareness that sees revelation in progress all around him and a parable to be entered into around every corner) places him appropriately along our continuum of Beloved Community. As a kind of visionary, grounded yet awake to mystery in all things, his unique brand of watchfulness reflects a love for the American landscape and the renewable resource of countercultural possibilities still at work, though often untapped, within the national character. He looks hard and humorously at everything we're becoming with an eye for every virus of unfreedom that might corrupt our endlessly impressionable imaginations. He seems particularly interested in all the ways in which a population will kid itself concerning its own history (recent and ancient) and all the madness that inevitably follows. If the price of liberty is eternal vigilance against unstoried tyranny and death-dealing impulses played out as necessities, Pynchon's creative labor involves enough overtime to leave readers feeling dizzy. But the charges of pessimism and paranoia often leveled at those who deem the practice of paying attention a civic duty are unfair, and in Pynchon's case, betray a misunderstanding, perhaps willful, of what he's up to.

In each of his novels, Pynchon goes back, *way* back, in a sometimes maddeningly thorough attention to specifics concerning who thought it would be a good idea to subjugate someone else and how the subjugation was accomplished. In 1969, he noted aloud a trajectory between the displacement and death the German government brought down on the Herero people of German Southwest Africa (now Namibia) at the turn of the twentieth century and America's foreign policy:

> I feel personally that the number done on the Herero head by the Germans is the same number done on the American Indian head by our own colonists and what is now being done on the Buddhist head in Vietnam by the Christian minority in Saigon and their advisors: the imposition of a culture valuing analysis and differentiation on a culture that valued unity and integration.[40]

Stay with that last part in spite of the fact that it sounds like a line from a textbook. What's the number being done on people's heads? A culture that privileges analysis and differentiation imposes itself—silences, shuts down, appropriates for its own dark purposes—a culture based in unity and integration. That's Toni Morrison's schoolteacher in a nutshell. If we have the eyes and ears for it, the Clearing of Baby Suggs, holy, is on offer among human beings here, there, and everywhere, but the monetizing, weaponizing impulse—also here, there, and sometimes seemingly everywhere—has other purposes: analysis over unity, detachment over relationship. A myth of critical detachment versus a myth of unity. If America is to remain, in any living sense, an extended conversation about what human beings owe one another, what the myth of critical detachment does to a sense of living unity, the violence it imposes has to be our subject. Or, as the ghost of Walter Rathenau, a Jewish statesman who was also the German foreign minister of the Weimar Republic, put it to Nazi officials who sought his counsel in a séance in Pynchon's *Gravity's Rainbow*: "What is the real nature of control?"[41] What does critical detachment, as a faith conviction, do to human beings who believe they wield it over others?

One televised exchange once brought this distinction to my mind in a peculiarly helpful way. The poet Allen Ginsberg is in conversation with the pundit William F. Buckley on PBS's *Firing Line*. Ginsberg has held the floor for an unusually long time through the recitation of a poem, all the while holding Buckley's gaze. Buckley praises the beauty of his word choice but includes a (to his mind) crucial qualifier: "Well, you know what in my judgment is unsatisfactory about this analysis, I really don't think—incidentally it is not so much analytical as it is poetical . . ."

Ginsberg interjects, "Oh, poesy is the oldest form. . . . Analysis is a later form."[42] Buckley analyzes away, but the point is a palpable hit to the claim of detached judgment. Analytic posturing, let the reader understand, is the late-comer in the human barnyard, and the seat of judgment is perhaps the most folkloric and dangerous myth of all. The lyrical precedes the analytical. Poetry, in fact, generates analysis as a form. Our perception of reality is relentlessly narrative, just as every fact is a function of relationship. Spirit, we have to understand, knows no division.

It is within this movement of beatitude that Pynchon dropped his first novel, *V.*, upon the world. Amid tales of the Herero, plastic surgery, wars, and barroom brawls, we receive the motto "Keep Cool, but Care," which per-haps might serve as a guiding ethos throughout his fiction.[43] It's uttered by McClintic Sphere, who, depending on your interpretation, might be viewed as a stand-in for Ornette Coleman or Thelonious Monk, and it's an increasingly necessary word for reading Pynchon as you come to suspect he's never met a conspiracy theory he didn't like. It speaks against the cynicism of ignorant bliss as well as for the desire to know the complex histories in which we live and move and have our being. As Fred Friendly understood, learning to live with the tension of what you'd rather not have known concerning the interconnect-edness of the workaday world is the beginning of wisdom. While dipping fur-ther into the book of what really happened always risks feelings of defeat and despair, any sense of coherence that depends on an aloof posture of disregard for the actual world is, for Pynchon, a poor showing for the still sometimes possibly righteous promise of America.

Trying to care against despair will involve, among other things, a deter-mined wit that can overcome melancholy, a turn for the comedic that won't let tragedy have the final word. Incidentally, comic consistency, in Pynchon's work, is a conspiracy of hope requiring constant satirization of the merry band of resisters who appear throughout his novels. In *Vineland*, for instance, his liberation force concludes a planning session, ready to tackle fascism and every form of totalitarian thought encroaching upon the realm of liberty, and the moment they make for the door coincides with the theme from *Ghostbusters* suddenly breaking out on a nearby radio. Every moment of emerging serious-ness eventually finds itself in a larger comic context, a funnier parable than whatever gravitas momentarily held the stage.

When Pynchon terms his resistance movements (against "Them") the Counterforce or the People's Republic of Rock 'n' Roll, he can bring to mind the odd, moral authority of Jack Black in *School of Rock* or Lear's Fool or Tom Bombadil. As absolute power corrupts absolutely, it becomes increasingly intolerant of the playful word and the honest though seemingly powerless tes-timony. In *Vineland*, Pynchon's freedom fighters believe that corrupting power keeps "a log of its progress, written into that most sensitive memory device, the human face,"[44] and filming the unsympathetic powerful, with an emphasis on the close-up, will dethrone and unmask them slowly but surely. The subject of his lamentation and the object of his lampoon is whatever comes only to steal and destroy, seeking whom it may devour, inevitably appearing to its host bodies (Pynchon's "Them") as an absolute moral necessity, duty, what-we-have-to-do, doublethink. Naming the Adversary ("the persistence of structures favoring death. . . . This is the sign of Death the impersonator"[45]), mocking power and speaking truth to it, would seem to be the purpose that, in some way, links all of his work. Celebration of life, not letting the Caesars or multinational cartels or whoever talks most loudly and expensively about freedom define who you are, is the driving method of a prose that kicks at the darkness. It's cynicism's opposite: coolness and caring.

As the witness of Beloved Community never stops reminding us, a nervous breakdown is at large, always advertising itself as normalcy, and that which gets called sanity might sometimes be nothing more than the agreed-upon madness of the global kleptocracy. Pynchon's characters, meanwhile, represent a humankind who can't bear much manufactured reality, and their inability to fit in or get with the program begins to look like a much-beleaguered stronghold of freedom. Morrison, Melville, and Faulkner have taken us here before. There is, even now, a contagion of power and pride and endless self-justification that will spread out in every direction, disguising itself as something to which all who believe in decency will gladly pledge allegiance. It has a nasty habit of confusing itself for the voice of God. It believes in its own sincerity so powerfully that it will feel violently offended at any question concerning its well-rehearsed script of goodness and sacrifice in all that it does, in all that it's ever done. It will mistake its towers of Babel (cooperatives of concentrated lies) for the light that shines in the darkness.

To see that which passes for history as a diversionary tactic or "at best a conspiracy, not always among gentlemen, to defraud" is to bring Beloved Community to bear on the way we think about the past.[46] It is to stand firmly within the sacred insight that evil doesn't come to us self-consciously, introducing itself and offering us a choice ("Join us in our evil"). It's more like a kind of sleepwalking, an unself-consciously Faustian bargain, a narcissism in which we believe our fantasy to be the only real, unbiased version of events. We surround ourselves with voices that will affirm our fantasy and dismiss as treacherous (or evil) any witness that would dare to call our innocence into question.

As our pantheon of elders insists, combating evil in all its impersonations will begin with a refusal to cooperate with it. In *Gravity's Rainbow*, Pynchon notes that evil will usually assume a "calculated innocence" ("It's part of Their style"[47]), and the ancient curse of western culture is its "dusty Dracularity" made all the more inimical by its ability to publicize itself as progress, "even to the point of masquerading, a bit decadently, as mercy" (350). Taking the power of collective delusion seriously, Pynchon follows Ginsberg's lead by understanding that the high places of Baal and the logic of human sacrifice to Moloch aren't limited to biblical history. Its investigative lore still has work to do, and Pynchon appropriately locates unacknowledged alliances with unholiness close to home. Like Emily Dickinson, he understands that our failures aren't compressed in an instant. They're consecutive and slow and well-intentioned, and tracing them well, the comedy and tragedy of it all, will require some careful storytelling, a clear eye, and some redemptively meandering confabulation. Above all, tracing our world out truthfully will involve salvific doubt concerning our ability to know and the abandonment of domineering knowingness for the more biblical justness that only lives by faith. Cultural revolutions are always housed in stories. Revolution is story. It will be told. "Once upon a time . . ." "The kingdom of God is like . . ." Enter Reverend Cherrycoke.

TELL IT SLANT

Among the numerous characters who come and go in *Gravity's Rainbow* is an unnamed German girl who spends an evening with the novel's confused American protagonist, Tyrone Slothrop, who's found himself wandering around postwar Germany in a pig costume. Their conversation turns to the topic of her father, a printer, missing since 1942, whose union had resisted the Nazis while all the others were getting dutifully in line. The tale of his existence inspires a state of liberty-loving reverie in Slothrop as he contemplates the commitment of his Puritan forebears who once dared to speak and write down the truth as they understood it, under the threat of persecution and even death. He also considers the righteous possibilities of a printing press and the threat a paper supply will always be to the prospering wicked: "It touches Slothrop's own Puritan hopes for the Word, the Word made printer's ink, dwelling along with antibodies and iron-bound breath in a good man's blood . . . did he run off leaflets against his country's insanity? Was he busted, beaten, killed?" (571).

Exiled to a pre-1776 America in response to similar crimes against authority, the Reverend Wicks Cherrycoke is our primary narrator and spirit guide in Pynchon's later novel, *Mason & Dixon*. Charged by the British with the crime of "Anonymity," Cherrycoke was discovered printing and posting unsigned flyers outlining injustices he'd observed, "committed by the Stronger against the Weaker."[48] He had said what he saw—or written it all out, named the guilty, and been locked up, and as he began to protest the notion that his own name, not his to give or withhold according to the law, belonged to the British authorities, he was declared insane ("or so, then, each in his Interest, did it please ev'ryone to style me" [10]) and shipped off to the New World for treatment.

Just in case we need reminding, it is the Hebrew scribe who dared to assert in writing that one day the mouths of liars will be stopped, that the one who oppresses the weak despises the Maker, and that the Lord opposes the proud but gives grace to the humble. The biblical collection ascribes a voice of moral authority to the refugee, viewing the disenfranchised of history as the custodians of human seriousness.

Excommunicated for his own commitment to truth and justice, Cherrycoke, a kind of American Baron Munchausen, holds forth in the household of his sister and her husband, John Wade LeSpark, a weapons merchant who has made his fortune selling arms to the British, the French, settlers, and native peoples with no particular concern over what becomes of his wares. Hosted within a domestic economy comfortably situated within the emerging military-industrial-incarceration-entertainment complex, the Reverend is allowed to subsist with the LeSparks as long as he keeps the children amused with stories. His audience will include LeSpark's brothers and their children as well. The year is 1786, and the place is Philadelphia.

Cherrycoke is an expert in circumlocution. Truth, as he sees it, demands as much. Like wisdom, it will have to dazzle gradually. He'll tell it slant. Easing it with explanation, he spins his yarns in the direction of moral instruction. But as the properly received parable will often dislocate (rather than reinforce) the personal peace of mind of the hearer, exposing the ways we go about betraying our most publicized values, it shouldn't surprise us to find that the Reverend is ever a prophet without honor, possibly too much the enemy of the state for his family's tastes, and the charge of insanity will continue to be placed in his direction by those whose interests are threatened by his truth telling.

Needless to say, the family values that come through in the conversational storytelling that constitutes the novel do not always coincide with one another. Given the fact that arbitrary weapons sales fuel the LeSparks' bread and butter, young nephew Ethelmer imagines that any Day of Judgment that has an eye on the armed assault on the human form divine will be bad news for his uncle. Despite these realizations, all are reluctant to directly insult their host. While Cherrycoke is inarguably a man of faith, he understands that LeSpark's devotion to the notions of Adam Smith are no less a faith-based initiative than his own vocation. As he sees it, LeSpark lives a cozy existence deep inside an unwavering faith as impractical as any far-fetched doctrine you can dream up, and his travels as an arms dealer are performed in blind obedience to the spirit of free enterprise and all the human sacrifices it requires. Although it is Cherrycoke's own version of America that has the floor, he knows that he lives in close proximity to LeSpark's regime, which thrives everywhere unnamed, understanding itself by way of the sacrosanct dogma of private property.

THE LEGACY WAS AMERICA

Twenty years after the fact, Cherrycoke tells the tale of an act of delineation he once witnessed, a line he saw drawn straight through the heart of a wilderness. In his account, Charles Mason and Jeremiah Dixon function as the Rosencrantz and Guildenstern of the Age of Reason, following their orders as duty seems to require while wondering if there's any particular duty motivating the Charter'd Companies (Factory, Consulate, Agency) whose interests are consistently served by the work they've undertaken in good faith on behalf of the Royal Society. Mason sees that Charter'd Companies now bend the world according to their purposes and wonders what his responsibilities might be within this peceeived inevitability. Can we ever know completely what ends we're serving? Dixon notes that erring comes with being a human in history, but folly can occasionally be curbed by the presence of a God who remembers or, if the notion's too figurative, a functional conscience. As a Quaker, Dixon believes such mindfulness is accessed through silence in worship, a wisdom beyond the immediate evidence of our eyes and memories, but Mason doesn't quite see the point of mixing up their jobs with religious questions. Like many future citizens of the land he's unwittingly defining, he believes he has the right and the preternatural ability to step back from religion when he thinks there's a job to do.

"Are we being us'd by Forces invisible?" Dixon fondly asks (73). And as the novel ostensibly addresses science, technology, and cartography, we're led to wonder if the surveyor of land might prove to be, biblically speaking, the purveyor of mass delusions. Reverend Cherrycoke accords the right of division to God alone, who, he will admit, probably did well to divide the waters with the firmament. But he wonders if the man-made divisions that follow aren't sometimes a little presumptuous, a machinery that claims authority without the proper reverence for, in Blake's phrase, the human form divine (that would be everyone who's ever lived). Having narrowly escaped the fading, secularized lights of Europe, he hopes for epiphanies of American Illumination not yet received, viewing the land as a space of prophetic possibilities. (361).

As storyteller and Remembrancer, Cherrycoke places his characters in the company of various movers and shakers on the eve of the republic's founding. When Dixon drinks a toast to "the pursuit of happiness" (395), a young Thomas Jefferson asks if he might borrow the phrase. They'll encounter Washington and Franklin on their journey as well, but the America that Cherrycoke celebrates is "the America of the Soul" lying beyond the presumption of deism and the arrogance of enlightenment "into an Interior unmapp'd" (511).

It is in witness to this, a countercultural, unmapped world of Word made flesh in spite of the domineering claims of royalty or a corrupt Christendom, that the Reverend printed and posted his flyers in the first place. His America serves as "a very Rubbish-Tip . . . for all that *may yet be true*" But there is also a spirit of reduction and devastation at work that transmogrifies "Possibilities [in]to Simplicities that serve the ends of Governments" (345). And as the experience of Mason and Dixon demonstrates, this demystifying machinery was doing its business some time before 1776.

Having witnessed the horrors of the slave trade during a visit to the Cape of Good Hope and their arrival in Maryland (not unrelated to the notion of Proprietary Happiness), Mason and Dixon begin to see a pattern at work in Lancaster, Pennsylvania, where a massacre of native people had occurred. Given the alleged civilizing mission of the colonists, they find it peculiar that "the first mortal acts of Savagery in America" were "committed by Whites against Indians," and they're dismayed by the manner in which the settlers transform into the very agents of savagery they fear (307). While otherwise priding himself on his dedicated participation in the Age of Reason, Mason is moved to pray at the site of the massacre. And as he prays, he experiences a troubled premonition concerning future generations whose skills in remembering righteously he imagines might prove perversely diminished. He imagines the land he's surveying might come to be inhabited by the most forgetful people the world has ever seen.

As they anticipate an engagement with representatives of the Mohawk nation, they're prepared to answer any number of questions about their strange instruments, but they come to dread the possibility that anyone would put the more straightforward query of why they're doing what they're doing. As they progressively doubt their labors will ever serve any human good, the question of who they're working for and why remains unresolved to the end.

REMEMBRANCE BELONGS TO THE PEOPLE

Cherrycoke's prophetic distrust of concentrated, unchecked power marks his revolutionary Americanness. And as he tells this story of the Founding (or as some Pynchon readers put it, the Anti-Founding) Fathers, his listeners, especially the older LeSparks, are continually put off by what they take to be his bias. But bias is as difficult to prove as objectivity, and those who claim to be the most fair and balanced in their reportage, like those who would boast of their humility or sincerity, undermine their own credibility. Truth, like beauty, is its own credential. Like wisdom, truthfulness doesn't go about promoting itself. It cries out in the street, raising its voice in the marketplace, extending its hand, but it can't exactly heed itself or force anyone else to heed. It will only witness and testify. Like poetry, it doesn't make anything happen. Ethelmer listens to the Reverend and the LeSparks' protestations and smiles at how easily offended those who profit off endless war can be. They're hell-bent on denying any data, any body of evidence, that might call their own integrity into question.

Cherrycoke, meanwhile, aspires to truthfulness, but he knows that claiming to own it is a heresy (who can know the mind of God?), and believing yourself capable of seeing it undimly is a crime against humanity: "Who claims Truth, Truth abandons. History is hir'd, or coerc'd, only in Interests that must ever prove base" (350). Cherrycoke was run out of old Europe for his insistence on bearing witness freely, on being one human voice that aspired to speak to the people for the people. And the beauty of a trustworthy witness is that it doesn't come with signs and wonders. In the land of Cherrycoke's dream, it is freely given and freely ignored. Let anyone who has an ear hear. Keep cool, but care.

On *The Simpsons*, when Montgomery C. Burns, threatened by the ability of Springfield's citizens to make of him what they will, decrees the age of his own first person singular by crowning himself king of all media, Lisa Simpson procures her own printing press and goes to work on the Red Dress Press. In spite of the manufactured crises of Burns's news-product monopoly, young Lisa crafts her own transmissions, asserting authorial authority one act of reportage at a time. This is how it works. As Karen McDougal once observed: "Every girl who speaks is paving the way for another."[49] There is yet another word to be had. Another human angle to be posited against the efforts of brutalizing forces to dictate meaning.

Predictably, Burns cracks down on Lisa's operation without mercy, but it's too late. Lenny, Barney, Flanders, and all of Springfield are following suit. Echoing Martin Luther, Homer remarks, "Instead of one big-shot controlling all the media, now there's a thousand freaks Xeroxing their worthless opinions."[50] So be it. This is the way the work gets done in the land of a thousand freaks. We get to hear one another again, awaking power to its pretensions. "Remembrance," Cherrycoke instructs, "belongs to the people" (349).

Chapter 4

The Freeway of Love

A poet . . . is constantly talking to himself, inside of himself, constantly approximating and evaluating and trying to grasp his experience in words. And the "sound," inside his head, of that voice is not necessarily identical with his literal speaking voice, nor is his inner vocabulary identical with that which he uses in conversation. At their best sound and words are song, not speech. The written poem is then a record of that inner song.

—Denise Levertov

Punk teaches the same inversion of power as the Gospel. You learn that the coolest thing about having a microphone is turning it away from your own mouth.

—Julien Baker

Art and music are a resource from which we can pull for self-care, to continue to engage. . . . Music made me realize that we engage in political acts everyday.

—Chelsea Manning

"Soul to me is a feeling," Aretha Franklin once explained. "A lot of depth and being able to bring to the surface that which is happening inside, to make the picture clear. Many people can have soul."[1] As I understand her, she's describing a way of being in the world, a way of approaching a vocal performance, certainly, but also a way of coming out of hiding, of holding your hopes and your hurts with open hands. Many people *can* have soul, we might say, but whether or not we're going to access it, enter into it together with others in the way we carry ourselves, is an everyday do-over type of phenomenon.

I think soul is shorthand for Beloved Community, and music is its movement. Music puts the question of who we really are and what we might yet be back in play over and over again. Rumor has it that hardly any American musician of note was willing to risk the forfeiture of soul and long-term credibility that might follow by allowing their own gifts to be employed in Donald Trump's inauguration ceremony, but music operates in that drama, which is the American taxpayer-voter's drama anyway. Trump himself once mused aloud that his favorite song is Peggy Lee's performance of "Is That All There Is?" It gets to him somehow: "It's a great song because I've had these tremendous successes and then I'm off to the next one. Because it's like, 'Oh, is that all there is?'"[2]

And . . . *scene*. Perhaps future musings on the existential futility of getting what you want without delving deeply into why you want it on the part of this particular president will come to light at a later date, but the song remains the same. It's an invitation to join the movement of soul, of registering the fact of how we feel, be it good or ill. We're members, meanwhile, of Beloved Community whether we take up the work of recognizing our membership or not. Music, whether we experience it as a help or a haunting, says so.

Beloved Community is the long realization of the biological fact of relationship as much as it is an ethic, a sensibility, and a way of inhabiting your own life with intense attentiveness to the lives of others. It's going public with your affection. It's Lisa Simpson's Red Dress Press, and many a Red Dress Press equivalent, insofar as it ennobles us enough to realize that we can write our own headlines as we test the spirits, believe our own eyes, and draw on the genius of other people as we live and act on the knowledge that the whole world is kin.

I'm tempted to say that music is the primary currency of Beloved Community. It houses, like no other form, the realization of the organic fact of other lives and the accompanying spirit of solidarity with people gone, here, and yet to come that nobody, as far as I can tell, can live without. Music has a way of changing the subject and, thereby, whatever we thought we had in our sight as *the point*. Consider for a moment that rhetorical pivot one can hear deployed to gaslight our sense of what's true: "That's not the point" or "The point *is* . . ." or "You're missing the point." Music, just by doing its thing, puts the question of *the point* back in play, flipping the script one more time, complicating the presumed and presiding narrative again and again.

Song and dance make a way when it feels as if there is no way. Song can admittedly be put to angelic or demonic use, because it is, after all, a form of enchantment, but even one designed to entrance and exploit can be differently—even healingly—deployed at any time, given a new and freer context. Any and every song is potentially a song of myself, if I'll let it be. In fact, it doesn't operate according to my conscious consent. Song simply sneaks up on me, bypassing my defenses, seizing by rhythm or lyric my train of thought and transforming my first person singular into a sudden someone else or something unexpectedly plural, a song of ourselves, yourselves, and many other selves. Songs contain multitudes. What once was can suddenly be again in song, and what's never yet been might now have a living chance.

Trying to trace continuums and influences in song is a deeply edifying and engrossing guesswork of who heard what when and how exactly it hit them when it came their way. What all happened in the two thousand or so years between Jesus' death outside of Jerusalem and Tom Waits's mad, howling performance of "Jesus Gonna Be Here" on an album called *Bone Machine*? Is he thinking of Memphis Slim? How exactly does he find himself singing like that? What's he trying to do? What's the history?

Phrases like "old, weird America" and "the secret history of rock 'n' roll" can get the mind working on and imagining perceived continuums. There is much discussion, for instance, on the matter of whether it was Ann Cole of Newark, New Jersey, or Muddy Waters of Rolling Fork, Mississippi, who first broached the topic of getting one's mojo working. Did Elvis ever hear the Golden Gate Jubilee Quartet's lively praise song "Rock My Soul" of 1938? What's with Screamin' Jay Hawkins singing about a little demon running through the world in an effort to understand his own pain? And where does Roy Orbison fit into all this mess? Does the absence of recorded hymns in his opus reflect his denomination's opposition to musical instruments in worship? Does it get any weirder than "In Dreams"?

Of course it does. The weirder, the truer, the more righteous the perception of self and others. And as ever, weirdness is only that which has yet to find a slot within our categories and paradigms, and maybe nothing human ever should. If America is a crime scene full of displaced agrarians responding sometimes horribly and sometimes beautifully to their own trauma, we're right to listen hard for the nascent clairvoyance Bambara insists resides within us all, each of us endowed with an authorial authority, blue with longing and desperate for a word—any word—of observational candor.

Something gets unlocked in song. There are times when I feel almost dumbfounded that Marvin Gaye's enunciation of the word "brutality" in "What's Going On?" hasn't turned the world completely around yet. But maybe it has here and there and will again, one broadcast at a time. Maybe Tracy Chapman is right, and talk of revolution has to sound like a whisper first, or an insinuation. Bikini Kill spies it in the movement of a woman's hips. The lyrical "I feel like . . ." can go absolutely anywhere: a stranger in your own house, a motherless child, a walking contradiction. Songs are subtle. They aren't even necessarily hidden ways of saying something else. They're their own brand of saying. Like the psalms, they don't contain principles or messages, exactly, but are witnesses and testimonies and guesswork. They're just saying how it feels and what happened and wondering if it had to go that way. The world seems to be falling apart; something's got to give, and there is plenty to tell of passion, guilt, oppression, and perplexity in the meantime. It takes a worried man. There are heartaches by the number. And nobody has to look too far to spot a cheating heart or two. There's a riot going on. Or as Dolly Parton puts it, "It's All Wrong but It's All Right."

THE TABLE IS SPREAD

As I understand it, Beloved Community is a wider-ranging and more open-ended communion of consciousness than we tend to imagine if we mistake it for a movement strictly confined to a few popular key figures in the late 1950s and early 1960s. A similar mistake occurs when people who rode to power on a wave of white supremacy offer perfunctory praise of Martin Luther King Jr. without paying heed to anything he said, acknowledging the school of prophetic consciousness from which he received instruction, or recognizing that King himself was formed by generations of unknown people whose righteous actions informed his own. Ella Baker addressed this failure of discernment most famously when she observed that "the movement made Martin rather than Martin making the movement."[3]

To say as much is to point to a whole life ethic out of which Beloved Community generally (and the civil rights movement in America specifically) arises. Baker points to it as the vision King and others knew themselves to be drawing their witness from: "As far as Martin was concerned, as far as anybody else is concerned, they were only a part of a whole. . . . The most important thing was, and still is in my mind, is to develop to the point that they don't need the strong, savior-type leader."[4] This development of human spirit has to override the impulse to credit any one individual for something as determinedly communal as lunch counter sit-ins or bus boycotts. When we skip straight to hero worship, we avoid the invitation to a moral realization concerning what was— and can be again—a common hungering and thirsting after righteousness that has a claim on each of us, calling us to reorient our concerns in the here and now. Beloved Community is a cultural revolution that's obscured whenever we try to tie it too closely to a single person or era. It's a movement of the spirit that brings Frederick Douglass to Seneca Falls and the Dixie Chicks to Beyoncé's "Daddy Lessons." Beloved Community is a millennia-old movement of righteousness that makes these moves possible, dissolving whatever demonic distinctions stand in our way.

Music facilitates such phenomena in a sneakily preemptive fashion. Before we even know it's happening, it spreads the table so widely that we're made to know *feelingly* that our divisions don't work, that one thing has to do with another, and that Beloved Community isn't an issue or an ideal but, in the phrase of W. E. B. DuBois, a gift of spirit, a communion within which we come to know and hear ourselves in relationship to others. This communion largely draws its life from the candor and courage of song and the embodied ethic of deep affection to which it gives rise. It also ennobles the transparency, that leveling with oneself and others, that lyrically expands the space of the talkaboutable.

"Be it life or death," Henry David Thoreau observes, "we crave only reality."[5] I believe something like this craving is at work in our reception of song. It's a way of paying deeper attention to ourselves, our search for the sound of fuller disclosure, an unveiling, an unmasking that might challenge the deception that, as Howard Thurman warns us, we're often in danger of becoming. In music, we're casually experimenting with an Amen we can live with in spite of the signals and sounds that would otherwise lull us into denying the fact of our own bodies, the bodies of others, and the ever-loving fact of our sweet old world.

"If you bring forth what is within you, what you bring forth will save you. If you do not bring forth what is within you, what you do not bring forth will destroy you." This sacred insight, attributed to Jesus of Nazareth in the *Gospel of Thomas*, names the healing game as I understand it. Through indirection and misdirection, music evokes and provokes contemplation, an engagement with our own inner dramas like nothing else, playing past our strategies of avoidance and the cordoning away of one realization from another, strategies that, if I'm not vigilant, will eventually leave me estranged from my own soul, the part of me that remains undivided, the spirit that knows no division. Music addresses my craving for reality, bringing to light the dramas which, left unaddressed, fester and toxify. Music, then, is the starter kit of Beloved Community, urging us to speak up, to spill all the beans before it's too late. Like a well-cast spell, it summons us to let ourselves know—to *try* to know—what we don't want to know we know.

RIGHTEOUSNESS IS ENDLESSLY COMPLICATED

If I might draw on one icon to better contemplate another, I think of the Pulitzer Prize–winning artist Kendrick Lamar as an Elvis of reality among us, a psychic pioneer of sorts whose determination to be honest with himself and others is his creative animus. His albums are missives of militant transparency, each chronicling afresh his tried-and-true conviction that giving lyrical voice to his deepest fears, anxieties, and resentments is the surest path to shaking free of them. This is the process he terms "Poetic Justice" on *Good Kid, M.A.A.D City*, a process of trying to right his wrongs by enunciating them in lyric, sound, and self-dramatization. Even when he mocks himself by measuring what he takes to be the moral distance between his own existence and the sacred standard of

Beloved Community, he still draws on it as a practical and poetical, communal life form, identifying himself as an Israelite struggling after righteousness. His rights, his wrongs, he'll write out, he tells us, till he's right with God.

On *To Pimp A Butterfly*, Lamar embraces this process of bringing it all forth with such exuberance, good humor, and relentless self-deprecation that no moment—be it anger, disillusionment, or megalomania—is allowed to dominate. He celebrates the high of being heard and beloved by an ever-widening listener base while dwelling hard in the sense that reaching the alleged top is to land decisively in outer darkness beyond the unbroken circle of human meaning. With "u," for instance, we're treated to a screaming hotel room meltdown in which he comes to the crushing conclusion that he's thrown away his ties to family and neighbor in exchange for a mass-market exchange of pseudointimacy with strangers. Amid warring and accusing accounts of who he really is at bottom, the shame spiral is suddenly interrupted by a knock on the door from a Spanish-speaking housekeeper who's trying to finish a shift. The drama of other lives goes on while those lives crowd themselves in amid the audio of his angst. One degraded self-conception is interwoven with another or made to counter it. Bouts of suicidal depression in "u" are referred to in "I" as one more mood—the war of the night before—now contended with, rebuked, and, at least momentarily, overcome. And the compassion he struggles to have for himself is offered as a clarion call, an imperative, to be communally applied in our own context, whatever that might look like.

Prince once posited that he *knows* there's a devil, because its voice is so loud on *Lovesexy*'s "I No." And where Prince named the deluding spirit Spooky Electric, Kendrick Lamar opts for Lucy (read Lucifer), who appears not only as a corrupting influence that would keep his imagination captive in comparison, competition, and condescension when it comes to his peers and predecessors; but also as the beautiful bearer of the promise of homeland security for friend and family in exchange for his soul. Righteousness, Lamar shows us again and again, is endlessly complicated. "For Sale? (Interlude)" serves as a public service announcement that evil (misuse of influence, abuse of power, estrangement from a righteous sense of self) is too elusive to ever be resisted once for all. If Lucy can quote Scripture with ease, the all-pervading confusion with which Lamar contends won't stop outside church buildings, because the calls to false worship are, it turns out, everywhere. Being true, or in Lamar's phrase "Mandela-like," involves deep discernment and consistent dismissal of every false signal. In this sense, Lamar's albums are like experiments in self-examination.

In her novel *The Dispossessed*, Ursula K. Le Guin makes a distinction between explorers and adventurers: "The explorer who will not come back or send back his ships to tell his tale is not an explorer, only an adventurer; and his sons are born in exile."[6] With a constant determination to dramatically lyricize his setbacks and missteps, Kendrick Lamar has long opted to be an explorer. As early as "F*ck Your Ethnicity" on his debut studio album, *Section.80*, he made clear that the table he spreads is set out for all comers also in process. Opening with the sound of a campfire burning, he explains that the fire itself represents his audience's passions as well as his own. He wants to offer the available data of his own life and what might be gleaned from it to those who pay him heed. *To Pimp A Butterfly*'s "Mortal Man" continues this vocation; he poses a question that's different from the question of fame, a question at work in all alleged receptions of song. He wants to know if his listeners are genuinely picking up the intelligence he means to lay down: Is his relationship with the audience fake or as real as the heavens?

Or as he also puts it: When shit hits the fan, are you still a fan? To put it this way is to lift our understanding of pop music into the realm of prophetic consciousness which is, as ever, at the core of Beloved Community. Are we really interested in the worlds to which he's bearing witness? What does our musical intake amount to? Are we receiving his witness at all? There's many a precedent for such a move, for turning the tables in this way and putting the question of reception to the audience, but an especially apt one is Ralph Ellison's *Invisible Man*, whose narrator offers his own singular experience as one black man in a world ordered according to the rules of white supremacy in the hope that readers might see or sense their own experience—their own voice in a tale candidly told, a door left open a thousand times before now made specifically visible. Radically openhanded telling true, he imagines, is probably his only possible method and his only hope. "What else could I do? What else but try to tell you what was really happening when your eyes were looking through?" asks the Invisible Man. Maybe we *will* see. Perhaps a call is being successfully transmitted across time from one more lonely heart writing his rights and wrongs unto another: "Who knows but that, on the lower frequencies, I speak for you?"[7]

This open-ended question is deeply in sync with an exchange with Tupac Shakur that concludes *To Pimp A Butterfly*. Having drawn Tupac's voice into the conversation through twentieth-century recordings, they talk sanity, survival, and what hope there might yet be for the human species. Lamar shares his own suspicion that the only remaining hope is "music and vibrations" and invites us to consider the human situation as scope and process in light of the life of the caterpillar, destroying its surroundings necessarily in an effort to get born, contrasting this sight with "the talent, the thoughtfulness, and the beauty of the butterfly." There's misunderstanding, resentment, and exploitation in the attempt, on the part of the caterpillar, to *pimp* the butterfly, to only see and use it perversely. *But*, as Lamar sees it, what's yet to be widely understood is that the caterpillar and the butterfly are one. Is there a fuller, more compassionate sense of self to be had here? What might Tupac—or Tupac's devotees—make of it?

With this kind of question, a gift of spirit is once more set in motion and a site is made ready and available for all takers. Perhaps the form of life Lamar conjures here and elsewhere will somehow *in*form our own. His hands are open and extended in the risk and hoped-for reception of song. Something is being passed on. It's the gift of spirit, the possibility of poetry, that June Jordan conceives as information, faith, and exorcism, made possible whenever some-one hazards the telling of truth. The song of *him*self might enter into the song of *our*selves. We can tell everybody this is our song too. Perhaps, on the lower frequencies, he speaks for you.

DEMOCRATIC DIGNITY

What's being passed on here, if we have eyes and ears and wit to receive it, is the clairvoyance of Beloved Community that is sometimes buried but now and then brought to surface. I take this to be what Walt Whitman spied and decreed in section 24 of "Song of Myself" as a never-quite-done deal some-times under way among human beings: the password primeval that is a sign of democracy to come. It speaks to the public and the alleged private, our hearts and our spending habits and our media feeds. It's the home and the landscape of international relations where whatever is said or done returns at last to each of us, military-industrial-entertainment-incarceration complexes notwithstanding:

> I speak the password primeval, I give the sign of democracy,
> By God! I will accept nothing which all cannot have their counterpart of
>   on the same terms[8]

Straining the boundaries of the bardic, Whitman here strikes a note of industrial-strength universalism. The human movement to which his senses bear witness draws on—but isn't confined to—each and every known effort of discernible righteousness ("This head more than churches, bibles, and all the creeds") among the pounding hearts of peoples past, present, and future (50). He wants to lift every voice, clarifying and transfiguring fellow humans lost, stolen, or hidden away. This is the remembering work that befalls anyone who knows themselves to be held aloft in an inescapable network of mutual-ity. Knowing his own consciousness to be a gift ("Seeing, hearing, feeling, are miracles, and each part and tag of me is a miracle"), he wants to keep the gift in circulation (49).

This is the relentlessly social, good-news ethic interwoven in the solidarity of song. We have within ourselves the actionable dream that change is afoot, and it will be a severe and blessed reversal of fortunes. Things are about to turn around. All oppression shall cease. Weapons systems will be beaten into plow-shares. Senseless pain, death, foreclosures, and crop failure can now be talked about with candor and passion and amusement. A place is made for telling it like it is—what Melville called a "democratic dignity."[9]

With the power of Herod, Pilate, Jim Crow, and Pharaoh somehow relativ-ized, music is free to operate under the assumption that the just prerogatives

of the Almighty will somehow ultimately prevail. The avenues for communication (of fear, worry, hope, and gospel) are expanded into a great wide
open. And here again, the dissent and truth telling of those about to rock
and roll can't quite be righteously characterized through our popular dichotomies. When Sister O. M. Terrell declares matter-of-factly that if the Bible's
right, somebody's wrong (in 1953 with a guitar sound that anticipates Jimmy
Page and a distinctly Little Richard–like howl), the powers that be are put
on high alert. The whole human and all of society are engaged with a mystical, prophetic power that knows no convenient divisions. The times are going
to change.

In a wonderful, provocatively messy meditation called *Mumbo Jumbo*,
Ishmael Reed describes the elusive quality of jazz/blues/freedom-chime-that-
shakes-nerves-and-rattles-brains as "Jes Grew." The phrase comes from James
Weldon Johnson's description of a "jes' grew" song: "A song which had been
sung for years all through the South. The words were unprintable, but the tune
was irresistible, and belonged to nobody."[10] For Reed, the "Jes Grew" factor is
the righteous practice of "HooDooing the dice" to make them roll sevens every
time, a sneaking in of good cheer and hilarity to deconstruct the trouble of
troubled times.[11] It isn't always received as good news by the gatekeepers but
it's a salt that's kept its saltiness, a mustard seed that contains multitudes. It's a
kind of liberating virus, spreading like a contagion and undoing death-dealing
seriousness and defensive posturing wherever it lurks:

> Jes Grew was unlike physical plagues. Actually Jes Grew was anti-plague.
> Jes Grew enlivened the host. Other plagues were accompanied by bad air
> (malaria). Jes Grew victims said that the air was as clear as they had ever
> seen it and that there was the aroma of roses and perfumes which had
> never before enticed their nostrils . . . Jes Grew is electric as life and is
> characterized by ebullience and ecstasy.[12]

As the anti-plague of Beloved Community, the transmission of Jes Grew
broadens the range of human expression. It teaches us how to keep cool and
care. It belittles our idols and channels stories of suffering and hope that remind
us we aren't strangers to other people's prayers. And an Easter consciousness of
escalating mutuality becomes a bigger reality than the oppressive present.

THE SLOW HOLY TRAIN

Theodore Sturgeon tells us that "morals are an obedience to rules that people
laid down to help you live among them."[13] Morality is lyrical and narratival
before it's analytical, and perhaps it loses its spirit as word made flesh whenever talk of right and wrong gets divorced, in the myth of critical detachment,
from bodies, the lived experience of story and song, the gift of spirit carried, as

DuBois claims, in the souls of black folk and the ever-expanding articulation of "the Sorrow Songs," which address everyone. This gift of spirit is sometimes termed "mother wit" as one more way of describing a fanciful, authority-deriding, improvised oratory that inhabits displaced communities. It is that which makes louder and livelier expression permissible and appropriate, a way of staring down madness with mirth.

I think of mother wit when I hear "Daniel Saw the Stone" (1931), by the Silver Leaf Quartette of Norfolk, Virginia. It traces a historical momentum that begins with Daniel staying the wrath of King Nebuchadnezzar against the wise men of Babylon by giving a description and an interpretation of the king's restless dream. The vision is that of a rolling stone, hewn out of a mountain and not made by human hands, that breaks through Babylon, becomes a mountain, and fills the entire earth. As the Silver Leaf Quartette tell it, a young David as well as Jesus got hold of the same stone, and now the singers, with their families, want to get hold of it too. The stone, turned mountain, turned inheritor of earth, is the only game in town. Call it what you like. This rolling stone breaks down crowns and thrones and all that oppresses and somehow encompasses all good, drawing in and redeeming all manner of things, making them well and whole. It's a matter of keeping your eyes on the prize that is the living, always-in-motion, always-healing stone, an inversion of power whenever and wherever it's really and truly beheld.

If the hope of the rolling stone is to be a complete orientation (a whole life ethic and a spirited concern without division), it will have to evade marginalization by that which boasts of itself as the "real world" and refuse the straitjacket of commodification. It has to reintroduce itself to the cultures formed out of it lest they assume they have it all down pat ("You have heard it said. . . . But I say . . ."). It's a matter of constant renovation and reform. "What do these Knaves mean by Virtue?" asks William Blake of the hardened hearts and minds of Christendom.[14] Would the prophets of old recognize in marble-columned evocations of "Virtue" anything resembling the unshackled hope of the living God? What abstractions are serving to gag the Holy Spirit? Woody Guthrie seeks out the ancient paths when he wonders what Jesus would make of America and what America really makes of him (in "Jesus Christ"). And when he nominates Jesus for the office of president of the United States, he's contemplating another faithful variation on this blessed theme, a comic joy that speaks prophetically to the concrete world.

On Woody Guthrie's guitar is inscribed the warning "This machine kills fascists," and this sensibility isn't limited to what was termed "folk" or "protest music." Twentieth-century America housed a white-supremacist terror culture with which to creatively and prophetically contend. Ma Rainey's "This Train" lyricized Beloved Community as a means of transport into future present glory. Wide-eyed Little Richard would boast of a healing to make the dumb and deaf hear and talk, and a young man named Bobby Zimmerman of Hibbing,

Minnesota, would long to join his band. The voices of the lonely hearts club were everywhere.

For his part, Johnny Cash said he was pleased to channel "voices that were ignored or even suppressed in the entertainment media, not to mention the political and educational establishments."[15] In this calculus, there are no sub-humans or irredeemable fools, no absolutely evil human beings beyond all help. And anyone who aspires to operate within its continuum can't take back its invitation to all who thirst, all the troubled, disenfranchised, mostly uninvited souls, without rendering themselves inhospitable to its flow. If it's by our own measure that we're judged, who can afford to measure self or other without mercy? Who can say to mercy, "This far, no further"? In speaking truth to untruth, Beloved Community invites us into a larger authenticity than that to which we've grown accustomed. It won't pause to be established, and it's always too far ahead to be completely respectable. The Love Supreme outshines all lesser loves.

Within three weeks of the assassination of John F. Kennedy, a slightly intoxicated Bob Dylan had the opportunity to speechify upon receiving the Tom Paine award at a fund-raising dinner put on by the Emergency Civil Liberties Committee commemorating Bill of Rights Day. Having played a voter registration rally or two in Mississippi as well as the March on Washington, his credentials for the moment were clear even if he felt a little out of place. After remarking that the audience should probably spend more time relaxing on the beach, he referenced Woody Guthrie (an idol for both Dylan and his well-dressed audience) and spoke dismissively of the notion that any person or gathering could claim to speak definitively on behalf of other people: "I've never seen one history book that tells how anybody feels."[16] A reasonable enough sentiment for a twenty-two-year-old guitar wielder, but he went on to speak more generally about the confusion and fear of the times, the loneliness and estrangement that a man can't help but feel, and the understanding that can't come without empathy. Taking it as a given that such empathy was the perceived task of the people in front of him (and probably that of any artist worthy of the title), he went on to express a word of pity (an "I can relate") for the most on-his-own-with-no-direction-home figure of the day, one Lee Harvey Oswald.

To say the least, this did not go over very well. And after the boos and an explanatory profile in *The New Yorker* ("Those people that night were actually getting me to look at colored people as colored people. . . . What's wrong goes much deeper than the bomb. What's wrong is how few people are free"[17]), Dylan no longer did much in the way of public speaking. The chimes of freedom, it appeared, weren't to extend so far as to speak to the troubled soul of Public Enemy Number One. Dylan reminded the audience that peace, love, and understanding have to have an actual object, that abstractions won't do. To be a carrier of—or to even be open to carrying—the gift of spirit of mother wit is to always go further. Steve Earle would make this kind of move on *Jerusalem* (2002) when he extended imaginative sympathy to the American citizen turned enemy combatant John Walker Lindh, on "John Walker Blues."

The stone that rolled through Babylon is always farther along than any person or group who would presume to speak on its behalf. When it's in danger of a pendulum swing too far away from one end of the multiple pilgrim species, a possible corrective (for anyone with an ear to hear) comes up on the airwaves. Take Merle Haggard's "Okie From Muskogee" (1969), which dares to lampoon the conformity of nonconformity while also envisioning a liberating space, a broader and braver America where "even squares can have a ball." What are the boundaries of our affections? Will the circle be unbroken?

FIXTURES AND FORCES AND FRIENDS

After the Bill of Rights Day fiasco, Dylan would carry his witness differently. The rolling stone, faithfully conceived, won't abide formalization. And any effort to categorize it as high art or low, folk or rock, spiritual or worldly would be dismissed as part of the soul-sucking establishment's attempt to debilitate it or, as Dylan put it in a short-lived *Hootenanny* column, "boundary it all up."[18] Upon winning the Nobel Prize for Literature, he would paraphrase Melville and opine over the self-understanding of Shakespeare, but even in this context, he would resist the suggestion that his song and dance can be helpfully conceived as literature. Making the music, living within it, and making it your own (without troubling yourself with whether you're country, Beat, hipster, gospel, hip-hop, or rock 'n' roll) is a vocation sufficient unto itself. Opening yourself up to the music and all its life-giving, sanity-restoring possibilities involves a receptivity toward more than the market or gatekeeper can know or understand. There's something more wonderful, open-ended, risky, and unyielding going on. As Dylan describes the music, "it's weird, full of legend, myth, Bible and ghosts . . . chaos, watermelons, clocks, everything."[19] Its truthfulness scandalizes, sanctifies, and enlivens every scene. Beloved Community begins in the imagination, dismantling structures of sorrow, oppression, hypocrisy, and enslavement. The liberating word won't be boundaried.

In 1964, as now, popular meaning-making gets policed. *Another Side of Bob Dylan* places such civil rights–era anthems as "Chimes of Freedom" right alongside "All I Really Want to Do." And "To Ramona" observes that the stratagems of unfreedom will defy easy description as sorrows stem by way of "fixtures and forces and friends," hyping and objectifying to enforce groupthink and deadened visions.

After Dylan already had burned a bridge or two with his ill-timed word of solidarity for Lee Harvey Oswald, *Another Side* received a cool reception from the folk music community, who, in turn, received a prophetic word from

Johnny Cash in a letter to the editors of *Sing Out!*: "SHUT UP!... AND LET HIM SING!"[20] (Sidenote: Dylan recently remarked that he still has his copy of that particular issue.) Add to this affirmation the beginnings of a friendship with Allen Ginsberg, an acquaintance with the mad genius of jazz, Ornette Coleman, and the earthshaking advent of the Beatles, and a different way of doing things emerges. Something's breaking through, and it could be that there's more than one way to transcend a genre, poke past a paradigm, and upset a subculture. What's a folk artist to do when the supposed folk establishment starts laying down what's "folk" and what isn't? Dylan biographer Robert Shelton suggests that these were the days when Dylan set out to become a mass-media poet.

I'VE GOT MY BOB DYLAN MASK ON

Kim Gordon of Sonic Youth once observed that live musical performance is a situation in which people will pay to watch other people believe in themselves. This is so true, and I imagine the confidence we pay to behold probably has something to do with our desire to be near freedom, real honesty, and the possibility of real community. We pay and hope.

If Dylan was to deliver at New York's Philharmonic Hall on Halloween night in 1964, he'd have to take on the forces of fake authenticity without getting preachy and tell it like it is without becoming a caricature of himself. After opening with the recent songs his audience would expect concerning the shaky ethics of boxing and anticommunist paranoia, he introduces a new, stranger number, "Gates of Eden," as "A Sacrilegious Lullaby in D minor." The fragmented, more elusive quality of his recent liner notes has now made its way into the music (cowboy angels, utopian monks on the golden calf, and lampposts with folded arms). But the song is just a song, like the ones that came before, another way of fitting words together, another attempt at story. The audience has carefully taken in his carefully enunciated phrases, and he won't trouble them with an explanation, but he will make fun of the idea that he's just shared something inaccessibly deep, complex, or scary: "It's just Halloween. I've got my Bob Dylan mask on. . . . I'm mask-erading."

Skipping the gravitas, mocking it even, he moves swiftly on to the more obviously ridiculous "If You Gotta Go, Go Now." Like Andy Kaufman, he will claim no particular job description save that of a song-and-dance man, and the question of whether he's to be taken more or less seriously is something with which he won't concern himself. That's someone else's business. It's on to another new one they've never heard before: "It's All Right Ma, It's Life and Life Only" will appear on *Bringing It All Back Home* as "It's Alright Ma (I'm Only Bleeding)." The audience laughs at the title and he laughs in response, "Yes, it's a very funny song."

But it isn't at all a funny song. While we can note that, for a "song-and-dance man," there is something amusing about the seven-minute "It's Alright Ma" on this particular evening, it is also the Dylan song that, possibly more than any other, would be regarded with the utmost seriousness. The song marks the day of judgment for every death-dealing abstraction, con game, and unjust ruler within view. Marshall McLuhan once observed that anyone who thinks there's a difference between education and entertainment doesn't know the first thing about either, and this song perhaps proves the point. One line that would be applauded for forty years of live performance through several administrations proclaims that even the US president will have to stand naked. Money doesn't talk so much as it swears (a George Harrison favorite). And a line savored by Jimmy Carter lays down the truism that anyone not busy being born is busily dying. Lest we think our young entertainer is getting too high-and-mighty and moralistic, Dylan ends the invective with the confession that if the authorities could see his "thought-dreams," he'd likely be duly escorted to the guillotine. Not bad for a twenty-three-year-old.

In recent years, when pressed concerning the meaning of a song, Dylan has noted, in mock exasperation, that nobody ever asked Elvis what he really meant when he sang about a hound dog. He's determined to be a "pop" entertainer. Social criticism as musical entertainment. Poetry for the people. When the audience needed it, he knew how to put his Bob Dylan mask on. In 1964, he began to create a media persona he could knowingly mess with. Within a year or two, he'd be telling his television audience, "Keep a good head and always carry a lightbulb." He could be Charlie Chaplin and Walt Whitman and Fats Waller all at once. There was never a need to boundary it all up. There still isn't. What could be more Americana than that?

And in another sense, he'd begun to learn the hard way that telling true (in metaphor or testimony or lyric) and letting the chips fall is the only way to bear witness, and, for his part, the song means what the song means. When asked to explain a particular song, Elvis Costello (an unashamed Dylan devotee) observed that, if he could have put it another way, in a sentence, for instance, he wouldn't have written the song. If he could have said it in a sentence, he would have. "This Land Was Made for You and Me" means, oddly enough, that this land was made for you and me.

Within months, "Subterranean Homesick Blues" (existential? surreal? nonsense? comedy?) would bust open expectations even further (with ripples reaching everyone from R.E.M. to hip-hop to Nirvana to Radiohead) and, in time, he would even "go electric" with what Dylan would call "thin wild mercury music." He would wear dark glasses and arrive for an interview with a lightbulb, silently daring reporters to ask him what it's for. A media blitz was simply another opportunity for a song-and-dance man to exhibit freedom and speak truth to the powerful and the people underneath. To name a few, Patti

Smith, Richard Pryor, and Michael Stipe would do it too. But in 1964, Dylan walked this particular tightrope in the public eye mostly alone.

Almost forty years later, *Love and Theft* would emerge with a seeming effortlessness from his Neverending (and still going) Tour. He tips his hat to Joan Baez, Buddy Holly, and Charley Patton, noting that affectionate borrowing and standing on the shoulders of giants is all any of us can manage when we try to speak out loud; pure, absolute originality is a bit of a myth. But something of an amused acknowledgment of his place along the continuum of folk/protest/punk/rock/entertainment might be coming through in "Summer Days" when he asks how we can honestly say we love someone else "when you know it's me all the time." Surely an icon is allowed to wax self-referential from time to time. And as he doubtless understands (as he's testified, in fact), it's all a masquerade.

RING THEM BELLS

"This is a fictitious story," Dylan once humorously noted concerning a song. Or even better, "This is taken out of the newspapers. And nothing has been changed except the words."[21] There are many ways, as Jeff Tweedy put it, to go about writing your mind the way you want it to read, trying to make sense of yourself to yourself, picturing a world gone wrong. In *City of Words*, Tony Tanner describes "a world of unprogrammed possibilities" that characterizes the creative impulse within much American creative expression.[22] And if we think again of the Silver Leaf Quartette of Norfolk's "Daniel Saw the Stone," there is always a more imaginative way to interpret the sounds and fury of the debilitating Babylonian present. The righteous stone will unmake the oppressive blueprints we've been handed into better, clearer, truer stories, making them signify something. When Sly and the Family Stone tell us we shouldn't let "the plastic" get us down or Beck dreams up ways of feeling less alone in "The New Pollution," they're giving a name to domineering presences that, left unnamed, will possess the minds of millions. Rock 'n' roll will often resonate with the many ways the Bible laughs at our unacknowledged idolatries. Once these bells are struck, the fire alarm of good news for the downtrodden and confused, they're very hard to unring.

The rolling stone not made by human hands has a way of bringing down the anxiety structures we've constructed in our fear and arrogance, mocking every manifestation of Ahab consciousness. This Jes Grew business will splinter into stranger forms, adapting itself to suit the times, unveiling all the new ways we've hypnotized ourselves into unawareness, boxing up our sympathies to better suit our comfort levels.

When Kris Kristofferson sings in his low, gruff voice about the wide assortment ("funky bunch of friends") that Jesus gathers about himself in "Jesus

Was a Capricorn," deriding the way that everybody craves somebody else to look down on, someone to feel better than, we can receive the good word that our fastidiousness (the easy habit of finding others hopelessly offensive) is of the devil. We seem to have a knack, Kristofferson intones, of hating anything we don't understand. "The Law Is for Protection of the People" testifies to the crucifying impulse of self-described "decent folks" who don't want "riddle-speaking prophets" disturbing the peace which is no peace. This is music for the country by the country.

To be people of amazing grace is to see ourselves as recipients of kindness and understanding not owed to us, and if we really believe it's been lavished upon us undeservedly, maybe we can lavish a little upon the people we find ourselves least inclined to view generously. If we're showering only the people we already love with love, do we really think grace is all that amazing? Are we any different from anyone else in our behavior? Do we really believe in amazing grace at all? Or have we placed a limit on it, somehow expecting it to abide by our national and cultural boundaries?

The amused affection that characterizes Beloved Community won't let us kid ourselves about our own ungraciousness or the common life of our multiple pilgrim species. I suspect we're often drawn to live musical performance in an attempt to somehow get in the mood of this ancient solidarity, something to enliven the daily grind. We want the company of mysterious tramps who know what it's like to feel strange, who seem unafraid to testify about feeling down and unwanted, who can sing a word of rebuke to our inner Ahabs.

On the Pixies album *Doolittle*, Frank Black (masquerading as Black Francis) begins a song called "Mr. Grieves" with a kind of reggae riff and the repeated hope that everything is going to be all right. As he makes this proclamation, he starts to laugh in a not-so-convincing manner, and as he tries again, the laughter becomes a sort of angry, barely controlled sobbing, and we know that everything isn't going to be all right. It's completely silly, of course. And it is, technically, only a performance, but it's deeply liberating to hear Frank Black play out a scene of lost composure, satirizing it by acknowledging it, letting a little air in. It almost hurts to hear it, but it's funny because it's true, and the recognition of severe dysfunction, the grieving of it (Lana Del Rey, Violent Femmes, mewithoutyou) can alleviate the pain. It brings it out into the open—songs of love and loss and nervous breakdown. We should be wary of being overly offended by comedic lamentation or poignant portrayals of screwed-uppedness. If we feel completely unsympathetic toward the silliness, it might be that we aren't sufficiently offended by ourselves.

Pixies enthusiasts have signed on for this brand of communication, recognizing themselves in the songs and the tensions to which they testify. Frank Black will cop a wide variety of attitudes to suit the neuroses of different songs. This is how the music works. It's an entering into a communal awareness, a partaking of the mother wit that resists the despair with nothing to say. If "punk" might be defined as a commitment to question everything, it, too, exists in the wake of the ancient rolling stone. There are a variety of countertactics to be pieced together in song and story against dehumanization on behalf of all things human, and we might not get it the first time around. We're welcome to be troubled by something we're shown by Jessie Reyez, Tori Amos, or Randy Newman, but if we're refusing the testimony of the truthful word, the witness, or the confession, we risk losing the ability to hear or love well at all. Only truthfulness can edify. And finding anything and everything interesting and worthy of song is a habit of the long, practiced, determined wit of Beloved Community, dethroning the mighty and chanting down Babylon at every opportunity and in all of its multiplying forms.

John Prine's "Your Flag Decal Won't Get You into Heaven Anymore" names a dawning awareness concerning a white-supremacist alliance with a demonic stronghold that mistakes itself for Christianity. It's not knocking flag decals exactly, but it does name a confused association rather aptly, juxtaposing the Sermon on the Mount with the militant ignorance of nationalism ("my country right or wrong"). And as we're inundated with all kinds of antiwisdom, disinformation, and unexamined thinking, we need sanity-restoring ways of looking at it all. We need finer work songs to better keep out the chill. Songs that might possibly serve as a moral compass as we look over the maps, legends, and blueprints we've inherited and all the rage and irritability that proffer themselves as integrity and virtue.

WELCOME TO THE OCCUPATION

Our music houses an underground ethos of good-humored resistance that speaks back to everyday chaos, songs and sounds that somehow describe what we're going through. Prine's "Angel from Montgomery" gives powerful expression to a woman who pines for a word, any word, from a husband who won't even tell her about his workday as her hopes and dreams for a loving future diminish. A familiar story turned prayer. In R.E.M.'s "New Test Leper," Michael Stipe puts the words of Jesus on the lips of an embarrassed guest on a television sideshow. It comes out awkwardly, but he'd hoped to illuminate the minds of the audience in the studio and the people at home with the dictum "Judge not, lest ye be judged." As we would expect, this doesn't go over well, and he's made to sit silent as he's cut off by commercials and the host's "index-carded" wit. Identifying with the postmodern leper, Stipe lyricizes life outside the conventionally telegenic, whose aching smiles feel too unattractive to look upon. That would be all of us.

This music of democratic dignity is possessed by an ethos of everyone invited and every testimony worthy of a kind, interested, sympathetic ear. It's scandalously open to the notion that anybody anywhere might have a worthwhile vision. It trusts that a revelatory word can come from the least among us at any time, that those we're least likely to want to listen to might have one. The music assumes that there is no human life unworthy of our affectionate interest. I think a young Bob Dylan bore faithful witness to this Beloved Community, of and for the people, when he voiced a word of insistent empathy for Lee Harvey Oswald in 1963. A moment's reflection might bring to mind a number of examples of this sort of thing in Dylan's catalog (Hattie Carroll, "Hurricane" Carter), Springsteen's invocation of working-class heroes and the ghost of Tom Joad, or Pearl Jam ("Jeremy," "Daughter," "Better Man"). But for my money, the career of R.E.M., hailing from the local culture of Athens, Georgia, is especially noteworthy for self-consciously democratic, resiliently compassionate music that spans decades as it speaks for, to, and despite the times.

R.E.M.'s 1986 album *Lifes Rich Pageant* opens with a call to heed the insurgency that was and is America ("Begin the Begin"), and the summons to look harder in the eyes of our neighbors and consider again the histories we've inherited is indicative of their entire catalog. With an eye fixed on all that might yet make American culture somehow righteously unique in the history of nations, R.E.M. rages against the machinery that will always feel threatened by an unconditional affirmation of all human beings as infinitely worthwhile. This is perhaps especially evident on "Exhuming McCarthy," which laments the loss of a sense of decency in public discourse as the general welfare is sold off to the highest bidder. According authorial authority to a disabled child ("The Wrong Child"), Montgomery Clift ("Monty Got a Raw Deal"), a traumatized soldier ("Swan Swan H"), and a confused, angry television viewer who saw fit to physically attack CBS News anchor Dan Rather ("What's the Frequency, Kenneth?"), their music imaginatively documents the visions of the unheeded and bewildered.

While "Everybody Hurts" off *Automatic for the People* (1992) is probably their best-known ballad (a finer anthem for the democratic solidarity of all things human is hard to come by), a favorite of mine is the deeply uplifting "Try Not to Breathe." As legend has it, the phrase of the title was stumbled upon in the recording studio when Stipe was instructed to maintain silence behind the microphone. "I'll try not to breathe" developed into the musings of a citizen of advanced age who doesn't want to burden the young with too much in the way of caregiving or worry while nevertheless entertaining the hope that someone somewhere down the line might want to listen to some stories. The citizen wants someone to remember his or her testimony. An odd accomplishment for what we usually expect in a pop song, admittedly, but "Try Not to Breathe" challenges the listener to look more generously and believe more widely and richly concerning the value of a stranger. They've seen things we'll never see. The stranger will often be a warehouse of wisdom and stories, an endless supply of human interest only so long as humans go to the blessed trouble of finding one another interesting. Remembering each other and paying attention is what we get to do. It's of and for the people. Wouldn't it be something if we did it automatically? Might we make it a habit? Might we learn that trustworthy witness will usually come from unexpected quarters? There's something very R.E.M. about this sensibility, the stranger as an occasion for joy. And a nation of diasporas gets to be especially adept at listening to one another.

R.E.M. concern themselves with the kind of people we find in country songs, shopping malls, daytime television, and overlooked photographs. Their music assumes that we're not yet young, that there's always a better way of putting things. This righteously curious attitude is captured particularly well in the band's fascination with Andy Kaufman ("Man on the Moon" and "The Great Beyond"), who could make the outrageous appear doubly ridiculous by portraying it as it is in the world of Wrestlemania or any and all entertainment media. When Stipe imitates Kaufman imitating Elvis Presley, we're made to think about celebrity, nostalgia, and public performance very differently. Popular entertainment is demystified long enough to be beheld in all its strangeness as a mode of social interaction. Our mean ideas can have us feeling pretty psyched at concerts, political rallies, and wrestling matches, but we're called to hold one another dear and with calm belonging. We need something to help us remember as much, something to keep us thinking kindly and carefully. If we believe there's something worthy of song up every stranger's sleeve, then maybe everyone's cool.

The music of Beloved Community articulates the otherwise unarticulated testaments of troubled souls ("great" and "small") in troubled times. Johnny Cash's "The Ballad of Ira Hayes" describes the drunken death of a Native American soldier who helped raise the flag at Iwo Jima and returned to a racist homeland. Beck's "It's All in Your Mind" describes the dismay of gradually discovering a dear friend has gone scared stiff and demon possessed. And Tom Waits gives voice to countless castoffs, respectability long lost, who note in Orbisonesque fashion that you're "Innocent When You Dream." We're all more than a little human, and there's nothing especially simple or straightforward about humans. Folk music always says so.

When Dylan speaks of first hearing Woody Guthrie ("Last Thoughts on Woody Guthrie") or Michael Stipe recalls hearing Patti Smith ("E-Bow the Letter"), we're reminded of how democratic solidarity makes its way through the masses. They're offering lyrical accounts of how the genius of being awake to your own life gets handed down, over, and passed on. They're describing the moment they happened upon an undercurrent of liveliness and sociability that they felt compelled to seek out and make their own. Better ways of being free and speaking truthfully to and about the world invigorate the listener, putting words, expressions, and images to an otherwise mostly undescribed existence. People need to know that they're not alone in their awkwardness as they struggle to find their skin. They want to hear their own hopes and dreams interpreted in new, truer fashions. And the truer ways of carrying oneself will build righteously on the old ones. Not better stories than their own, but explanations more dignifying and liberating than the prisons and paradigms in which they find themselves. Prayers and songs that cover everything, even the sadness that seems to defy sense and all the strangeness that doesn't seem to bother anyone else. A music of the misfits, by the misfits, for the misfits.

EVERYTHING IS EVERYTHING

Beloved Community reminds us that any language that presumes proprietorship over the authentic, the free, the godly, or the truthful is a bearing of false witness, and I don't believe we can entertain such language for long without going off the rails. As I understand it, good music summons us to revere ourselves, the people nearby, and the history we're standing in with a bit more tenderness, awe, and amusement. It also inspires an imaginative vigilance, dislocating the fixations that keep us thinking and speaking falsely; a vigilance that anything approaching emotional health thrives on. With a watchful eye on history that is the present, the right now what's-going-on in the world, the songs are written by and for people who want to have a go at not losing their souls. We write and recite psalms and songs to keep from losing it, to regulate our dramas, and to make sense of the senseless. We listen, watch, and pray as a form of crazy-prevention. We're not alone.

When we talk about the music or any history of faithful witness or truthful testimony, nobody gets to be an absolute authority, an expert, or a theologian who can see undarkly. No nation, culture, or political party can claim to speak definitively for freedom itself. Who claims complete, undivided truthfulness, truth abandons. And there is no professional opinion on the human soul. But we can aspire to be true to the songs of lone pilgrims, apostles, poor immigrants, and escaped slaves. We do well to be haunted by them, and we can hope that our own words won't sound hopelessly untrue, unwise, or dishonest beside them. All we can do is hope.

"All doors are open to the believer. It is the lesson of the Samaritan woman at the well."[23] This is Patti Smith offering a mantra for seeing and living well, for locating oneself along a continuum of human honesty, the lyrical current of someone else's drift. Where life has been finalized, absolutized, and shut down, music drops in as an antidote to whatever momentary feeling of inauthenticity might plague us. It's one more way to *get real*. A way out and in.

One can try to tune in well and be an echo among other echoes, more or less faithful, in a landscape of power and greed and seemingly endless defensiveness. We get to add to the heaping collection of testimonials and eyewitness accounts of weird goings-on and broken dreams. To add or to even amplify is to take on the task of the hierophant, the person who elevates others into an experience of holiness. Consider the way Aretha Franklin managed this feat for years in her cover—we forget it's a cover—of Otis Redding's "Respect." I've noticed that, almost whenever it's played, many listeners young and old drop their decorum and feel compelled to put on a furrowed brow and join their voices and postures to her enunciations. It's like a call to arms. What could and should have been between women and men and all of us has gone horribly awry and requires—we feel it—immediate attention. This very kind of cultivating work occurred in 1967 when Franklin performed a jujitsu move on Redding's song, deploying its demands in the direction of a specifically feminine, ethical insistence on decency, care, and demonstrable affection. And if its summons for lived attentiveness to the bodily needs of one's partner weren't already sufficiently explicit, Franklin and her sisters sealed the deal in the studio with their insertion of the famous "sock it to me" line. The hierophant's space-making enterprise occurs in new and unexpected contexts. Love's proof is in the pudding or nowhere at all.

Go public or go home, we might say. Bring your God-given clairvoyance to the surface and think! Gather what remains. All justice is social. All righteousness is relational. We have to get granular in thinking it all through. This deep soul work has been lyrically undertaken for centuries. It's all around us in the land of the free.

I lately spy it in the witness of the hierophant Chance the Rapper, whose album *Coloring Book* functions as good-news catechesis for all comers. In Chance's art, the inescapable network of mutuality (classroom, church, family, neighborhood, fans) is always in view. There's no love to be had or life to be lived outside it. On *Coloring Book*, heaven—like hell—is always other people.

ARE YOU READY?

Consider "Nostalgia" from his first formal mixtape, *10 Day* (2012), a track that can be meaningfully paired with *Coloring Book*'s "Summer Friends." Chance sets the eschatological scene by recalling schoolmates lost to gun violence in his native Chicago and the hope that, when God's kingdom comes and God's will is done, all of these lost people will be restored to one another in a citywide healing. We know there's a way of separating God and gospel from the fact of lived reality, divinity from the everyday, prayer from bodies, praise from protest. See yesterday, today, and tomorrow's news cycle. But like the Beloved Community that forms him, Chance will have none of that. "Nostalgia" envisions the lost and found companions within his childhood community engaged in a long-haul game of hide-and-seek which gives way to heads bowed in "Seven Up" and raised again on earth as it already is in heaven.

In chorus and verse, the promise of longed-for restoration in the future is forever tied to the land of the living, a seeking out of righteousness within—and in spite of—the beleaguered present. While the *10 Day* of the title refers to Chance's ten-day suspension for on-campus marijuana possession during his senior year of high school, even here Chance's sense of vocation as a neighborhood conjurer, an articulator of much-needed perception, is in play. Witness "Brain Cells," which features Chance entering the listener's ear as a "tab of acid" turned animorph bearing "the passion and the magic in the air" amid "the labyrinth of Pan's Lab." Amid the reigning dysfunction and disinformation, this is the shape his lyrical attentiveness will take. The hoped-for future will have an animated representative in the metamorphosis of verse. Chance will give to airy nothing a local habitation and a name.

So into our fevered labyrinth comes *Coloring Book*. And there's so much to feel good about. Salvation, we're made to see repeatedly, is a *this-worldly* process. And blessedly so. The work of holistic discernment, Chance's phrase, involves a spirit of mirth (giving "Satan a swirlie," for instance") as well as Harry Potter–like perseverance (Scars on his head, Chance decrees himself "the boy who lived"). And music, which is all any of us have got, is ever before us as the vehicle of love, insight, and energy.

Meanwhile, the righteousness for which he hungers and thirsts has nowhere else to happen but his life on earth, because right relationship is all. He prayerfully insists that the mother of his child will increasingly have in him a righteous partner and lover (they're "on a marathon" they "can build a marriage on"). Here too, the thriving he has in mind is inescapably communal, because the Chicago inextricably connected to his fame (he's got his "city doing front flips") is the space he wants to keep safe for the sake of his daughter, the campers for whom he volunteers his time, and the elderly of his neighborhood. As "Finish Line/Drown" envisions the end of days, there's a final righting of creation when God's kingdom comes on earth as it already is in the heavenlies with Kirk Franklin intoning that one day "we'll all be free." But the universal hope is preceded by the local concern: One day "*Chicago* will be free." The context of later is now or not at all. The word must put on flesh.

With "Blessings," Chance voices a state of mind reminiscent of Bob Dylan's response to the question of his own happiness, put to him by *Rolling Stone* on the occasion of his fiftieth birthday. Dylan refused the terms: "You know, these are yuppie words, happiness and unhappiness. It's not happiness or unhappiness, it's either blessed or unblessed. As the Bible says, 'Blessed is the man who walketh not in the counsel of the ungodly.'"[24] Blessedness, we understand, is a very different game from the pursuit of happiness. Similarly, Chance lays out a sacred economy that flips the script on power, prestige, and profit as they're popularly conceived. He doesn't "make songs for free," he makes them "for freedom." He doesn't "believe in kings," he believes "in the kingdom." And for what appears to be a purposefully slow jam, "Blessings" does an awful lot of work, placing a punchy, James Brown–like "Good God!" directly next to a smoothly crooned, slowly enunciated "Good God" as if mulling over the wide spectrum of emotions out of which the goodness of God might yet be evoked.

A sound-bite won't do. A life of praise takes time, and you'll know one by its fruit. Chance is at war with his wrongs in an industry demanding "four minute songs," but what's needed is "a four hour praise dance" broadcast "every morn." True praise is a long haul, a lifelong embodiment of ups and downs. We're never not worshiping in Chance's world.

And in this sense, the blessing game will require a relentlessly tender imagination of self and others. The question of lived tenderness, of holding oneself, everything, and everyone dear is at the center—is, in fact, the moral heft—of *Coloring Book.* Hence the inclusion of "D.R.A.M. Sings Special," which features Shelley Massenburg-Smith, a.k.a. D.R.A.M., singing a rounding blessing over the listener as if we're all children recovering again a realization of how special we are by looking into one another's eyes. But again, Chance has offered this insight before. I certainly have in mind "Everything's Good (Good Ass Outro)" from *Acid Rap* but primarily "Everybody's Something," which strikes the same insistent note of human kinship in the context of white-supremacist violence: everybody is somebody else's everything, and nobody, in the final measure, is nothing. On both albums, it's as if a universal law of tenderness, an ancient imperative of mutual affection often instilled in children, is being brought to the sing-song surface like a forgotten catechism, a long-distance call from our best selves.

We might begin to spy a deep orderliness in Chance's work when we recall an adage afforded us by Ursula K. Le Guin, who observed that an artist, a truly creative personality, is a child who has survived adulthood. Like the busy, enlivening animorph he promised he'd be on *10 Day*, Chance brings out of his treasury items ever ancient and ever new in his speechifying on soil and promised lands and "wondrous unfamiliar lessons of childhood" that teach us "how to smile good." Against the division of flesh and spirit, Chance speaks of God in public testifying, in fact, that he believes God and he are "mutual fans."

There's a boldness here, a kind of chutzpah, that might challenge popular conceptions of piety, but Chance's faith in a God who accepts every emotion and welcomes every form of candor and good humor is every bit biblical. His expression defies marketing and genre, but this too is a blessed thing. The divisions of sacred and secular dissolve upon contact with the way a heart really works. But we've received that wisdom already from one luminary after another, right? Lauryn Hill knows it. Toni Morrison lays it all out. Every prophet in our sacred chronicles says so. We forget so easily. True witness knows no division. Labels be damned.

Coloring Book won't be boundaried up. It's composed of songs of innocence *and* experience, and full humanity requires both. This is William Blake's Doctrine of Contraries as well as what Judee Sill refers to as a union of opposites, light and shadow. We need a profound and ongoing recognition of both to keep from becoming hopelessly estranged from ourselves. It's a process Chance the Rapper chronicles with wit and wonder. We might have "missed the come up," he says, but he's a "Mister Mufasa" trained to "master stampedes." If he can, maybe we can too. In Chance, we have a chronicler determined to be a living and loving witness to his own experience. We also have, on the authority of Irenaeus of Lyon, a second-century church father, that a glory of God is a human being fully alive. Maybe there's glory to behold here. Maybe there's glory everywhere. Are we ready for our blessing?

Chapter 5

The Signposts Up Ahead

Ignorance is expensive.

—Octavia Butler

What helps for me—if help comes at all—is to find the mustard seed of the funny at the core of the horrible and futile.

—Philip K. Dick

The Universe is not only stranger than we imagine; it is stranger than we can imagine.

—J. B. S. Haldane

So at the dinner table when I was very young, I was boring to all those other people. They did not want to hear about the dumb childish news of my days. They wanted to talk about really important stuff that happened in high school or maybe in college or at work. So the only way I could get into a conversation was to say something funny. I think I must have done it accidentally at first, just accidentally made a pun that stopped the conversation. . . . And then I found that a joke was a way to break into an adult conversation.

—Kurt Vonnegut

If we take a moment to imagine a young Kurt Vonnegut sitting at a busy, chattering dinner table wondering how he might get in on the fun, we might begin to feel something universal, seeing ourselves with him, trying to figure out a way to jump perceived barricades into the joys of observational candor. Vonnegut (like everyone I know) wants in. We want attention, a way of relating, some excuse to be heard, an avenue for placing our limited perspective alongside the limited perspectives of others. How to do this? How might we get someone to say, "That's interesting! I never thought of it that way," and look at us with an appreciative smile? How do we get in on the act?

With "The Fire Balloons" (1951), Ray Bradbury offers a "once upon a time . . ." featuring a couple of Episcopal ministers trying to share Jesus with "the Old Ones" of Mars. How's this going to work? An interesting thought experiment, to say the least, and it can get the mind wondering about a lot of other things as well. Such confabulation isn't merely a story; rather, it's a way of describing the present world (the stranger and livelier the better) to a world in danger of being disenchanted with itself. It's not a prediction so much as a way of talking about what's going on, a living reminder that we're free to think about things differently at any point. Orwell's *1984* isn't rendered irrelevant by the fact that we aren't divided into Oceania and Eurasia at the moment. Doublethink, Reality Control, and Thoughtcrime describe lived experience. And *Slaughterhouse-Five* (chronicling Billy Pilgrim's relationship with his green friends on Tralfamadore and his prescription of corrective lenses for Earthling souls) is one way Vonnegut can try to bear witness to his experience as a soldier reflecting on the destruction of Dresden in World War II. And so it goes.

When we first begin to share or even compose songs and poems and science fiction, we begin with the hope that we might have something to say, but it isn't as if the stories are simply vehicles for morals or messages. As a thought experiment, Boots Riley's *Sorry To Bother You* gets us thinking more practically and even prophetically about what the successful channeling of a "white voice" does to people, planet, and the possibility of a discernibly human future. What started out as one man's mulling over a telemarketing gig gives way to an industrial-strength parable for our times. It tells the truth—the crushing truth—by telling it strange. A people with no appetite for such telling are a people estranged from their own existence. Shannon Hale describes this state of stupefaction most effectively: "If we don't tell strange stories, when something strange happens we won't believe it."[1]

I treasure in my heart an early memory I take to be a moment of initiation in my own life to the work of recognizing what's strange in the existence we share with others. I was a five-year-old home sick one day when my mother brought home and placed before me what would become my earliest visual memory of a comic book cover. It was the Incredible Hulk standing at the mouth of a cave holding an unconscious woman and weeping. I needed my mother to read the caption aloud ("SOMEBODY HURT HULK'S FRIEND . . . AND WHEN HULK FINDS THEM . . . HULK WILL SMASH!"), but the image was all I needed to begin to be awakened to art, creativity, and an openness to strange new worlds that awaited my emotional engagement. I imagine my mother simply spied the image on a spinning metal rack at a gas station and figured it might lull me away from television for a while. For me, it was an entry into lore that, truth be told, serves my self-understanding even now. One more artifact in a pop culture catechesis which, to my mind, expands the space of the talkaboutable and serves the righteous ends of Beloved Community wherever it's received.

PEACE OFFENSIVE

Following news reports of the alleged facts on the ground during the Korean War, film producer Julian Blaustein became preoccupied by the oft-repeated and contradictory phrase appearing in headlines and spoken by self-respecting world leaders everywhere: "Peace Offensive." Looking for a story to speak to the paradox, he eventually found the piece (Harry Bates's "Farewell to the Master") that became *The Day the Earth Stood Still*. And from the intergalactic calm and moral authority of Michael Rennie's Klaatu to the stalwart grandeur of Gort, this word on worldly ambition stands rather well. The publicity that preceded its release in 1951 ("WHAT IS THIS INVADER FROM ANOTHER PLANET . . . CAN IT DESTROY THE EARTH?") plays to the very paranoia that the film mocks and derides, and the film's enduring appeal testifies to the American public's hunger for a perspective-enlarging word.

It is only after the American military shoots and wounds the newly arrived Klaatu ("We have come to visit you in peace and with goodwill") within seconds of his landing in Washington that the enormous robot Gort slowly exits the spaceship and begins to obliterate tanks and cannons and machine guns with a laser located behind his head visor. Blaustein once recounted that, in a preview screening, he was horrified to note that audiences laughed at the first sight of Gort. But in time, he realized that they weren't amused by Gort so much as the presumption on the part of anyone "in power" that this impasse had a military solution or that the arrival of an extraterrestrial required an adversarial posture to begin with. When a radio announcer solemnly proclaims, "We are dealing with forces beyond our knowledge and power," and the president reluctantly concedes, "We may be up against powers that are beyond our control," we see again that science fiction creates a space for seeing our limits-denying hubris anew.

Like *Star Trek*'s United Federation of Planets or Ursula K. Le Guin's Ekumen series, *The Day the Earth Stood Still* offers the possibility of a larger ethical order within which our sense of polity and profit will have to reorient itself, and, in this sense, science fiction can serve as a mode of apocalypse if we'll let it. Le Guin's Ekumen (a sort of democratic, intergalactic Vatican) won't presume to define freedom for the rest of the universe ("from the top down," as it were), but her descriptions can get the imagination working and expanding beyond the perceived necessities of the Washington Consensus and the suggestion that history is nothing more than the memory of states. These moral visions challenge our overweening faith in our own alleged realism. Klaatu brings tiding of peacefulness and words of admonition concerning Earth's escalating aggression. Even if all sides inevitably term themselves "peacekeepers" and "freedom-fighters," Klaatu assures them that, however they might choose to name their evil, any spread of their hostilities will earn the wrath of Gort.

The president sends a secretary to meet with Klaatu in a closed room, and he tries to articulate the fact that his homeland security concerns won't necessarily coincide with Klaatu's desire to take his gospel to all of Earth's nations. Klaatu wants the president to think of him as a neighbor, but the secretary explains that it's difficult for his fellow Earthlings to think of Klaatu as a neighbor, true neighborliness between anyone being a rather delicate matter. "I'm afraid in the present situation you'll have to learn to think that way," Klaatu replies. He will take his errand of mercy outside of the nation's security apparatus and travel under the name "Carpenter" (get it?). Needless to say, his influence campaign will be confronted by certain challenges.

A strange neurosis with Gort alongside, the image of Klaatu wishing us well and looking compassionately but knowingly at our hysteria is an enduring one. It's indicative of the interest in human moral progress (and recidivism) at work throughout classic science fiction. To be able to laugh at the human foibles made manifest in the debilitating fear we feel before the unknown is to enter into a kind of ecumenical laughter that privileges no party or tribe. And yet there's also a less amused, antitotalitarian impulse pervading these thought experiments, a hypersensitivity for the more elusive forces of unfreedom.

Philip K. Dick had a powerful aversion to anything that seemed to justify the reduction of human beings to their "use" value. Viewing people (or training them to view themselves) as machines existing for someone else's purposes struck him as "the greatest evil imaginable." And resisting "pseudohuman behavior" or "inauthentic human activity" struck him as the most pressing need in our society.[2] Borrowing Tom Paine's complaint about Europe, "They admired the feathers and forgot the bird," Dick remarked, "It is the dying bird that I am concerned with. The dying—and yet, I think, beginning again to revive in the hearts of the new generation of kids coming into maturity—the dying bird of authentic humanness."[3] The fear that the inhumane has come to pass as standard procedure or a basic requirement for living in "the real world" is a recurring theme throughout American science fiction.

One of the early classics dealing with communal dehumanization is *Invasion of the Body Snatchers* (1956). Describing the plight of Kevin McCarthy's Dr. Miles J. Bennell, the preview declares, "AN ACCURSED, DREADFUL, MALEVOLENT THING WAS HAPPENING TO THOSE HE LOVED." His patients come to see him in droves, complaining that their loved ones aren't themselves, that they've been replaced by impersonators. But gradually, fewer people are complaining, and most apologize for having been so unreasonable. His psychologist friend, Danny Kauffman, explains it as "a strange neurosis . . .

evidently contagious—an epidemic of mass hysteria. In two weeks, it's spread all over town."

"What causes it?" Miles wonders.

"Worry about what's going on in the world probably."

But Kauffman, as it turns out, is one of them. It's the pods. While the citizens sleep, the pods absorb their minds and memories, grow into exact replicas, dispose of their bodies, and assume their identities. To learn to stop worrying about the world means being replaced with a soulless counterpart with no affections, passions, or fanciful notions. Blissful sameness rules. "You're reborn into an untroubled world," the pod people assure Miles and his girlfriend, Becky Driscoll ("I felt something was wrong, but I thought it was me").

Against the commonsensical notion that too much concern over what's going on in the world is unseemly and mildly neurotic, there's a sensibility here that suggests we should be worried if we aren't unsettled and awakened to the strangeness of what we've settled for every so often. A nation that flees any and all unsettledness is a nation that wants to be brainwashed. If we resent troubling news that fails to verify our lifestyles, learning to reflexively improvise it away with words like "bias" and "politics," we're narrowing the zone in which we can see, think clearly, or confess wrongdoing. When we fail in the obligation to be vigilant against our own worst instincts, we're an easy target for whatever news products or election campaigns will confirm our already-made-up minds. This is how ideology operates. It's what we have to believe to not feel quite so bad about what we've already decided to say and do. It's a product that sells itself by slipping smoothly into the already-underway improvisations we undertake to avoid hating ourselves. Science fiction is bad news for ideology.

HUMANS FROM EARTH

When Karl Barth spoke of the strange new world of the Bible, he was noting the manner in which the Bible undoes the reigning takes on reality, undermining our tendency to paint the world in our vanity's favor and speaking a particular kind of earthbound, kingdom-coming hope to our anxiety-stricken landscape. When the Bible is made perfectly normal or obvious to anyone who shares our perfectly natural status quo values, we might do well to suspect we're in the presence of false witness. Properly received, the Bible has an annoying way of unsettling our sense of what's fair and balanced. It resists the tidying-up mechanism that Flannery O'Connor viewed with such disapproval. It frees us up to view ourselves strangely again.

As a young person, I was taught to read the Bible as if my life depended on it, but what I felt to be the intensity of its witness was only rarely reflected in the words and sensibilities of those whom Hawthorne describes with some degree of bemusement as professional teachers of truth. To my young mind, the supposed authorities never struck me as being sufficiently freaked out by the escalating stakes involved in the endless varieties of human screwiness at work in the world. And then came science fiction. I'd felt that something was wrong, and without these stories and images, I was at risk of assuming I was the only one. Enter Rod Serling.

With his odd and chronically underestimated witness, Serling insisted on viewing television as a medium of broad sociological possibilities. In the 1950s, his writing for *Kraft Television Theatre* and *Playhouse 90* had earned him a living, but teleplays that spoke directly and unambiguously to such events as the murder of Emmett Till had just about put him out of a job. But he still maintained that television was potentially a mother lode of storytelling, consciousness-expanding, artistic expression. With *The Twilight Zone*, Serling would keep the airwaves weird and wonderful while noting how effectively words that couldn't be uttered by a Republican or a Democrat could be said loud and clear by a Martian. He would stand in front of the camera and narrate us through the weirdness of the world we're living in. As something of an antifascist crusader, Serling was unwilling to leave the biggest game in town, television (the drug of the nation), to soap and aspirin companies.

As a moral tale that lingers in the imagination, one of the most famous episodes, running a close second behind "To Serve Man," is "The Monsters Are Due on Maple Street." There is a power failure in the suburbs. For the denizens of Maple Street, the absence of evidence is not the evidence of absence, and the loss of electric power combined with some hearsay concerning out-of-the-ordinary behavior among seemingly upstanding people will lead to every-person-for-themselves, murderous mayhem. In their desire to root out the evil they suspect in one another while noting nothing threatening or amiss in their own hearts, they will destroy each other in the name of security. Above the fray, one invading alien remarks to his apprentice that they've long learned that the most effective weapon of mass destruction is the random manipulation of electricity in one community at a time, whereby they conquer those who are more than willing to conquer themselves. (Serling's final thought: "The pity of it is that these things cannot be confined to the Twilight Zone.") It can all seem a little quaint, but, then again, so much depends on an American electorate that wants to know what's true, even if it involves the realization that the rally you attended or the visual you shared or the op-ed you read was the creation of people operating a mind control app under the dictates of a billionaire whose perceived self-interest is threatened by climate realization or a Russian oligarch. Or as Alexander Nix, former CEO of Cambridge Analytica, once observed, "It doesn't have to be true. It just has to be believed."[4]

Serling was haunted by our disinclination to imagine the motivations, the mind-set, or the hopes of whoever it is we regard, from one year to the next, as our adversary. "A Quality of Mercy" features a Lieutenant Katell (played by Dean Stockwell of *Quantum Leap* fame) whose eagerness to lead an assault on some starved Japanese soldiers holed up in a cave on the Philippine Islands (in 1945) is suddenly put in a different light when he's inexplicably transformed into Lieutenant Yamuri, a Japanese officer contemplating an assault on wounded Americans on Corregidor (in 1942). As he pleads with his superior to forgo an attack, he finds himself back on the Philippine Islands, driven by newer, larger motives than that which had seized him previously. Serling ends the episode extolling a wisdom (in this case borrowed from Shakespeare) applicable to all nations at all times: The quality of mercy is not strained.

THOUGHT LIVES

My favorite *Twilight Zone* episode, "The Obsolete Man," casts Burgess Meredith as a librarian on trial in a totalitarian state for the crime of "obsolescence," with Fritz Weaver's Chancellor presiding. In a fine characterization of the genre, Serling explains, "This is not a new world, it is simply an extension of what began in the old one. . . . It has refinements, technological advances, and a more sophisticated approach to the destruction of human freedom." Logic that fails to buttress the will to power is an enemy, and voices that don't coincide with the stratagems of that power (echoing an occasional characterization of the United Nations on the part of the occasional American president) are dismissed as irrelevant. In this vein, the Chancellor decrees Wordsworth a breed of vermin without purpose or meaning.

"I am a human being!" Wordsworth retorts against the judgment of the state with that authority of earth-inheriting meekness characteristic of Burgess Meredith in so many of his roles.

And after being assured that his speech is without substance or dimension, weight or meaning (less than nothing, according to the Chancellor), as it's out of tune with the state, Wordsworth declares, "I exist! And if I speak one thought aloud, that thought lives! Even after I'm shoveled into my grave."

The execution will be televised. And in a McLuhanesque observation, the Chancellor remarks that capturing these moments on camera serves to educate the populace. But Wordsworth has an idea in mind for his televised, final moments, and it will involve an engagement with the principalities and powers of this present darkness. After Wordsworth stages a demythologizing epiphany for the Chancellor and the viewing public, Serling has a word on the state of the State that all, save Wordsworth, worshiped: "Any state, any entity, any ideology that fails to recognize the worth, the dignity, the rights of man, that state is obsolete. A case to be filed under *M* for mankind . . . in the Twilight Zone."

As we've seen, Beloved Community is a politics that views every human being as a bearer of infinite value. And as a word-fraught species, our politics can never be separated from the way we talk about each other, the words we use and the stories we tell to explain and justify our policies, decisions, and lifestyles. In a lifelong study of human behavior and the actions that are now and then described as "war crimes" (from My Lai to Abu Ghraib), Robert Jay Lifton developed the term "atrocity-producing situation" in an effort to name the way words speak actions into being and the way stories about absolute good and absolute evil can create the conditions (the scripts, if you like) for confusion and gray areas over the very good and evil supposedly at stake, with generally well-meaning people playing maniacal roles that radically differ from the heroic self-conception they've taken to be at work in their title or office.

Serling doesn't name nation-states in his narration, but I can imagine he would note a certain degree of Orwellian applicability in the assessment of a bipartisan Senate Intelligence Committee concerning intelligence failures preceding the September 11 attacks: "groupthink." Their report, endorsed by all nine of the Republicans and eight Democrats on the committee, pins this atrocity-producing thought habit on the Central Intelligence Agency, stopping far short of the admission that politicians themselves had much to do with producing this herd instinct. Hostility toward honest questions and rejection of advice that doesn't coincide with our already-made-up minds will often call itself patriotism while sneering at any insight that seems too sensitive or nuanced. But the whistle-blower is the real patriot when groupthink has silenced all hope of moral realization. Wordsworth will give everything for his culture as a minority of one. Is his public still capable of being moved? Are we?

The tale of Romney Wordsworth's assertion of the sacred power of one human voice against the fundamentalism of the state deprives the language of redemptive violence of its emotional appeal and credibility. It moves in the flow of the moral continuum that this book hopes to identify and celebrate, a movement of truthfulness making people free. The memory of the story (Wordsworth vs. State) can serve as a reference in our ethical dilemmas (required viewing for public service?) and a source of illumination concerning our tendency to find peacefulness offensive when we're in the grip of the power of pride. We don't have to look far to find Romney Wordsworth equivalents in our own world. Decorated Air Force veteran Reality Winner and the former Israeli nuclear technician Mordechai Vanunu are among those whose righteous witness has been made to slip through the cracks of competing interests.[5] It's as if mere mention of their acts of conscience shakes the credibility structures of the military-industrial-entertainment-incarceration complex.

In the wide world of sports, brand names, wrestling, and presidential campaigns, we won't usually go broke selling a sense of belonging. But just because we can sell merchandise and win elections with a sense of outrage doesn't mean we have to give in to its tactics. When America's public discourse is reduced to two parties trying to outshout each other concerning how angry they are about other people's evil, the mantras inevitably work their way into our conversations with spouses, neighbors, brothers, and sisters. We need a Romney Wordsworth who reminds us that we live our lives under the gaze of a just God who knows our innermost thoughts as if we were shouting them, who opposes the proud but gives grace to the humble, and who notices our hateful words even after we've learned to surround ourselves with people who talk the same way. It costs him his life, but Wordsworth offers the demystifying, prophetic word. It's always costly.

THE WORD IS FANCY

The realization that we are all the time seeing and speaking in a state of moral myopia, all too often equipped with blinders that obstruct the possibility of wider visions, can be a liberating one. Serling isn't a pessimist or a cynic but a hopeful realist. Living up to the moral breakthroughs of history requires a determination never to rest from trying to break through further. A community that operates under the mostly unspoken assumption that we've somehow reached a plateau (or that, as an old beer commercial puts it, "It doesn't get any better than this") shouldn't be characterized as optimistic, positive, or morally uplifting. From the perspective of the sci-fi sensibility, that would mean that the pods have won, and the status quo is the carefully defined sanity of wordless despair and plastic smiles.

The alternative mind-set present throughout much science fiction is one of Always Further to Go, endless frontiers, and strange new ways of describing a creation whose strangeness knows no end. As Philip K. Dick insisted, "Joy is the essential and final ingredient of science fiction, the joy of discovery of newness."[6] And the discoveries invite us to forget our defensively held views long enough to sympathize with other people and possibilities that aren't as comforting or familiar as we might prefer. But without these discoveries, we can't learn, forgive, or be born into anything we aren't already. We can't develop or change our already-made-up minds.

In Dick's *The Man in the High Castle* (1962), we're treated to a world in which the Axis won World War II, and the United States has been divided up between Germany and Japan. In a reversal of fortunes, an American-born merchant struggles to live up to the honor codes of his Japanese occupiers, deferring to their superior wisdom not far from the honky-tonk jazz slums of San Francisco, overseen, like the rest of California, by "puppet white" governments. Copies of the *I Ching* appear everywhere like Gideons' Bibles while Germany and Japan are engaged in a race to colonize the planets (with no Cold War nuclear weapons proliferation, the money's available). A man named Baynes (an undercover Jew who has infiltrated the highest echelons of German power) wonders over the innate motivations of the Nazis:

> They want to be the agents, not the victims, of history. They identify with God's power and believe they are godlike. That is their basic madness . . .

> It is not hubris, not pride; it is the inflation of the ego to its ultimate—
> confusion between him who worships and that which is worshipped.[7]

This kind of analysis is vintage Dick—an analysis afforded us by way of his out-rageous scenarios (technological or historical). Do we have a sympathy pain or two as we try to imagine what it might be like to be overcome by an archetype? Do we know the look and feel of an inflated ego?

When Baynes makes contact with a Mr. Tagomi, in concert with whom he hopes to reveal a Nazi military operation in the interest of preventing global conflict, he is presented with a gift numbered among the last vestiges of long, gone American culture. Sitting on a pad of black velvet, it's a 1938 Mickey Mouse watch (one of only ten surviving). Mr. Tagomi will later risk his career by speaking frankly to a German diplomat of the wisdom he's learned from the diary of a Puritan whose insights appear increasingly relevant in these ego-inflating days: "Therapeutic possibility nil. . . . In language of Goodman C. Mather, if properly recalled: Repent!" (237–38).

To top it all off, there is growing unrest in the occupied lands following the appearance of a book (banned in German territories) called *The Grasshopper Lies Heavy*. Written by a certain Hawthorne Abendsen, it conjectures a world in which the Axis lost the war and the structure of society came out very differ-ently. Alternately dismissed as outlandish and ridiculous and read by any and everyone whenever they can find a private moment, it seems to be sparking a revolution in thought. The Nazis suspect Abendsen is probably a Jew.

When characters contemplate American artifacts and revel in the aura of historical authenticity they carry, we can note that we're neck-deep in philo-sophical investigations . As we've already noted, Dick believed a failed appre-ciation for weirdness or the ways in which total reality eludes us will lead to totalitarian, inauthentic human behavior. Just before Tagomi issues his call to repentance, he experiences a sort of satori concerning the biblical understand-ing of knowledge that haunted many an American mind:

> Saint Paul's incisive word choice . . . seen through glass darkly not a metaphor, but astute reference to optical distortion . . . our space and our time creations of our own psyche. (233)

Uniquely fit for the health of democracy, the elaborate thought experiments of science fiction can woo us toward a recognition of our incompleteness of vision. As we strive to pay attention to the world, we need constant reminding that just because we feel something (imminent threats or anger) doesn't mean it's there. It, as Run-DMC and all ancient wisdom testify, is tricky. We have terrific trouble acknowledging facts that won't fit our scripts, our paradigms, or our self-congratulatory mythologies. As an American voice that won't let us hold off the biblical word on these matters as merely metaphor or primarily a "faith issue," Dick amuses us into higher awareness.

MAD AMERICA

As we noted concerning Klaatu and the United Federation of Planets, Ursula K. Le Guin's Ekumen gives us one possible means for imagining ourselves righteously beyond the rhetoric that fills our minds concerning necessity, duty, goodness, and glory. Ideally, reading the Bible should perform this function, but all too often we read the words and assume they're affirming all that we hold as good, true, and glorious instead of letting it exorcise our elaborately conceived delusions. If we take seriously the possibility of a larger frame of reference than the sovereignty of nations (a given within the biblical worldview of world without end where God alone is sovereign), we might be able to examine our language and our well-laid plans with an enhanced vigilance.

In Le Guin's *The Left Hand of Darkness* (1969), Genly Ai brings good tidings to the planet Gethen on behalf of the Alliance of the Ekumen (eighty-three habitable planets, three thousand nations), but he has to engage Gethen one nation at a time, and as we might guess, the health of all other nations, as a unity, isn't necessarily a top priority for the people "in power." And worse, King Argaven of the nation of Karhide, in the king's own eyes the perfect patriot, mistakes his own perceived self-interest for that of the health of the nation. Patriotism as selfless love of one's homeland makes sense to Genly Ai, but he comes to understand that Argaven will always mistake love of power for love of country. This patriotism, in practice, is nothing more than the fidgeting fear of a cornered animal.

Needless to say, communicating with King Argaven is a difficult task. The fact that Genly Ai comes offering fellowship, one conscious being to another on behalf of millions of others, is incommunicable. He offers space travel and cosmic community to the king, country, and planet, but Argaven can only think in terms of power and perceived threat to it. Argaven only speaks the language of career ambition and survival strategy and is genuinely befuddled over why anyone with power would ever want to share their resources. To the query as to why the Ekumen wants an alliance ("this kingdom out in nowhere, this Ekumen"), Genly Ai responds with words that could well suit the modus operandi of Wikipedia: "Increase of knowledge. The augmentation of the complexity and intensity of the field of intelligent life. The enrichment of harmony and the greater glory of God. Curiosity. Adventure. Delight."[8] But these phrases have absolutely no appeal to the king and add to his sense of escalating insecurity that feels bullied at every turn.

As if wrestling with an insight increasingly difficult to suppress, King Argaven wonders how the Ekumen would define the word "traitor," and after sending the question via interstellar transmission, Argaven receives an answer that only serves to madden the royal mind-set further: "To King Argaven of Karhide on Gethen, greetings. I do not know what makes a man a traitor. No man considers himself a traitor: this makes it hard to find out."[9]

When we bring this logic to bear on words like "evildoer" and "terrorist" as well as the less generously applied terms like "good man," "friend of freedom," and "great American," we see that science fiction is tackling some rather enormous issues. King Argaven angrily dismisses the Ekumen's wisdom as the kind of thing that could have been procured from any religious crackpot. But this is only the beginning of Genly Ai's ministry to Gethen and only one of Le Guin's Ekumen novels. Bringing good news to busy minds (like ours, often unyieldingly culturally captivated) will ever prove a complicated, costly business.

In *Slaughterhouse-Five*, Vonnegut recounts a conversation with Harrison Starr in which he reluctantly conceded that *Slaughterhouse-Five* was probably "an anti-war book." To this, Starr hauled out his all-purpose response to the prospect of anti-war books: "Why don't you write an anti-*glacier* book instead?"[10] And if we're looking for an anecdote to characterize science fiction's tragicomic preoccupations, I believe this one will do nicely. It's not a completely cynical take on social criticism, but it does offer an amused perspective on the question of its effectiveness.

Yet effectiveness, narrowly defined, does not always have in mind the realpolitik of the Lord's Prayer, that great cosmic equalizer of all our talk of markets, necessity, and justice. Absolute effectiveness, like unassailable security and total information awareness, is one of those mythologies no less mythical for its ability to bring up poll numbers and sell units. But the Lord's Prayer invokes that which is beyond our control, unflattering to our pridefulness, but salvific in its appeal to determined mercy and compassion as an eternal imperative for mere mortals. Vonnegut once remarked that while Einstein's theory of relativity might one day put Earth on the intergalactic map, it will always run a distant second to the Lord's Prayer, whose harnessing of energies in their proper, life-giving direction surpasses even the discovery of fire. The universe-altering phrase he has in mind is "forgive us our trespasses as we forgive those who trespass against us." There are no zero-sum relationships in the cosmos, and every fact is a function of relationship. What do we do with this knowledge, this red-hot casserole of the present?

MENTAL COMFORT ZONE

Though she hesitates to term it science fiction, in *Kindred* Octavia Butler addresses the complications of the living fact of kinship and its histories more powerfully than any one book I can think of. It's the story of Dana, a black female writer in modern-day California who, without warning, is inexplicably pulled back in time to save a drowning child, the son of a plantation owner in pre–Civil War Maryland. It is neither a hallucination nor a dream, and this rupture occurs repeatedly and unexpectedly throughout the child Rufus's growing-up years whenever his life's in jeopardy at various stages of his nineteenth-century existence. Mere days can pass in Dana's time when she's abruptly transported into the path of Rufus, who may have aged months or years while she's been away, and her return to her own time can occur just as randomly. "I don't have a name for the thing that happened to me," she explains to her bewildered but believing husband. "But I don't feel safe anymore."[11]

Each trip back in time adds up, for Dana, to a life-threatening rescue operation. The candor she risks constantly endangers her own life. Saving Rufus the first time, when he is a child about to drown, is easy enough, but as he ages her commitment to save him and to even attempt to educate him against all odds becomes increasingly problematic. "Not all children let themselves be molded into what their parents want them to be," she hopefully muses aloud at one point (83). But what chance does anyone have of overcoming the murderous ideas upon and within which they're raised? How do we bring ourselves (or anyone) to a realization that the world that is isn't the world that has to be? If we get there at all, even for a moment, how do we remain true to that realization once the moment has passed? As Dana observes, "a lifetime of conditioning could be overcome, but not easily" (118).

Like all science fiction, *Kindred* can kick-start conversations about what we've normalized and why and what it might mean to try to turn things around. We will always have our own ignorance to contend with, but Butler powerfully dramatizes how we cannot even begin to do so without also addressing the infrastructure of bad thinking we are born into and which we often unwittingly fund with our silence.

In a scene that's almost comically sad, Dana has managed to bring a book on the history of slavery back in time to Rufus as a part of his continuing education. If there's some way she can make him see the world to come before it's too late, he might become less likely to torture the people he holds captive and more likely to give his own children their freedom. "This is the biggest lot of abolitionist trash I ever saw," he exclaims as he reads about Sojourner Truth.

"No it isn't," she says. "That book wasn't even written until a century after slavery was abolished."

His reply: "Then why the hell are they still complaining about it?" (140).

As someone who's been conditioned by and within the ideology of white fragility, I can note that these dots appear before me already connected. I've heard it all before. This is a young man for whom lynching and rape are the law and order of the day, whining about political correctness. This is a woman trying (and failing) to talk the young man out of his own murderous madness. As people will do, Rufus is derisively waving away the living fact of the history he is sitting in and perpetuating. Sound familiar? What is political correctness if not the pressure of realities that call me outside of my own mental comfort zone, my own feverish feed of self-legitimation?

"A gift of God may sear unready fingers," Butler assures us in *The Parable of the Sower*.[12] And her work functions in just this way, jarring us toward revelations, actionable intelligence. Butler banks everything on the hope of bringing a light of revolutionary awareness to a dark time that can barely comprehend it. Her tales can hardly be said to contain easy resolutions but, like all art, they offer themselves as a cause for moral reflection and a profound vision of how the past impinges on the present, as it always has, despite whatever psychosis of denial and forgetting we bring to our conceptions of history. There are so many ways to avoid moral realizations in feeds of endless self-legitimation, but there also gifts of God for the people of God, deeper visions of Beloved Community to be had one true story at a time.

Chapter 6

True Garbage

We are what we pretend to be, so we must be careful about what we pretend to be.
　　　　　　　　　　　　　　—Kurt Vonnegut, *Mother Night*

They worship death here. They don't worship money, they worship death.
　　　　　　　　　　　　　　—William Faulkner on Hollywood

If I love you, I have to make you conscious of things you don't see.
　　　　　　　　　　　　　　—James Baldwin

Among the means by which I try to encourage my students to consider the Bible a living witness of actionable intelligence for overcoming evil with good in their own lives and the lives of others is the near completely common lore of *Star Wars*. There's almost inevitably one or two folks who will court the mock derision of others by announcing aloud that they've never seen a single episode and don't plan to, but they know the tradition, the characters, and the stakes in a general sense. I stand before them as a true believer who's followed the thing from the beginning and who, as a child, had to wait to see what was foreshadowing and what wasn't when it came to claims of paternity and what really befell Luke Skywalker's father.

I recount aloud feeling, at the age of ten, every bit as schooled as Luke himself in *Episode V: The Empire Strikes Back* when he realized that the robed, pointy-eared, dried-out, amphibian-looking sprite he'd screamed at and imagined was delaying and even impeding his destined meeting with a Jedi master was—it's so embarrassing—Master Yoda himself. ("I cannot teach him," Yoda says with a sigh, "The boy has no patience.") Once his training is under way, one helpful way of conceiving Jesus' temptation in the wilderness is placed before us when Luke's exercise regimen takes him to the mouth of a cave.

We wonder aloud together what to make of the differences in the Gospels' account of the temptation of Jesus. In the earliest, Mark, we're told he was tempted by Satan for forty days among angels and wild beasts and . . . that's it. Matthew transports him, with "the devil," to Jerusalem and a high mountain, and all of this with visions of stones turned to bread and global domination. The same goes for Luke, which casts it as a time of testing, while John has no temptation account at all. What's going on here, and how did the report of Jesus' vision quest make its way into these three Gospels? Was it something that, with time-travel technology, could have been filmed with a video camera, or was it an inner journey of the kind Aang and Korra regularly undergo on *Avatar: The Last Airbender*?

This is where reports of strange happenings in the Dagobah system can come to the rescue in reading the Bible well. In the middle of his training, Luke has been running through the swamp with Yoda on his back urging him to feel the power of the Force running through him while responding to his own fear that he won't be able to rightly discern good from evil when it counts. When they pause to rest, Luke senses something amiss: "There's something not right. . . . I feel cold."

Yoda gestures in the direction of a cave: "That place is strong with the dark side of the Force. A domain of evil it is. . . . And you must go."

"What's in there?"

"Only what you take with you."

Spoiler alert: Luke encounters Darth Vader in the cave and cuts off his head with a light saber. My literalistic, ten-year-old mind actually followed the story in precisely this way for a few pregnant seconds. Was Yoda in cahoots with Vader himself? The helmeted head, however, rolls over, the mask dissolves, and Luke confronts the sight of his own face. The apparition ceases. Yoda shrugs at something R2D2 tells him outside the cave. The saga continues.

That "only what you take with you" line, though; is that not one for the ages? Is it not just as true for Jesus in the wilderness as it is for Siddhartha under the Bodhi Tree or Buffy the Vampire Slayer realizing that slayers have the power to wrestle the earth from fools? Is it not also true for each of us when we open a Bible or look at a screen or read a news feed or enter a moment of silence before going to sleep? Not a bad line at all for naming the risk and reception of media intake, the thing I enter when I try to escape it by reaching for my phone. That cave, that hole, that dark and brooding abyss is before us, in one way or another, at all times, and—another spoiler—it's a mirror. Projection is, it turns out, nonoptional. Jung could even spin it positively: "The cave you fear to enter holds that treasure that you seek."

I imagine this is why my pulse quickens whenever I enter a movie theater. It represents a space of deep emotional engagement, of leveling with myself, and of experiencing something that will sneak past my defenses with sight and sound. I find that this occurs even when the film itself strikes me as kind of horrible. One person's well-manufactured fantasy is someone else's moral revelation. Same as it ever was. The unconscious doesn't care. What will you experience? Whatever you take with you. We become what we behold.

I have an example. There is a moving scene in *Patch Adams* (1998) in which Robin Williams's Hunter "Patch" Adams, a medical practitioner, has painstakingly arranged a dream come true for an elderly woman whose confinement to hospitals has, in recent years, stood in the way of almost every form of sensual pleasure. She has long dreamt, for instance, of swimming in a pool of noodles, Patch discovers, and as I sat in the dark theater watching the slow-motion sequence in which her fantasy is finally fulfilled, I turned to my partner with tears in my eyes and said, "I hate this movie."

Please understand, I didn't begrudge the woman her moment or wish that the tale (based on a true story) had never been told, but there was something in the sequencing that felt a little like an insult, a way of cuing sentiment, and a pressing of certain heart buttons that had me feeling more than a little tricked. When Peter Coyote's Bill Davis, a notoriously recalcitrant patient, watches his family leave the room with the understanding that he wants to die alone in the company of Patch ("You're killing me, Patch," he says through pained laughter), something might strike the viewer a little amiss. I'm not saying it didn't work, because it did. The carefully programmed eliciting of my emotions, we might say, had me at hello. Nevertheless, I wouldn't trade this teachable moment for anything. I've been mulling over it ever since.

Often accused of misanthropy for, among other things, his utterly desentimentalized way of telling stories, Stanley Kubrick once surprised an interviewer by expressing unqualified affection for Frank Capra (director of *It's A Wonderful Life* and *You Can't Take It with You*). As Kubrick saw it, artists aren't confronted with an either-or in which they have to decide for or against emotion, but honesty probably requires a broader consideration than whether or not an audience will be immediately gratified emotionally: "The question becomes, are you giving them something to make them a little happier, or are you putting in something that is inherently true to the material? Are people behaving the way we really behave, or are they behaving the way we would like them to behave?"[1] This standard can be made to inform all media intake. Are we falling for confirmation bias, an easy affirmation of our preconceived notions about life and how to live it, or are we looking for what's true? What do we mean by "objectionable subject matter"? Would that include an examination of our own lives and our own behavior? Who among us isn't, to some degree, objectionable? Do we avoid mirrors? Kubrick understood that the hopeful realism of unfiltered honesty is a more comprehensive stance than optimism or cynicism: "You don't have to make Frank Capra movies to like people."[2]

It might seem strange to lift up film as a way of liking people, of being more honest ourselves, or as an avenue for the restoring of the senses, but I believe this is how it works. I don't know what I would do—or who I would be—without it. As a form of ringing true, it's essential to my own sense of seeing my own life in Beloved Community with others. It's a refuge, if you like, from the reigning disinformation. Philip K. Dick defines disinformation as "noise posing as signal so you do not even recognize it as noise." It can leave hearts and minds in dire need of a clarifying cave or a darkened theater. Disinformation deadens the possibility of a genuinely informed electorate and, therefore, righteous governance. Dick names the situation this way: "If you float enough disinformation into circulation you will totally abolish everyone's contact with reality, probably your own included."[3]

And then there's the soul-restoring work of film. As a viewer, I hope to be up to the same work the director Kelly Reichardt says she's up to behind the camera: "You're opening yourself up to the living thing that's happening in front of you."[4] This opening of self occurs, it seems to me, as a kind of circle that includes viewers and makers and facilitators of cinema, a righteous cultural work of recognition among people who mean to speak and act freely, the work—surprise, surprise—of Beloved Community, the work of people who hope to be exceedingly informed and aware, the work of neighborliness.

WHAT'S IN MOUNT ZION?

As a challenge, a comfort, a remembrance, and a possible facilitator of such neighborliness, David Lynch's *The Straight Story* (1999) holds a unique place in American film. Based on a true story and adapted by Mary Sweeney and John Roach, it follows the determined, long-distance love of Alvin Straight (a representative of what Tom Brokaw once referred to as the Greatest Generation) and his bold and costly decision to focus on the family. It is a testament to a particular, radically moral character type within American culture that sometimes escapes notice.

It opens with the sound of myriad insects chirping to the view of a starry sky, inviting the viewer to contemplate a universe hypnotically open, infinitely mysterious (think Hubble telescope images), and bearing a beauty we've hardly begun to fathom. We're then given an aerial view of an Iowa cornfield, drawn down to the particulars of a small town's layout, and made privy to the disorder breaking out in the life of a community as it's discovered that seventy-three-year-old Alvin Straight (played by Richard Farnsworth) has fallen down on his kitchen floor. His daughter Rosie, declared mentally incompetent by the state and separated from her children, expresses her distress in halting phrases. There is humor (neighbor Dorothy: "What's the number for 911?"), but in typical Lynchian fashion, there is no judgment in the camera's observation of eccentricities. We're made to think again concerning all the seemingly discordant elements that make up our every day.

At the doctor's office, Alvin refuses to go in until Rosie (Sissy Spacek) reminds him that he promised to cooperate, and his considered, long-practiced contempt for the sterile, obtrusive complexity of institutionalized health care will not allow the hip replacement his doctor recommends. Listening to a thunderstorm later that evening, he sits and contemplates his brush with mortality (he can no longer walk without the assistance of two canes), as he overhears his daughter's side of a telephone conversation and realizes that his brother, Lyle, has had a stroke. She notes that both men have been horribly stubborn. And we begin to realize that the larger disorder haunting Alvin is his relationship with his brother. They haven't spoken to each other in over a decade.

Alvin announces that he has to make his way to Lyle. But the goal is complicated by Alvin's eyesight (he hasn't had a driver's license in years) and their lack of funds (Rosie sells birdhouses for a living). After a few hours of soul-searching, Alvin decides to drive to his brother's home in Mount Zion, Wisconsin, on an ancient riding lawn mower. Toward the end of a late-night, backyard conversation in which Rosie realizes he won't be talked out of it, he tells Rosie to stare at the sky with him, as if the universe bears wordless witness to an order he can ignore only at the risk of his own soul.

Alvin's friends ask him what he hopes to accomplish, scandalized by the sight of him processing, with his getup, out of the small town and onto the road. Lynch will take us across the land inch by inch, making us see the beauty we've sacrificed in exchange for our hurry-up-and-matter, psycho covenant of haste and alleged "development." There are many stops and starts, including the need for a slightly less antiquated lawn mower (Alvin calmly shoots the old one with his rifle once it's failed him), and Alvin subsists on processed meats and cheap cigars. One of the most moving scenes occurs in his interaction with a young female runaway with whom he shares his fire and his food. When she can't talk about her family, he discerns that she's with child. She says her family hates her and will only hate her more when they hear her secret. Alvin conjectures that they probably wouldn't be so mad that they'd want to lose her or her child. She says she's not so sure about that.

Alvin recounts Rosie's loss of her own children to the custody of the state and remarks that each day, for her, is an exercise in lifelong pining. He then describes handing each of his children a stick and asking them to break it, which was easy enough, and then instructing them to tie the same sticks in a bundle and try to break them then. "Of course, they couldn't. Then I'd say, 'That bundle—that's family.'" They talk a little more while looking at the stars before retiring, and Alvin awakens to find the girl gone and a bound bundle of sticks beside the fire.

The film might be viewed, in one sense, as a slow-motion affirmation and celebration of, for those who like to speak this way, enduringly American values, but Lynch has been quick to point out that these long-term decisions for humanity are at the core of communities around the world. And the historical continuum of Beloved Community along which they're located (lest we need reminding) is not the property of any one human-group. To claim otherwise is to invite deluding spirit possession. Alvin's witness is shared in some way with everyone he encounters, and like a Tiresias or an awakened American Lear, his presence is an invitation to rethink our private pursuits of happiness to accommodate the hopes of the old man on the lawn mower. The desire of the people he meets to be a positive presence within his story is intensified by his explanations. "What's in Mount Zion, Alvin?" one woman asks.

"My brother lives there," he responds, as if turning their exchange into the lyric of an ancient song. While they worry for him ("There's a lot of weird people everywhere now") and advise him to forgo the lawn mower in exchange for an easier ride, he politely asserts, "I wanna finish this one my own way." And we know that his intuitive suspicion of easily acquired reconciliation, a high-speed moral shortcut, is right on the money.

After a harrowing account of a friendly fire incident with a fellow veteran of World War II, he offers a bit of neighborly counsel to a pair of angry twins: "My brother and I said some unforgivable things the last time we met, but I'm tryin' to put that behind me, and this trip is a hard swallow of my pride. I just hope I'm not too late. A brother's a brother." As he nears his destination, a minister asks about the source of trouble that led to the stalemate. Alvin explains that it's a story as old as any. It's Cain's resentment of Abel and the ensuing cycle. None of it matters as much as seeing him again: He wants peace. He wants to sit alongside him and look at the stars like they used to as younger men.

"Amen to that," the minister affirms. The tenderness and power of the short scene in which Alvin reaches Lyle (a brief but Oscar-worthy performance by Harry Dean Stanton) is a centering moment worthy of constant meditation. The reckonings we avoid hold the treasure, the gifts of insight, we seek, the homecomings we long for. Same as it ever was.

RECOGNIZING INSANITY

Though it's mostly addressing it in regretful retrospect, *The Straight Story* invites us to consider the damage our tiny avoidances of conflict add up to, yielding with humiliating exactness the state of our hoped-for unions. Divinity opposes our pride—on our behalf—but manifests beautifully when we're humble, when we know and feel and act on the biological fact of kinship with others. But as the demoniacs of the New Testament demonstrate ("What do I have to do with you, Son of Man?"), our manic obsessions—deluding spirits, in their own way—don't respond well to identification. Until they're recognized and talked about (painted, portrayed, put in song), their power is unchecked, dictated by their own mad logic, and veiled in an air of surface propriety. And that which expands articulation is gospel. The good news is that the exorcism of recognition is under way. To acknowledge a difficult or even crushing truth is to step toward Beloved Community. Kubrick again: "A recognition of insanity doesn't imply celebration of it; nor a sense of despair and futility about the possibility of curing it."[5]

In Kubrick's *Doctor Strangelove or: How I Learned to Stop Worrying and Love the Bomb* (1964), Peter Sellers's Captain Mandrake has to order the shooting of a Coca-Cola machine to procure the coins required to telephone a warning of a preemptive strike on Russia to a White House that won't accept collect calls. And President Muffley (also played by Peter Sellers) tries to prevent a fistfight between George C. Scott's General Buck and the Russian ambassador (Peter Bull) by crying out, "Please, gentlemen, you can't fight here; this is the War Room!" In our day, calling attention to these contradictions and the ways in which our words are often an assault on meaning is as easy as accessing and discussing a Twitter feed, but the work of attempted truthfulness is the same. Without a culture of truthfulness, there can be no democracy. Kubrick found the work of the artist within the human barnyard to be rather straightforward, "The only morality is not to be dishonest."[6]

Unfortunately, our commitment to truthfulness is often co-opted by our concern over who benefits from which truthfulness. This is an understandable concern, but a radical commitment to what's true will have broader interests than who's made to look good and who looks bad when truth is spoken. If we only think in these terms, our imaginations are hopelessly sealed off from the truth that would name our idolatries.

On the release of *Doctor Strangelove*, one newspaper proclaimed, "Moscow could not buy more harm to America." But this alarmist critique is a distraction from the vocation of any culture alert to its own contradictions, eager to be spoken to, as the proverb says, in its ridiculous folly. The truth that makes us free won't necessarily accommodate our armchair offendedness or do well in a box office that only thrives on the stories that can advertise themselves as "feel-good." Who can deliver us from our inner Mickey Mouse?

I'M READY FOR MY CLOSE-UP

"Cast out this wicked dream which has seized my heart." This, as it happens, is neither Kubrick nor Shakespeare. It is, in fact, a line from a film within a film, a caption actually from a silent film starring a young Norma Desmond whose older, sadder, madder self is the central character of Billy Wilder's masterwork *Sunset Boulevard* (1950). It chronicles a breakdown that exceeds its ostensible subject by speaking to our stumbling around the mouth of the opening (cave, screen, abyss) that can hold a nation in thrall. It's a cinematic consideration of Hollywood as a symbol, a place, and a culture that can melt everything that was solid into thin air. David Lynch has remarked that *Sunset Boulevard* is a film he watches obsessively and repeatedly, seeing something new and instructive with every viewing.[7]

But back to Norma Desmond, as played with extreme tragicomic effect by Gloria Swanson, in real life a former silent-film star. The prime witness to her decline is also the film's narrator, William Holden's Joe Gillis, who describes the rotting mansion in which she sits alone in the dark watching reels of her former alleged glory on a screen: "The whole place seemed to have been stricken with a kind of creeping paralysis, out of beat with the rest of the world, crumbling apart in slow motion." It's a slow burn, but we're gradually made privy to the process involving investors, producers, writers, directors, and (lest we forget) audiences that's put her in the state she's in, screaming, "Say you don't hate me!" when she doubts a man's affection, reading fan letters forged by her butler as a daily peace offensive, and endlessly readying herself, as the famous line has it, for her close-up. There are and were so many hearts and minds involved in the degradation of her soul and the transmogrification of her person.

Cecil B. DeMille (played by Cecil B. DeMille) politely plays to her vanity in her presence but privately grieves what's been lost when he recalls that, when he met her at seventeen, she was more full of hope and bravery than any young person he'd known. The film industry, he notes, "can do terrible things to the human spirit." Something sacred has been commodified and rendered unrecognizable, desecrated even. And we won't be allowed the hope of critical detachment from the situation as we're made to understand that we're complicit too and also, in myriad ways, equally enthralled. Before it's over, Gillis addresses us in an aside as "those wonderful people out there in the dark." Who will deliver us from this wicked dream that has seized our hearts?

To be a great star is to possess "great pride," intones mad Norma in her calmer moments. But it's back to begging people not to hate her as the possibility of candor and intimacy begin to elude her again. And even when she's back in the company of Cecil B. DeMille, she can't stop herself from proclaiming, "You don't know what it means to know that you want me." Joe Gillis's slow recognition that her fan letters are forged, that her friends "aren't friends in the usual sense of the word," and that Hollywood doesn't want her anymore is described as a "sad, embarrassing revelation." Watching the film fifty years on, it's hard not to notice a Norma Desmond epidemic making its way through the tuned-in Westernized world.

As Gillis watches her go to any length to make herself appear more youthful while her spirit wastes away under the torment of impossible hopes and expectations, Gillis tries to speak against her delusion: "There's nothing tragic about being fifty; not unless you're trying to be twenty-five." But the wicked vision won't let go.

It seems obvious to me that, with one film in particular, David Lynch has set out to address the possibility of release from this wicked vision. If art is a feat of attentiveness, perhaps this could be said of all his creative efforts, but there's one I believe succeeds on the level of exorcism (or public service announcement) like no other. *Sunset Boulevard* seems to me to operate as a kind of a template for *Lost Highway* (1997) and *Inland Empire* (2006), but it also performs the function of the call—perhaps one of many calls—that has elicited the *response* I believe to be Lynch's masterpiece, *Mulholland Drive* (2001).

THERE WAS AN ACCIDENT

Here's Lynch on what cinema can do: "Cinema is a language. It can say things—big, abstract things. . . . It's not just words or music—it's a whole range of elements coming together and making something that didn't exist before. It's telling stories. It's devising a world, an experience, that people cannot have unless they see that film."[8] If describing a film as an exorcism or a freeing spell seems a little overwrought, let's at least accept viewing a film—taking in cinema—as the purposefully orchestrated experience (following Lynch) of a world. Consider again Reichardt's dictum of filmmaking as opening yourself up to the living process in front of and within you. Lynch is famously articulate when it comes to teasing this out. What's the message of the film? The theme? The film *says* it. It's all there, *holding* abstraction. Lynch again: "When something's abstract, the abstractions are hard to put into words . . . unless you're a poet. . . . Cinema is a language that can *say* abstractions. Cinema can say these difficult-to-say-in-words things."[9]

I don't think there's any getting to the bottom of what *Mulholland Drive* says, but I have a wide range of thoughts concerning what I take it to be. It is, for instance, a beautiful dream vision and a gift of sacred insight to anyone interested in taking it on. It can be meaningfully paired with Kendrick Lamar's "The Art of Peer Pressure" as a signal flare alerting us to our inner jihads. Taking his cue from the promise and thoughtfulness of *Sunset Boulevard*, Lynch is giving us a view of something that happens to people, something—we begin to sense—that's probably happening to us. (We're made to *feel* it happening before the closing credits.)

What's happening? I draw on proclamations peppered throughout the film itself: Something bad's happening. Someone's in trouble. The girl's *still* missing. An *accident* has occurred. Who is speaking to whom and to what end? It seems that we're being invited to a scene of recognition in which Hollywood is itself the crime scene, and the criminal activity is simultaneously a global export, with its powers of proselytization like no other, *and* a local economy, an illusion factory, in Blaise Cendrars's phrase, that functions as a mecca of fantasy, drawing lonely and hopeful souls unto itself for a hundred years or so. But, to be clear, Hollywood might also be said to function primarily as a symbol to encapsulate liturgies also concentrated in places like New York and Nashville and Washington, DC. In this broader sense, *Mulholland Drive* is a vision of what the entertainment industry can do to the human psyche, a chronicle of a few of the terrible things it works on and within people, and an alarmingly coherent consideration of, as Joni Mitchell has it, the star-maker machinery at work behind the most financially profitable pop-culture offerings. If we care to zoom out and slow the tape a little, it's also a vision of what happens when an unrepentant sexual assailant wins an election with the help of a Twitter account. There are no lanes for a military-industrial-entertainment-incarceration complex that would weaponize all available souls in our one human barnyard.

But Lynch is in Los Angeles, and he has a principality to unmask as he confronts Hollywood as a spiritual reality (from one angle, a demonic stronghold) that claims lives, often absorbing its most fervent pilgrims into a felt oblivion. The scene that centers this realization involves an exchange between a man who's arranged to meet another man (possibly his therapist) to discuss and contend with a deeply disturbing dream that occurred in the very café in which they're sitting. The café is called Winkie's and it's located—you guessed it—on Sunset Boulevard. Initially, their exchange seems to have no relation to other events in the film, but in time, it becomes clear that it draws into daylight the monstrosity—the very psychic chaos—Lynch tries to somehow expose.

The man with a dream to recount and somehow summon up the nerve to engage, played by Patrick Fischler, speaks as one who can barely contain his own fear. It's broad daylight. They're surrounded by talkative customers. But he's embarrassed and so clearly shaken by the memory of the dream that it's as if he's still stuck within it. With wide-eyed trepidation, he describes the experience:

> I had a dream about this place. . . . I'm in here . . . it's not day or night. It's kind of half night, you know? . . . And I'm scared like can't tell you. . . . I realize what it is. There's a man in back of this place. He's the one who's doing it. I can see him through the wall. I can see his face. . . . I hope that I never see that face ever outside of a dream.

And now, his hope is that he'll be able to regain his equilibrium if his friend will just accompany him on a quick trip outside the restaurant to look behind a nearby dumpster to verify that this man, the one who's *doing it* and whose face is so cosmically unsettling, isn't there at all. If he can only have a corroborating witness alongside, he imagines the apparition will lose its hold. Slowly and nervously (his friend is a little creeped out now), they make their way to the troublesome spot.

What lurks behind the dumpster is the guiding centerpiece of this purposefully fragmented, often necessarily nonlinear film. That man (Creature? Power? Principality?) in back of the place—the one who's doing it—represents the sad and horrible realization, for Naomi Watts's character Diane Selwyn, of what's been done to, by, and through her. The wicked dream that has seized his heart—and that constitutes the majority of this extraordinary film—is hers. And if we're open to receiving the revelation, it's ours too.

IT'S STRANGE TO BE CALLING YOURSELF

Within the first few minutes of *Mulholland Drive*, we're treated to music and dancing a little reminiscent of the ritual Luis Buñuel's Satan in *Simon of the Desert* (1965) refers to as "Radioactive Flesh." Amid the frenzied dancing, we also have Diane Selwyn (or more specifically her dream-self Betty) gazing with adulation upon the Arrivals section of the Los Angeles airport alongside an elderly couple who will assure her, with what we might come to regard as a malevolent, lying optimism, that she's going to be a star. (We'll see them behind the dumpster and soon driving her to final despair before it's all over.) We also discern the sound of Selwyn's labored breathing when the camera assumes her perspective as she drops her head (our head?) on a pillow for something close to the last time.

Something bad is happening. Diane Selwyn has been defeated by her own despair. In her dream, her name is Becky, and she's come to Los Angeles to stay in her aunt's apartment while trying to break into acting. Hailing from Deep River, Ontario, she exclaims that she feels as if she's in some kind of dream. And in fairy-tale fashion, a beautiful and kind woman suffering from amnesia awaits her there, having wandered in and fallen asleep following a head injury from a car accident (which prevented her murder) on Mulholland Drive. Spying a poster for the film *Gilda* (1946) starring Rita Hayworth, she decides her name is Rita when asked.

But this is all the dream of someone hopelessly and tragically estranged from her own intuition. Slowly and surely, the dream is playing to Selwyn's best fantasies about herself while simultaneously breaking the news about what's really happening. Someone's *still* in trouble. The girl is *still* missing. Time for a little sleuthing. Betty knows just the thing for it; they'll pretend to be someone else, like people do in movies. Why? To discover what exactly occurred on Mulholland Drive. Betty *winks* at Rita as she tries to glean information while also misleading the police concerning her own identity on a pay phone at Winkie's. Sitting at a table for a bite to eat, Rita sees a waitress's name tag, Diane, which suddenly brings to mind the name of Diane Selwyn. Maybe *that's* who Rita really is. As they try to call the Diane Selwyn in the phone book, Betty remarks how strange it is to be calling oneself.

We begin to see that there's hardly a moment in *Mulholland Drive* that *isn't* Diane Selwyn somehow calling herself in one way or another. Not every episode in her dream draws on real-life events to which we're eventually made privy, but we can easily guess at their referents in reality. For instance, her beamingly expectant smile as she exits a taxi, having perfected her lines as she arrives for an audition, is accompanied by powerfully sad music that wouldn't have been out of place on the *Elephant Man* sound track. Upon entering, she's surrounded by a small crowd of polite film professionals presumably on hand to observe her promise as an actress. The leading man they've invited to help her demonstrate her mettle is a smarmy actor who's clearly her senior by decades. He lets Becky and the director know the way he'd like to operate. He wants to play it up close like he did with another young actress whose name he can't recall.

In an achingly awkward scene that is, to my knowledge, without precedent in cinema, we watch Becky respond to his groping advances with such convincingly passionate enthusiasm (seemingly lost in erotic abandon) that the actor and the onlookers are left in a state of shock. But just before their scripted scene concludes, she fixes her tear-filled eyes upon a man she's only just met and made out with and delivers her line: "Get out of here before I kill you. I hate you. I hate us both."

While we can't say for sure that Becky's eye-rubbingly degrading audition is based in events that occurred in Diane's waking life, we know all too well that these words of murderous self-hatred were spoken and acted upon by Diane in one of her last exchanges with Rita's real-life self, Camilla Rhodes. We know that they were intimate friends and sometime lovers, and we're made to see, in the gradual unfolding of the moral vision of the film, how one beautiful and gifted woman is reduced to a state of trauma, betrayal, and diminishment so isolating that she makes arrangements to have the love of her life murdered.

And most movingly, Lynch tells the long, complicated, numinous tale of Diane's failure to hide from herself the fact of what's happened to, in, and through her. The film is, in this sense, a chronicle of tragic realization. It is also, in more ways than anyone can keep track of, an intense work of mourning. By way of phone calls and extensive sleuthing, Betty and Rita together make their way to Diane Selwyn's own apartment, where they behold and grieve her decomposing body. And guided by the totem of a mysterious blue box (arising, it appears, from the real-world blue key Diane's contracted killer leaves as an agreed-upon sign of the murderous deed done), they make their way to an exotic and darkly lit theater where they listen to Rebekah Del Rio singing Roy Orbison's "Crying" ("Llorando") with what looks to be her last breath. In sync with the song, Rita weeps, Betty shakes uncontrollably, and our lead characters mourn the loss of their own lives, crying over each other, themselves, and the whole sad surreal situation.

As I see it, the scene, the song, and the film as a whole mourn a failure (personal, collective, and cultural) to somehow turn longing into *be*longing.

It marks the absence of Beloved Community among a people made for it. As we know too well, this psychic disgrace and the toll it takes on human life is in no way limited to the alternative realities of Los Angeles. The thoroughness of Lynch's meditation on Diane Selwyn's life constitutes a prophetic summons to attentiveness and care in our relationship to one another. And in its unveiling of certain processes that would and do break down human souls, it performs the work of apocalypse, challenging the systemic evil that's been normalized as harmless, inevitable, and relentlessly profitable.

"Nothing can stay hidden forever," Lynch insists.[10] And if we receive this mantra as a trustworthy adage, we might begin to see that the time to enlarge our sympathies, to increase the scope of what we feel, of what we know, of what we might yet do in the way of regarding ourselves and one another more compassionately and imaginatively, is now. There's many a Diane Selwyn among us (without and within). And it's never too soon to undertake this sacred work. One can develop a taste for it. It's the name of the human game, after all. Or as Lynch puts it, "I love seeing people come out of darkness."[11]

I'M BUSY!

Show business, we understand, is the long and ancient work of our species as we come out of hiding or pretend to come out of hiding only to hide away again. If Thoreau is right that, in the final analysis, we only crave reality, and Bambara is right that we're all clairvoyants sometimes—or practically all the time—estranged from our own intuition, then we all have careers in show business of one kind or another. We're never not broadcasting. We're each showing or unsuccessfully trying not to show our hands. Viewer discretion is advised. Nothing stays hidden.

Mulholland Drive, like a fable or a parable or a poem, conjures a space for feeling, seeing, and addressing the ways we hide from ourselves what we're doing to people with and in our imaginations and, therefore, our words, deeds, and general devaluing of self and others, the desecration and disgrace that begins with a misconception, a tiny betrayal of the mind, a corruption. Perhaps paradoxically, it's an evil rooted in lack, a misperception of the good and therefore beautiful that isn't ever inevitable. James Joyce channels Augustine very helpfully here: "It was revealed to me that those things are good which yet are corrupted which neither if they were supremely good nor unless they were good could be corrupted."[12]

If we receive this instruction, we see that everything depends on framing, editing, context, and angle of vision. Footage we think of as garbage, because there's nothing that's *just* garbage, can be cast in a manner that allows the living fact of it to ring true. Sound and slow-motion video, for an auteur like Vic Berger, can turn a Jim Bakker infomercial or Donald Trump's appearance on Jimmy Fallon's show into a deep-dive meditation on the way we kid ourselves into oblivion. There's a holiness in our heart's affections that might yet be engaged differently if we have an ear to hear or an eye to see. The treasure is there amid our patterns of avoidance.

I see it in the mass-media-generated pathos of Martin Scorsese's *King of Comedy* (1983). Paul Zimmerman's story of amateur comedian Rupert Pupkin (a movingly uncharacteristic role for Robert De Niro) features a life lived in a basement with cardboard cutouts of late-night talk-show host Jerry Langford (Jerry Lewis) and his lively guests. He fantasizes scenes in which he assures Langford, "I know, Jerry, that you are as human as the rest of us if not more so," and Langford tells Pupkin how talented he is: "You've got it. . . . How do I know? Because I envy you." All the while, his mother calls him from upstairs, asking him what he's doing, and he yells back, "I'm busy!" And in a deeply disturbing fashion, he is. Anyone who knows what it's like to lose all sense of self in the spiraling pseudointimacy of a social media feed can relate. In time, he'll form a kind of fan club with Sandra Bernhard's Masha (who will engage a bound Jerry Langford in the kind of conversation she'll continue in real life with David Letterman), and certain dreams, for better or worse, will come true.

It's completely ridiculous on so many levels, but, like *Sunset Boulevard* and *Mulholland Drive*, it stands up well in an age in which commodification of all things human seems to know no bounds. When Pupkin imagines being a guest on Jerry's show, with his high school principal appearing to apologize on behalf of everyone who ever doubted him (thanking him now for all the joy he brings to the world), we might be right to sense that an economy that instigates, facilitates, and preys on our heart's misperceptions, amplifying our most estranged selves, is perfectly calibrated to yield today's crises. One nation's unaddressed neuroses can spell catastrophe for the rest of the species.

If covetousness and competition inevitably drive the American economy and if campaigns for public office increasingly depend on gangs of hypnotists paid by oligarchs, it might seem inevitable that the closed dream systems they foist upon us will eventually possess our hearts, minds, and nervous systems. But we have films that demystify, inspire, and speak against the wicked dreams that have us plastering our preconceived notions over other people's faces while weighing humans out to see how they might fit within our fantasies. Alvin Straight knows that neither life nor death matter more than being reconciled, and the weak mantras of pride and personal security won't lure him away from trying to be his brother's keeper.

Our preference for imitation of life over the real thing did not begin with the advent of electronic media, but some media might suit our phantasm consciousness with particular intensity. In 2 Peter 2:3, the early church is warned against the machinery of covetousness that makes people into merchandise, the false witness that makes us think falsely of ourselves and others. Learning to recognize the more righteous visions among us is a life's work of Beloved Community never quite done. "Not everything that is faced can be changed," James Baldwin teaches us, "but nothing can be changed until it is faced."[13] The film is on.

In a recent re-viewing of *The Wizard of Oz* (1939), I found myself taken aback by little signals of magnanimity that moved me before I had a word like "magnanimity" with which to say why. Consider the man behind the curtain who eventually gets worn down by his destructive efforts to hide his own fear by shouting people down and keeping them chasing down treasures they had all along to begin with, eating their own tales, rutting in a shame spiral that mirrored his own. Give it up, wizard. Let go. Make resignation great again.

And then there's the woman whose own trauma had her wanting to do all kinds of cruel and unusual things to Dorothy, her friends, and that dog of hers. As she melts, the Wicked Witch of the West is not unaware of how strangely her well-laid plans have gone awry, and the filmmakers allow her a word of amazement concerning how her sense of justice was too simplemindedly pursued: "What a world! What a world!" Nothing like the lyrical dismay of an alleged villain.

We won't unfailingly consume media for the purpose of being humbled by the tragedy, comedy, and paradox of real life, but if we're to evade the throes of groupthink, mob fury, and other wicked dreams, we need to cultivate and sustain a taste for media that will challenge us. We do well to make sure we aren't simply tuning in to whatever will confirm our already-made-up minds or harden the patterns of sentimentality we're apt to mistake for soul. We need the rifts that restore an alertness to that which has been wrongly normalized in our minds, rifts that interrupt our prejudices and our shortsightedness. If we're constantly angered and defensive against anything that challenges our view of the world thus far, we're right to wonder if we're growing increasingly incapable of perceiving Beloved Community and any means by which divine grace and the moral realizations it affords us might sneak into our always-in-danger-of-being-hardened hearts. Maybe nobody ever gets away with anything. Maybe full disclosure doesn't depend upon our attentiveness. It's coming anyway. What a world.

Chapter 7

An Imagery of Infinite Possibility

Your truth is more powerful than your mask.

—Jordan Peele

Outside the margins, you have to get your power from somewhere!
—Thi Bui

The only poetic tradition is the voice out of the burning bush. The rest is trash and will be consumed.

—Allen Ginsberg

Let us not disdain, then, but pity. And wherever we recognize the image of God, let us reverence it, though it hung from the gallows.
—Herman Melville

Publick Occurrences Both Forreign and Domestick was the name of the first American newspaper. It was published by Richard Pierce and Benjamin Harris of Boston in 1690, and because they hadn't applied for the required government license, they were shut down after one issue. But a professed reason for starting the paper is worth preserving as an early freedom-loving impulse in American history and a worthwhile motivation for unsanctioned expression in any culture: "That something may be done towards the Curing, or at least the Charming of that Spirit of Lying, which prevails amongst us."[1]

Words to live by, right? One person's truthfulness is someone else's impropriety, and a moment's consideration of a White House press conference, the demonizing of anyone with an honest question, and the general history of whistle-blowing might lead us to conclude that the termination of Pierce and Harris's operation involved more than a question of proper paperwork. Attempted truthfulness is costly. Omnipartisan alertness to what's real—to what really happened—is a risky affair. When it comes to the sexual assaults of the powerful, Jessica Hopper once asked, "Who do you excuse and why?"[2] To live and think freely is to live with such questions. We have to put aside the question of who's made to look good or bad by the truthful utterance if we're ever to be made free by it. This is a difficult work for human beings, but there is no apprehension of Beloved Community or any good news for democracy without it. The limits of my curiosity are the limits of my life.

There's a moment in the book of Jeremiah that describes King Jehoiakim in his palace, listening to the words of the prophet read aloud off a scroll (36:20–26). The text denounces the king's power of pride and insists that his leadership is not pleasing to the Lord ("Yet neither the king, nor any of his servants who heard all these words, was alarmed, nor did they tear their garments" [36:24]). In a fit of disgust, Jehoiakim responds by cutting off portions of the scroll as they're read and burning them in the fireplace, and he orders the arrest of Jeremiah and his secretary Baruch.

Commenting on this story, Northrop Frye once observed that the king's palace would, as Jeremiah had announced, disappear in no time while "the Book of Jeremiah, entrusted to the most fragile and combustible material produced in the ancient world, remains in reasonably good shape."[3] This is an important word, in my view, concerning the prophetic witness of God's order spoken to all our well-advertised, "high-impact," lesser orders and their, to borrow a phrase, record crowds. Jehoiakim was king of Judah (God's chosen, we might say) and could easily lay claim to a "God bless Judah" while outlining a doomed foreign policy and ordering the arrest of all prophets. Who appears to have been put in charge, after all? But then there's little beleaguered Jeremiah, Baruch, and their pamphleteering, zine movement, ministry-revolution. Aren't they just asking for trouble? Why, they can write up whatever they want without anybody's say-so. Fake news! Exile that Reverend Cherrycoke! Arrest Lisa Simpson and shut down that blasted Red Dress Press! Somebody oughta do something.

If we're among those who affirm, as I do, that "the Word of the Lord endures forever," are we thinking of a caravan of asylum seekers scribbling away under the shadow of a not-always-receptive empire? My fear is that many Americans think of something more along the lines of "my understanding of reality endures forever" or "me and my kind will prevail." In our praise of the strong-headed, endlessly self-justifying personalities who think they're elected to project power and buttress their own brand of national confidence at all costs, we would do well to contemplate the spirit of lying, the atmosphere that makes it seem perpetually necessary for survival, and the means available to us to be delivered from it and somehow detoxed.

GOOD ALONE IS GOOD WITHOUT A NAME

Submitted for your approval, this chapter offers some brief sketches of some of America's pioneers of the new seriousness. And in the spirit of Jeremiah, they all remind us, in one way or another, that the righteousness of God stands in contrast to all nations and their histories. In our temptation to view God as the blessed, profound, sacred center of what we say and do, these figures assert, often unself-consciously, that we don't know the half of it. Reinhold Niebuhr, for instance, believed that history is moving toward the realization of God's kingdom, but he also insisted that God's judgment (God's larger standard) is above and upon each new realization. Or to put it another way, we must not congratulate ourselves prematurely when there's so much further to go. We have yet to learn fully the ways of the Lord. We have only begun, if it's right to say we've begun at all, to say yes to God's purposes. An unsought awareness of our unprogress will sometimes be a jarring experience, but the new seriousness requires it.

For these figures, there is no theoretical faith, no religiosity that minds its own business, and no ideas except in actuality. No unincarnate word or disembodied belief. They're practitioners of Beloved Community who won't let us get away with our tendency to misconstrue the Scriptures in such a way that they no longer witness against our lifestyles (while being more than happy to use the Scriptures to speak critically of everyone except ourselves). Because they are people on whom nothing is lost, they're wary of being softened up for someone else's death-dealing program, and they all hold to the creed, through word and deed, of each and every person as "a soul of infinite metaphysical value," a phrase drawn from the theopolitical imagination of Martin Luther King Jr.

When Allen Ginsberg cries, "Slaves of Plastic!" or the Student Nonviolent Coordinating Committee (SNCC) of 1960 asserts that "nonviolence, as it grows from the Judeo-Christian tradition, seeks a social order of justice permeated by love,"[4] we might begin to envision an arsenal of mostly unused imagery and inspiration in the resistance of humanity against the nonhuman. These are a few voices of communal credibility, and I suspect they'll occupy some role in any ecumenical history of the future that considers the significance of American culture in the experience of the holy catholic church. Being a living mystery, as Cardinal Suhard says, is more effective than engaging in propaganda or rabble rousing, and these people fit the bill. And as I try to believe that all persons are living mysteries whether they realize it or not, I find the pro-human culture described here an invigorating injection for believing this way. These individuals are only too aware of the deafening propaganda of the principalities and powers of the present darkness, but they refuse to let it drown out the Word of God in a world they insist belongs to God. In the face of all the evidence to the contrary, they believe that the kingdoms of the world are being and somehow will be redeemed by the kingdom of God (Rev. 11:15). They're convinced that it is the vocation of all of God's people to start acting like it in word and deed and attitude. This is what I call apocalyptic witness, though it isn't always televised. But if our bandwidth is our worship space, we'll do well to allow them in as we try to righteously orient our own lives.

CLARIFICATION OF THOUGHT

As a young woman who experienced a moral awakening to the possibilities of communal thriving in the San Francisco earthquake of 1906, Dorothy Day had a preoccupation with the downtrodden that was further enhanced by her reading of Upton Sinclair's *The Jungle*. After dropping out of college, she found work with New York's socialist paper *The Call* and interviewed everyone from butlers to labor activists to Leon Trotsky.

Jailed in 1917 for her role in a suffragist protest in Washington, she undertook a hunger protest and was surprised to find herself reading the Bible for comfort and encouragement. After being released with other women by way of a presidential order, her late evenings with the likes of Eugene O'Neill in a Greenwich Village saloon nicknamed "The Hell Hole" would end in the back pew of St. Joseph's Church. She'd long viewed the Catholic Church as "the church of the immigrants, the church of the poor,"[5] but her fascination with Christianity was something many of her peers found incomprehensible at best and distressing at worst.

A relationship with another journalist led to a pregnancy ending in an abortion, and she wrote about the experience in a novel, *The Eleventh Virgin* (which she later called "a very bad book"). With the proceeds, she bought a house on Staten Island and entered into a common-law marriage with Forster Batterham, an Englishman. With Batterham, she shared a love of nature, but her interest in Catholicism did not resonate with him. When she became pregnant again in 1925, he did not share her interpretation of the news as a miraculous turn of events any more than he approved her decision to have the child baptized into the Catholic Church.

"I knew that I was not going to have her foundering through many years as I had done, doubting and hesitating, undisciplined and amoral,"[6] she later wrote. And after a year, her insistence upon joining the church herself would finalize a break with Batterham. It wasn't something she described as a great awakening, but rather a decision she felt she had to make in the direction of life for her child, her own health, and her moral vocation. During the years that followed, she would work for the Anti-Imperialist League and continue to write, supporting herself and her daughter while hoping that clarity would come.

In 1932, Peter Maurin, a French immigrant, would enter her life, and out of their conversations, the Catholic Worker movement was born. He termed the purpose of conversations and the discussions that would spread around the world out of their interaction "clarification of thought."[7] And he envisioned houses of hospitality founded for the purpose of equipping and caring for the downtrodden. In the era of the Great Depression, he felt that Christians should be less concerned with what government is up to and more occupied with how they might embody new creation, new ways of being human, in the shell of the old, dying orders. Beginning with the two of them, the Worker movement would consist of whoever showed up.

They began with the *Catholic Worker* paper (sold then and now for one cent), and when homeless people showed up at Day's apartment asking for the location of one of the houses of hospitality described in its pages, Day would tell them to rent an apartment and get started. In time, the Catholic Worker movement had its own building. An alternative community that wasn't waiting on funding or government license, it could be undertaken anywhere, and it was. By 1936, there were thirty-three Catholic Worker houses across the country.

"We believe in an economy based on human needs, rather than on the profit motive,"[8] Day would state on behalf of the movement, and wherever there was social upheaval (reaching out to Hispanic migrant workers in California, participating in sit-down strikes in Detroit), she would show up to say that there were Catholics somewhere on their side and that Christianity, in case someone somewhere needed reminding, did not belong solely to the rich, the powerful, or whatever political party might most shamelessly quote Scripture out of context. The paper went out and the communities formed in the interest of "the rights of the worthy and the unworthy poor" and as a witness that wherever two or more are gathered, "we can work for the oasis, the little cell of joy and peace in a harried world."[9] The shared life of even a few is a witness of Beloved Community and an enlistment of the mostly untapped dynamite of the gospel. We start small if we start at all.

To the oft-deployed question of "Did not Jesus say that the poor would always be with us?" Day had a quick reply: "Yes, but we are not content that there should be so many of them. The class structure is of our making and by our consent, not God's, and we must do what we can to change it. We are urging revolutionary change."[10]

This wasn't the only time Day drew from America's founding documents to articulate her points. The Catholic Worker movement would often have a word to say on the government's abuse of power, and a 500-page file of the Federal Bureau of Investigation concluded that Day was being used by Communist groups, describing her as "a very erratic and irresponsible person." But run-ins with government and church authorities simply afforded more opportunities for clarification of thought. And at the other end of debilitating praise, she didn't like language that suggested imitation of Christ as something that wasn't the business of all Christians: "Don't call me a saint. I don't want to be dismissed that easily."[11] Doing what one can is radical enough, and what we can do is always more than we're accustomed to imagining. She often pointed out that anyone at all can hand out sandwiches and soap, and in this sense, the gospel waits on nothing.

According to Day, "The mystery of the poor is this—that they are Jesus, and what you do for them you do to Him."[12] But she wouldn't sentimentalize the difficulties of trying to love well. On the issue of her own shifting moods, she'd quote Saint Teresa: "The devil sends me so offensive a bad spirit of temper that at times I think I could eat people up."[13] And salvation as a process (saved, being saved, will be saved) is a daily occurrence: "It is by little and by little that we are saved."[14] The long haul of neighbor love, of being good news to the poor and to the enemy, is best undertaken where two or more are gathered. Gospel happens.

CREATIVE TROUBLE

I'm not sure that we could call it a thought experiment exactly, but in 1942, Bayard Rustin, a young Quaker from West Chester, Pennsylvania, who'd toured with Leadbelly, decided to try something unexpected.[15] Boarding a bus in Louisville, Kentucky, bound for Nashville, Rustin sat in the second seat from the front of the bus. When the driver noticed and told him to sit in the back, he responded with the potentially world-altering question "Why?"

"Because that's the law," he said. "Niggers ride in the back."

"My friend, I believe that is an unjust law. If I were to sit in back I would be condoning injustice." Perturbed, but unsure how to respond, the driver repeated the routine at each stop. In time, Rustin realized the driver had made a phone call when he heard sirens and saw a police car and two motorcycles. Four policemen got on board, conversed briefly with the driver and then approached Bayard's seat, shouting at him to get up. When he asked why again, they kept shouting.

"I believe that I have a right to sit here," he said softly. "If I sit in the back of the bus I am depriving that child"—he gestured to a nearby child of five or six years—"of the knowledge that there is injustice here, which I believe it is his right to know. It is my sincere conviction that the power of love in the world is the greatest power existing. If you have a greater power, my friend, you may move me." As he wouldn't move they started beating him, and after being knocked to the floor, he was dragged out of the bus, where the beating and kicking continued. Reminding himself that resistance would lead to more kicks, he forced himself to be still. Once they slowed down, he stood up and with his arms spread out said, "There is no need to beat me. I am not resisting you."

At the sight of this, three Southern white men became agitated, got off the bus, and loudly objected to Rustin's treatment. One smaller man grabbed a policeman's club and said, "Don't you do that!" When another policeman moved to strike the smaller man, Bayard stepped between them and, facing his advocate, said, "Thank you, but there is no need to do that. I do not wish to fight. I am protected well."

An older fellow asked where they were taking him and, upon hearing that he was Nashville bound, said, "Don't worry, son. I'll be there to see that you get justice."

In the car, Rustin sat between two policemen, with two seated in the front. As they shouted at him, trying to get him to lash out, he took out a piece of paper to calm himself and began to write out a passage from the New Testament from memory. "What're you writing?" a policeman beside him asked, taking the paper, reading it, crumpling it up, and pushing it in his face.

At this point, Rustin caught the eye of a younger officer in the front before he looked quickly away. Describing this moment, Rustin wrote, "I took renewed courage from the realization that he could not meet my eye because he was aware of the injustice being done." After a moment he leaned forward, touched his shoulder, and asked, "My friend, how do you spell 'difference'?"

Upon arriving at the police station, he was pushed down the hallway to the captain's office, where they searched his bag and examined his copies of *Christian Century* and *Fellowship*. Eventually the captain summoned him to the desk: "Come here, nigger."

"What can I do for you?" Rustin asked.

"Nigger, you're supposed to be scared when you come here!" the captain shouted.

"I am fortified by truth, justice, and Christ. There's no need for me to fear."

The captain looked at his officers and said, "I believe the nigger's crazy!"

As he then waited at the courthouse, he heard a voice ("Say, you colored fellow, hey!") and realized it was the older man from the bus. "I'm here to see that you get justice," he explained.

Brought before assistant district attorney Ben West, the policemen were asked for their side of the story and gave it with much embellishment. When Rustin was asked if he would offer his account, he replied, "Gladly. And I want you," looking at the younger officer, "to follow what I say and stop me if I deviate from the truth in the least." Holding his eyes the whole time, he'd stop and say, "Is that right?" "Isn't that what happened?" "Did I tell the truth just as it happened?" And West eventually asked him to step outside.

After Rustin had spent an hour in a dark room, West came in with a gently spoken word: "You may go, Mister Rustin."

Rustin would later note that the possibility of the truth being heard, of the other passengers leaping to his defense, the older man's advocacy, and the young officer's unwillingness to be entirely complicit in deception, was generated by the moment he said, "There is no need to beat me. I offer you no resistance." In 1947, he would help plan the first "freedom ride" in the South in what was known as the Journey of Reconciliation and be sentenced to work on a chain gang in North Carolina.

"I believe in social dislocation and creative trouble," Rustin once remarked.[16] And it is believed that his conversations with Martin Luther King Jr. were essential in the development of King's own commitment to nonviolence. (Rustin would later serve as deputy director and chief organizer of the March on Washington in 1963.) Harnessing the domination impulse (what King famously called "the drum major instinct"), redirecting it in the direction of goodness and the loving purpose that characterizes Beloved Community, can make the old world a new world. By way of improvisation, it cracks a moment open toward newer, better possibilities. Maurin's gospel of untapped dynamite starts to look like the only game in town: A healthy disrespect for human instrumentalities that demand exclusion and a radical reverence for human beings. A multipartisan witness that refuses to discriminate on the basis of any party affiliation. Realism redefined. Imagining the real world.

MR. JESUS IS IN THE STREETS

When Will Campbell—a white Baptist minister carrying a walking stick, a Bible, and a guitar case—arrived at the organizational meeting of the Southern Christian Leadership Conference in 1956, some of the younger organizers refused him admittance. But then Bayard Rustin spotted him in the hallway. "Let this man in," he insisted, "We need *him*."[17] Campbell, a former chaplain of the University of Mississippi who had accompanied students passing through angry mobs in an effort to integrate Central High School in Little Rock, Arkansas, would later meet John Lewis at a training session in nonviolent resistance at the Highlander Folk School, counsel and support Freedom Riders in the 1960s, minister to imprisoned Klansmen in the 1970s, and travel with Waylon Jennings as a cook in the 1980s.

Ordained in a small Mississippi church at the age of seventeen, Campbell found himself increasingly estranged from much of his family and the county he grew up in, but his affection for the culture too often cast in the broad net of "bigots" and "rednecks" often had him wondering over the subtle manner in which bigotry can cut both ways. Observing as much did not always go over so well, but he was quick to point out that the stumbling block of the gospel trips up his own imagination first and foremost.

The era of the Freedom Rides afforded him many lively conversations. In one such instance, he was challenged by a newspaper editor, P. D. East, to sum up the Christian faith in ten words or less. Rising to the challenge, he proposed a summation: "We're all bastards, but God loves us anyway."[18] Not long after in Lowndes County, Alabama, a special deputy named Thomas Coleman shot and killed an Episcopal seminarian named Jonathan Daniel. While discussing the tragic news, East wondered if Campbell's theology would hold up under duress: "What you reckon your friend Mr. Jesus thinks of all this?" Campbell said he reckoned he was pretty sad.

"Was Jonathan Daniel a bastard?" he asked. And when Campbell wouldn't respond definitively, he repeated his question.

"Yes," Campbell said.

"Well," he pressed, "was that deputy, Thomas Coleman, a bastard?"

"Yes—Thomas Coleman is a bastard."

Drawing closer to Campbell and looking him in the eye, East asked, "Which one of these two bastards do you think God loves the most?"

Campbell would later describe this moment, which followed a degree from Yale Divinity and twenty years of ministry, as his conversion experience. Through tears and laughter, he saw himself in deep danger of betraying his call as a disciple and, in his own words, he saw unmasked before him

> an attempted negation of Jesus, of human engineering, of riding the coat-tails of Caesar, of playing on his ballpark, by his rules and with his ball, of looking to government to make and verify and authenticate our morality, of worshiping at the shrine of enlightenment and academia, of making an idol of the Supreme Court, a theology of law and order and of denying not only the Faith I professed to hold but my history and my people—the Thomas Colemans.[19]

Campbell looked at East and observed, "You've got to be the biggest bastard of us all. . . . Because, damned if you ain't made a Christian out of me. And I'm not sure I can stand it."

Years later, he would attend a conference of the U.S. National Student Association and lead a discussion following the viewing of a CBS documentary, *Ku Klux Klan: An Invisible Empire*. Disturbed by the derisive laughter that followed scenes of a clumsy young Klansman nervously trying to find his way through a military formation, Campbell began the discussion that followed with a provocative word: "My name is Will Campbell. I'm a Baptist preacher. I'm a native of Mississippi. And I'm pro-Klansman because I'm pro-human being."[20]

When pandemonium followed and most participants left the room, Campbell tried to point out how the power of particular words brought people to a boiling point. He wanted to explain the lesson he'd recently learned himself, that pro-Klansman is not the same as pro-Klan, and being capable of making the distinction might be our only hope for civil discourse.

Campbell brought this scandalous sense of a difficult gospel to his every interaction. He was present, for instance, in 1998 when Sam Bowers, White Knight of the Ku Klux Klan, was sentenced to life for the murder of civil rights hero Vernon Dahmer. Campbell greeted Bowers warmly just before taking a seat in a Hattiesburg, Mississippi, courtroom with the Dahmer family. When a reporter asked how he could possibly befriend both parties, he said, "I guess it's because I'm a goddamn Christian."

"Be reconciled" sums up the ministry of Will Campbell. Borrowing the language of 2 Corinthians 5, he pursues his vocation on behalf of a God busily reconciling himself to sinners through Jesus, a work, in his view, not always undertaken primarily by efforts that advertise themselves as "Christian." Viewing self-perpetuating institutions as, in large part, a corruption of Jesus' purposes, Campbell has defined the church of Jesus Christ as "one cat in one ditch and one nobody of a son of a bitch trying to pull her out."[21] This is the work of reconciliation. And it is good news.

IMMORTAL URGES DO NOT COME CHEAP

To my mind, something all of these figures have in common is a steadfast refusal to view the alleged opposition as nothing more than opposition. Without the larger biblical confession (our problem, our child, our mess, our life together), speech about God and grace is all too often only a reference to someone's personal, private acceptance of personal, private forgiveness: God's love for me. Dorothy Day could speak powerfully of a "filthy, rotten, system" (the sum total, we might say, of everyone's personal, private sin), but she did not stand aloof from it. Or as Lenny Bruce would say, "I am a part of everything I indict."

Against the them-and-us formulations of every war on terror, we have the dazzling realism of Daniel Berrigan. "I don't believe that Christians are called to win anything," he once remarked.[22] And "unwinning" is a description I imagine he'd be more than happy to have applied to his career. There is a candor in his understanding of poetry and civil disobedience that is often missed in the haze of disbelief and conflicting feelings surrounding news of what he's said and done. And I'm not sure America has a surer and saner voice when it comes to leveling with ourselves:

> We would like to be able to say, I can judge the world without being judged. But we know it is impossible. Because disorder lies at our heart. The drama without is the drama within, at least in an exemplary way; the one is joined to the other by the undefeated possibility of evil—the human potential for self-destruction.[23]

Whether marching in Selma, pouring blood on nuclear warheads, or doing time as a prisoner of conscience, Berrigan never stopped dramatizing, for anyone with an ear to hear and an eye to see, the moral disgrace we sustain with our tax dollars, our votes, and our presumed consent. He charted a Christianity

worthy of thinking adults and was cheered—sometimes from the sidelines—
by many who were otherwise long inured against thinking such a thing possible. "For me Father Berrigan is Jesus as a poet. If this be heresy, make the most
of it," Kurt Vonnegut once remarked.[24] In an age of heartbreaking hypocrisy
on the part of so many a loud God-talker, Berrigan is remembered as a pioneer
of human seriousness, one who really meant it and believed it and took on the
cost of doing so again and again, come what may.

When Berrigan read the Scriptures, he was moved to note that "we are
unready for God; we are hardly more ready for one another."[25] And Scripture
that doesn't in some way dislocate our imaginings of success, victory, terror,
goodness, and beauty is scripture that has yet to be read properly. Scripture
calls us out of Egypt and every form of enslaving culture. But when we've
reduced its liberating word to our own terms, our own idolatries, we fail to
apprehend its summons to freedom.

Berrigan believed that art is that which "cries reality!"[26] As a Jesuit priest,
Berrigan was especially sensitive to language that offers itself as liturgy or words
of consolation when it's actually just a presuming of God's uncritical blessing
on "more of the same. More of war, more of war preparation, more of social-
ized death."[27] This sensitivity is similar to Campbell's concern over a culture
that speaks condescendingly of the Ku Klux Klan while, in word and deed,
behaving like "a nation of Klansmen." When Berrigan founded Clergy and
Laymen concerned about Vietnam with Rabbi Abraham Joshua Heschel and
Richard Neuhaus, this resulted in his temporary exile to Latin America by
Francis Cardinal Spellman (one of Lenny Bruce's favorite targets). Needless to
say, his sojourn south of the border did not lessen his convictions concerning
the demands of Beloved Community. He returned with renewed fervor and a
deep desire to disturb the alleged, official peace that is no peace.

One such opportunity arose in the form of a phone call from Tom Hayden
in January of 1968. It was an invitation from Hanoi. The North Vietnamese
government wanted to release three American prisoners of war in celebration
of the Buddhist Tet holiday to two representatives of America's peace movement as a joint goodwill gesture. Agreeing to the mission, he was joined by the
historian Howard Zinn. As welcomed guests in Hanoi, they hid in bomb shel-
ters, held infants, and took in the scenery. For his part, Berrigan experienced
the facts on the ground as a live-action lesson in all the ways "American power"
serves as "the active, virulent enemy of human hope."[28] A foreign policy of
murderous despair, the listlessness of the American electorate, and the suffering of the many on the wrong side of one nation's perceived self-interest were
rendered undeniable. A conviction concerning the psychic toll of endless war
he'd come to share with his brother and others within the Beloved Community was only intensifying. He would carry his vision of the dysfunction, this
mess wrought by all manner of misconceived human self, into the twenty-first
century: "Immortal urges do not come cheap, whether in lives or resources."[29]

JESUS IN PROTECTIVE CUSTODY

Meanwhile, Daniel's brother Philip (a veteran of World War II who'd become a Josephite father) had begun to take courage from younger men who refused induction into the military and suffered imprisonment for it. Wanting to engage the crisis himself in a way that involved risk, he walked with the artist Tom Lewis, the poet David Eberhardt, and the minister Jim Mengel into Baltimore's Selective Service Board at the Custom House. Mengel handed out copies of the New Testament while the other three opened draft files and poured blood over them.[30] Lest anyone misunderstand the meaning of their action, they also passed out leaflets containing the following statement: "This sacrificial and constructive act is meant to protest the pitiful waste of American and Vietnamese blood in Indochina."[31]

Philip would eventually receive a six-year sentence for this action, making him the first Roman Catholic priest to be tried and imprisoned for committing a political crime.[32] But in the meantime, he was free to confer with Daniel and propose an escalation of dramatic tensions. Before his case went to trial, he felt compelled by God to perform another prophetic action involving draft files. Daniel was unsure but was also committed to praying the matter through.

He would famously characterize his spiritual formation crisis in this way: "I was in danger of verbalizing my moral impulses out of existence."[33] Anybody know the feeling? I imagine these words name the danger we're all in—whatever the context—in a wonderfully specific way. It's a confession of the felt risk we sense when we're at the point of decision between a conscience that's on the threshold of eroding or becoming incarnate. I believe this was his point of decision (not that there aren't a multitude in any one life) when it came to going deeper toward embodying a community of witnessing discernment when it counted for a nation on the brink. What appeared before him was one solid and perhaps costly opportunity to speak justly to power and to gesture toward what human wholeness looks like in the shadow of our reigning geopolitical liturgies of domination and degradation.

If not them, who? If not now, when? The Christian tradition to which they'd vowed to be true and the very body of Christ they were called to be *in the world* was, by many indications, completely sidelined in popular discourse. Could they make a vanished inventory of sacrament credible again? Maybe authority was up for grabs. Daniel Berrigan later articulated the state of play:

> Who owned the tradition, anyway; and who was worthy to speak on its behalf? . . . Indeed, the issue was not simply that a tradition was traduced daily by those responsible for its purity and truth. The issue was a far more serious one. . . . The tradition was a precious voice, a presence, a Person. The war had silenced the voice, outlawed the Person. Church and state had agreed, as they inevitably did in time of war, that the Person was out of fashion, "for the duration." He had nothing to offer in the face of guns.

. . . He was a prisoner of war, this Jesus. He was in a species of protective custody.[34]

And yet, the earth is the Lord's and everything in it: files, designated areas, the whole of it. Could they keep their vows to be ambassadors of God's righteous order without publicly protesting—in some demonstrative way—the idolatrous ordering of the nation-state? They would bring the liturgical forms with which they'd been entrusted by their tradition to the war-making liturgies, the paperwork, for instance, of the US government, whose enlisting of young men to commit acts of indiscriminate violence and devastation upon the people and the land of Vietnam constituted, biblically speaking, a demonic stronghold. On May 17, 1968, they joined seven other activists and walked into a draft board in Catonsville, Maryland, removed papers with the names of young men scheduled to be conscripted, and conducted the prayerful burning of draft files with homemade napalm. Apologizing for their fracture of what they could no longer abide as "good order," and noting that they were no longer able to say "Peace, peace" when there is no peace, they observed that they thought it fitting to burn paper instead of children: "We could not so help us God do otherwise."[35] As the fire burned, they punctuated this purposeful ritual by reciting the Lord's Prayer.

In the name of the deeper, truer rhythms of God's greater economy and what it might yet mean to be formed by it, their action was a redemptive raid on the *sacrosanct*. A moment's reflection on that almost excruciatingly helpful adjective—sacrosanct—is a reminder that it is indeed *ever in play*: flags, borders, weapons facilities, private property, bodies, pledges of allegiance, wildlife preserves, water. Choose your own liturgy? We do. All the time. And the Catonsville Nine did one fine day: "Those draft files! They were, of course, more than they purported to be. They had an aura, they were secular-sacred documents of the highest import."[36] The Berrigans chose to be militantly transparent when it counted. And in this way, their *transparent* liturgy would serve to disrupt and destabilize, even if only in one neighborly instance, the *unacknowledged* liturgy of the draft. Were they wrong to do so? Our answer will largely depend on our sense of the sacrosanct. What's yours? This is an essential question for anyone who means to live according to the witness of Beloved Community.

What was accomplished? They went to jail, and the Berrigan brothers were placed on the cover of *Time* magazine. It was a *palpable hit* in the sense that it *made the news* for a time. Similar actions were undertaken and continue into our day, most recently by Sister Megan Rice and her companions.[37] These endeavors are often staged under the moniker of the Plowshares Movement and pose, as the prophetic always does, the question of authority. To whom and what are we rightly *subject*? What shall we *credit*? How shall we *adhere*? To what are we *devoted*?

In 1972, Berrigan asked, "How do we help Americans get born, get going, get growing, get moving toward recovery of intention?"[38] And we can carefully note that this question isn't a matter of personal spirituality or private faith. It's a question that assumes no such dichotomies of unhealth, and it isn't a comfortable question (especially coming from the likes of Berrigan), but it is a gospel question. It's a question about the nature of Jesus' good news, a God who is not an abstraction. Are we ready for it? Are we ready for each other? Is America ready?

A MEMBERSHIP THAT EXCLUDES
NOTHING AND NOBODY

To really recall or to consider following the lead of these figures is to invite a disruption, to recall the sometimes-unwelcome realization that everything has to do with everything else. But perhaps disruption is essential to right vision and right practice. Spirit, again, knows no division, and, when it's pursued with any depth at all, the question of Beloved Community naturally overflows whatever boundaries we've erected to somehow assert that one section of the human barnyard can be made definitively separate from the other. *This*, the saying goes, doesn't have anything to do with *that*, but Beloved Community, same as it ever was, insists otherwise as it invites us, yet again, to refuse the dualistic thinking that renders us sad and confused and very often angry. Perhaps there are others who've been here before, people who might help us out. Enter our saints.

The people we come to call saints are those who seem to have generally succeeded in overcoming dualism and somehow manage to stand—as perhaps everyone's called to stand—in the great divide. We praise them and cite them on solemn occasions, and we expect respectable people to nod approvingly when they're mentioned. But could it be that we cut their voice off a little and render their insight less immediately available when we confer sainthood upon them? Is there a further dualism or even a disavowal involved, a hiding away of something from ourselves, when we erect pedestals and place our fellow human beings out of reach with the attribution of saintliness? Are we trying to contain the disruption they bring to consciousness lest it spread to areas we would prefer to keep obscured?

Maybe Dorothy Day was onto something in this regard. ("Don't call me a saint. I don't want to be dismissed that easily.") She didn't like the suggestion that her own attempt at hospitality for and among the poor or her lifelong resistance to state-sponsored violence was something more than what the plain teaching of Jesus and the prophets and communities of sanity here, there, and yon demand of right-thinking people everywhere. We aren't really honoring or even taking seriously anyone's lived witness when we pretend to sanctify them in this way. And similarly, I suspect we lose the hard-won gifts of insight that practitioners of Beloved Community offer us if we're quick to speak of them as radicals, as people somehow beyond the pale of *normal* health and wholeness, *standard* spiritual formation.

"The whole world runs by rhythms I have not yet learned to recognize, rhythms that are not those of the engineer."[39] These are the words of the poet, monk, and correspondent supreme, Thomas Merton, a friend to many of the figures we've considered. One insight I imagine Merton might bring to each of us is this sense of deeper rhythms at work in everyday reality, deeper than the mind of any engineer—whatever the alleged specialization or expertise might be—can successfully ascertain. As witnesses to these ordering rhythms, Beloved Community is alive to all manner of *dis*order sustained and defended by the alleged upholders of right order. But Merton's example as a contemplative who resolutely viewed himself as a *learner* of the sacred rhythms of *true* order, as opposed to a master, an authority, or a copyright owner, can serve us in proceeding with care, specificity, and profound humility of mind in a rebelliously idolatrous world . . . or what we mistakenly think of as the world.

Merton's appeal to the *true* rhythms of the *true* world reminds us that what we think of as the kingdom of God has nowhere else to happen but here among our—to put it mildly—*less* orderly kingdoms, the sometimes dysfunctional power arrangements into which we're born. In its appeal to our imagination, God's kingdom comes little by little, one recognition—one feat of attentiveness—at a time. With an eye on *oikos* (Greek for "household" and at the root of the term "economy"; recall the psalmist famously hoping that he might dwell, as the Septuagint renders it, in the *oikos*/house of God forever), Wendell Berry suggests that we might occasionally free this sacred vision of its sectarian associations as well as our own tendency to assume we already know all about it by referring to the kingdom of God as the Great Economy, that sacred vision of a membership that excludes nothing and no one and within which everything we do or don't do signifies.[40] Such sacred visions beckon us to turn our imaginations back toward the human circle, to locate our existence within it, and to ask ourselves how far we'll allow our sympathy to reach, to *re*member despite the fact of a culture that often appears hell-bent on *dis*membering our understanding of ourselves at every turn. What might it mean to form ourselves and others as people who seek first the truer rhythms of the Great Economy and the right relations it engenders within the world God so loves?

FLIP THE SCRIPT

Faithfulness to the deeper righteousness of Beloved Community in the American scene assumes many forms only occasionally well publicized. It occurs when a woman like Therese Patricia Okoumou decides to climb onto the foot of the Statue of Liberty on the Fourth of July to publicly demand the return of the terrorized children of asylum-seeking families to their parents and thereby demonstrates more determination and energy and risk in the direction of seeing America's promised publicity through than any member of Congress. It's at work among the water protectors of Standing Rock. It's present in every act of conscience undertaken on behalf of the public good. It's everywhere.

But I do have one tale that speaks to all of the above for the wit and the improv and the genius of Beloved Community on which it draws. I'm thinking of the Reverend James Lawson, the leading theoretician of nonviolence within the civil rights movement in America, the man Congressman John Lewis often cites when he speaks of his own instruction as a self-conscious practitioner of Beloved Community. Having moved to Nashville in the late 1950s, Lawson trained Lewis and Diane Nash and others in the discipline of not reacting with anger or violence when confronted by hostile crowds and inevitable arrest for sitting in the "whites-only" sections of downtown Nashville restaurants.

One Saturday,[41] Lawson was on the scene in the thick of it to coach students, reminding them of their commitment and to dissuade white passersby from responding violently to young people wholeheartedly—and whole-bodily—committed to nonviolent witness. In the hope of deescalating the situation, Lawson approached one motorcycle jacket–clad aggressor at the center of a group who had kicked Bernard Lafayette and Solomon Gort. The man directed a racial slur at Lawson before spitting in his face.

Reverend Lawson regarded the aggressor calmly and asked if he might have a handkerchief. The man was so taken off guard that he handed it to Lawson before he knew what he was doing. As Lawson thanked him and wiped his face, he asked the man if a nearby motorcycle belonged to him. It did. And in no time, they were discussing horsepower. Within a few minutes, the man was asking how he could aid Lawson and the students in their work. The script had been flipped. I once asked Lawson how one might develop the habit of handling people so beautifully, and he responded, as if it was just then occurring to him, "You have to keep in your mind an imagery of infinite possibility."

I'm so grateful I was there to write those words down, because I think they name the game (the culture, the revolutionary summons) of Beloved Community as well as any directive I've heard spoken aloud. Live up to your bravest, most lyrical, clairvoyant, imaginative, and loving self at all times. Keep in your mind an imagery of infinite possibility. Let's do it.

Chapter 8

God Remembers Everything
Violence Forgets

Lift me up out of this illusion, Lord. Heal my perception, so that I may know only reality.

     —Bill Hicks, *Rant in E-Minor*

The Bible means justice or it means nothing.

     —Arthur Miller

The Americans may be as vigilant as they please, but they cannot be vigilant enough for the Lord, neither can they hide themselves, where he will not find and bring them out.

     —David Walker, *Appeal to the Coloured Citizens of the World*

You have to take out their families.

     —Donald Trump

Confession time. Like many Americans who pass time in churches, synagogues, mosques, and temples, I have sat in relative silence through thousands of sermons. During the sermons and under their influence, my thoughts have often wandered toward my ongoing worries over eternity, and my worries, from time to time, have often assumed the form of a manic obsession. What chance do I have of getting eternity right? If you're an infidel, will you know it? Can I ever believe the right things intensely enough to get infinity taken care of so I won't have to worry about it anymore? Can I get a guarantee? Might I be incredibly, tragically wrong concerning the age to come? Should anyone dare to presume, concerning eternity, that they're getting it right?

As a young teenager, I paid very little attention to the sermons I sat through on Sunday mornings and Sunday evenings, because I was too busy reading through the Bible. I wouldn't have said that reading the Bible would get me to heaven, but, if pressed, I might have explained that I wasn't willing to take any chances. I didn't like the thought of the Lord returning and finding me a wishy-washy servant who hadn't read the Bible all the way through, and, to be completely candid, I wasn't completely pleased to imagine the Lord returning at all. I dared to hope that such a return might be good news for me, but I didn't suspect it would be good news for most of humanity, the quick and the dead, who probably had even less of a chance of believing the right things than I did. I worried and prayed for the son of Yul Brynner's Pharaoh in Cecil B. DeMille's *The Ten Commandments*, because he had kicked Moses' staff and mocked him, not knowing the gravity of what he was doing, and was duly taken by the angel of death before he could repent or be baptized. In truth, I suspected he was not alone in his unfortunate ending. I imagined millions were similarly endangered, and I wasn't sure how I should feel about it.

In those days, I believed that the thirteenth chapter of the Gospel of Mark referred to the second coming, and I was especially intrigued by verses 32–37. They seemed to say that the only thing certain about that dreadful day was that no person would be expecting it. Matthew's Gospel said it would come like a thief in the night, and to my mind, this sounded like the one guarantee concerning a coming day with no reassuring guarantees and not much in the way of good news for most people. So in the thick of my obsessing over eternity, I devised a plan.

What if we organized an around-the-clock Keep Awake vigil? If the Scriptures promised that the Lord wouldn't come back when anyone was expecting it, why not make sure we had someone on the clock at all times, busily sustaining, on behalf of everyone else, a personal sense of anxious expectation, the better to stave off the inevitable? The burden could be shared in shifts just so long as each person understood and felt committed to their responsibilities. For the duration of a half-hour time slot, anyone who felt so inclined could sign up to take a turn imagining that the Lord might be coming back at that very moment. We could keep the vigil going until everyone everywhere had had plenty of time to start believing the right things about the Lord. We'd have more time to get ready. Most specifically, I'd have more time to get ready. For the love of humankind and the eternal fate of most people, it seemed like a good idea. And because I believed that loving other people was most obviously what the Lord required of us, I even entertained the hope that the plan might be pleasing to him. Maybe I wasn't the only one to notice this very helpful loophole. Maybe it had been put there to be lifted out by a clever, dutiful reader, a good and faithful servant, like myself.

I don't share this testimony as a joke or to denigrate anyone's eschatology. But I imagine there is something familiar here, for many Americans, in the suspicion that God's ultimate purposes will involve a vast ethnic cleansing to end all ethnic cleansings. Needless to say, I don't share this suspicion, but I wonder about the question of empathy in the minds of citizens (not always limited to those who consider themselves "religious") who feel sanctioned to view other people as target markets, hell fodder, collateral damage, infidels, or irredeemable nonsouls. Do we fancy ourselves somehow godlike when we deem our opponents (Republicans, Democrats, anti-American) beneath our contempt? Do we think we're doing the Lord's work when we steal a campaign sign from someone's yard or e-mail a cartoon that makes the person we'd never vote for look stupid? Do we assume God will "take care of" all the people who'll never understand how good we are? Do we hope God will happily dispose of all those unreasonable people who hate our freedoms?

The biblical witness, in my view, is a countertestimony to all our antihuman reductions as it calls us to pray for, love, and radically seek the welfare of anyone we've come to view as the enemy. And God's faithfulness to all generations will always surpass whatever we think we know about people and what they deserve. It is the vocation of Beloved Community to uphold the human as the bearer of the divine image against the drumbeat of nationalism, market devaluing of the human, and every form of mob hysteria. But as we've seen, the witness will often be subordinated as a side issue, a misplaced sensitivity, or an insane dissent that will only aid those we're told threaten our alleged security. Or else, the witness will be held off as irrelevant to the political sphere and reduced to that nebulous, harmless, vapid realm the market calls spirituality. How are we to go about properly valuing ourselves or others within these categories? What will be the content of our values talk? How might we hope to get control of our vain imaginings, wicked counsel, and lying tongues?

THE TROUBLE WITH GROUPTHINK

On this side of the coming kingdom, it could be that the closest a twenty-first-century world power will ever come to formally recognizing an instance of possession by a deluding spirit is the report, to which we've already alluded, in which the Senate Intelligence Committee invoked "groupthink" in an effort to describe the faulty decision-making process whereby certain government employees charged with the work of homeland security seemed incapable of correctly observing the evidence before their very eyes. On the issue of weapons of mass destruction in Iraq, we'd been told that the absence of evidence is not the evidence of absence and that we mustn't distinguish between Saddam Hussein and the Al Qaeda network in our talk of war on terror, but here was the use of Orwellian language to describe what had gone wrong, a name to describe the unseen forces that battle it out in the formation of public opinion. Do campaign operatives traffic in anything less than groupthink manipulation? Are their methods unsound?

A culture of groupthink will cultivate its own institutional belief structure (principality, power, team spirit), and our ability to think and see clearly will often fall victim to its persuasiveness. Neither Rod Serling nor the apostle Paul stands alone in his warnings of atmospheres in which honest questions provoke outrage, and testimony that fails to fall in sync with the herd is viewed with angry suspicion. But who benefits most from the careful manipulation and maintenance of these atmospheres? What becomes of the general welfare? Who watches the watchers?

I'm not calling for a Department of Exorcism, but I hope I've spied out and highlighted Beloved Community as one form of American culture, here and among us, uniquely fortified and committed to resisting the pleasures of groupthink. We don't have to look far to note that Beloved Community often strikes us as hard sell. I don't mean to knock the sense of belonging for which God's creatures naturally pine. But there is an intoxication available to us in the form of blissed-out lockstep, a strength in numbers, and a kind of pseudo-community united by escalating aggression toward whatever person or people-group it might momentarily brand the source of all unease. Groupthink works as a uniter, because we often want to feel safe and strong more than we want to be wise, and we often habituate ourselves to a laziness of thought that has us drifting toward whatever power can most aggressively ridicule all opposition while extending a word of "Come unto me" to the confused masses. The siren song of groupthink sells.

The New Testament provides numerous words of admonition and careful articulations of this elusive, multiheaded appeal to our self-preserving instincts, and the most provocative of them all is "antichrist." The term is so often abused that we're loath to use it, but we might do well to utilize the term when we're in the presence of mythic realities gone murderous; when hatefulness, buttressed by myth, begins to spread like a contagion; and when we're prone to mistake immoderate intensity of passions for strength of character. When we're willing to name antichrist thusly, we might discover that our mental furniture is better equipped to resist the magnetic pull of groupthink. Experience shows that groupthink works because it affords us momentary ease. Groupthink sells units and wins votes, but it can't make the world safer for democracy. It doesn't like authorial authority, Romney Wordsworth, or that pesky notion that no insignificant person has ever been born. We're all especially susceptible to antichrist when our sense of self-preservation outweighs the call to love and enjoy our neighbors, but we're deaf to the possibility of confession when we only see antichrist in other people claiming peace and justice and deliverance from evil.

Disenthralling ourselves from the elaborate mythologies of other people's power struggles is a tall order, but it's a crucial work if we're to avoid becoming an America that can't stand to be questioned, Americans more in love with their preferred mythic reality than the lives of people who have yet to fit within their side of the mythic Them and Us. To the extent that we're uncurious, uninterested in the differences between one country and the next, and unmoved by any testimony that doesn't confirm our advance publicity, we're caught in the throes of what Orwell called doublethink, the mind trick whereby citizens learn to deny freedom to their own minds. As we buy into the projections of strength, calm, and victory we demand of our elected leaders, we become tragically closed to the biblical witness against our pridefulness, and Beloved Community is no longer a living element within our vain imaginations.

As the Council of Bishops of the African Methodist Episcopal Church understood in their response to the lawlessness of the Trump administration in 2016 and the authors of the Belhar Confession maintained in their stance against white supremacy in South Africa in 1986, the confessions of the Beloved Community are a challenge to every form of groupthink, especially when those who claim an affiliation with God begin to rally hearts and minds under a nationalistic banner. When this occurs, it is the prophetic consciousness that brings a righteous skepticism to our reigning mythic realities. The confessing community can speak candidly and demand candor when career politicians and celebrity pundits feel constrained by a viewing audience that seems to demand false covenants, further proclamations (against all evidence) of America's moral superiority, and assurances concerning the innate goodness of the American people. The confessing community is called to disrupt the feedback loop of self-congratulation, to speak back to the Us-and-Them sales pitch, and to bear witness to the scandalously multipartisan posture of God's Beloved Community.

Karl Barth understood that the gospel of Jesus and the prophets is represented falsely whenever it is viewed as a truth among other truths, a novel opinion among others, a whispering chaplain to human instrumentalities, or a private faith option with nothing to say to anyone's national pride or spending habits. It isn't a position but a cosmic reality. And Barth believed that the love of God sets a question mark up against all our mythic realities, principalities, and rabble-rousing words. This love undermines all our death-dealing idolatries. It belongs to no nation, and it will allow no other allegiances to stand alongside it. Its scope is without end, and it is under way. It makes all things new. It's the love that is stronger than death.

FAILURES OF IMAGINATION

When the 9/11 Commission Report famously cited a failure of imagination as a central issue facing the United States in its response to the possibility of terrorist attacks, we might be prone to most immediately think in terms of the difficulty of imagining all possible threats and all the numerous stratagems by which hostile forces seek to threaten our health and property. And as we've seen, the script for the future that features seekers and holders of public office devising new ways to assure voters that they, and they alone, are capable of imagining every imaginable threat to America's perceived self-interest has not proven to be a promising prospect for public discourse. But there are larger moral possibilities in an acknowledgment of a deficient national imagination, and, as I hope I've at least begun to demonstrate in this book, American culture contains a greater arsenal of imaginative witness than we're liable to forget if we treat every exchange as a zero-sum game of conversation stoppers and escalating what-aboutery. The more unimaginative we become in our responses to conflict, the more we play into the caricature of chaos the rest of the non-American world rightly looks upon with fear and horror.

On the difference between a warrior community that lives by unacknowledged piracy and a compassionate people who fear their fortress impulse and seek to live according to a vision of Beloved Community, the good-neighbor impulse, because their souls depend upon it, Wendell Berry has a timely word. As we consider the state of Brand USA, Berry's words sit well alongside the findings of the 9/11 Commission:

> I think the only antidote to that is imagination. You have to develop your imagination to the point that permits sympathy to happen. You have to be able to imagine lives that are not yours or the lives of your loved ones or the lives of your neighbors. You have to have at least enough imagination to understand that if you want the benefits of compassion, you must be compassionate. If you want forgiveness you must be forgiving. It's a difficult business, being human.[1]

This imaginative work is itself a kind of alternative catechesis to so much that passes for knowledge and necessity in our popular discourse. At our best, Americans hunger for more effective ways of being positively human. We're drawn to stories and songs that help us make better sense of our own struggles, our successes and failures, and we're edified to see ourselves reflected in the infinitely valuable everyone else. But, to borrow Octavia Butler's phrase, there's also a lifetime of conditioning under the dictation of other visions of meaning, the myth of punitive violence as constructive, a myth that actively resists the call of Beloved Community to see ourselves as kindred to one another. Daniel Berrigan once recounted confronting, as a schoolteacher, the depth of its inculcation.

As a teacher of fifteen-year-olds at St. Peter's Prep in Jersey City in the late 1940s, he began to sense a tension in the pursuit of his vocation. From a long line of thoughtful people who'd inspired and taught him, he'd picked up the habit of mulling aloud over what he himself was discovering in his own reading, and the class discussion one particular day brought to mind Ronald Knox's book *God and the Atom*. Among the speculations entertained in Knox's text was one path not taken in World War II. Among a few Americans, conventional wisdom concerning President Truman's faith-based approach to defeating Japan, we might say, had yet to completely concretize, and Berrigan voiced aloud Knox's observation that the United States could have easily opted to drop the bomb on an uninhabited Pacific island as a show of force instead of incinerating thousands of people in Hiroshima and Nagasaki.

While he doubtless understood that it was even then a controversial idea, Berrigan was surprised by the knee-jerk hostility he'd provoked among these not-so-Christianly catechized young people. "We did good! . . . It was them or us!" they exclaimed. In just a few formative years, they had come to believe—and even insist—that the escalation of violence and the needful human sacrifice that fate sometimes decreed must never be questioned. What's done is done. No reflection, confession, or repentance allowed. And in a profound sense, they'd been formed to believe and know, with accompanying heat, that entertaining alternatives to the path of necessary annihilation, in this instance, was tantamount to treason.

Among these young thought police, he saw that a very different spiritual formation than the one he hoped to build upon had been long ago ingrained. Their hearts and minds had been enlisted in the direction of unreasoning aggression for some time, and the learning space was the entirety of American culture and its self-understanding on the world stage. As a young educator, Berrigan was himself receiving an education. Throughout his life, these clarifying moments in conversations with students, parishioners, superiors, and professional politicians would continue, and a picture would emerge: The deep formation of mistaken identity—we have to humiliate others in order to survive—has been deeply entrenched in many a human psyche. Berrigan's task as a minister of word and sacrament was emerging. He described the realization thusly: "We . . . knew who we were . . . in the act of war. Ancestors were, first of all, warriors; in that degree only, they merited honor. . . . Ancestor to child; it was presumed that violence needed no teaching, it took care of itself. It was nonviolence, civility, that required discipline and instruction, and was under perennial assault."[2] One generation's failure of imagination would be made to trump, at every turn, a more righteous sense of self and others.

It is one thing to note that human beings are often prone to reduce the world, other people, or a given situation to the size of their own fear. It's another to spy, describe, and bear witness against a relentlessly traumatizing (and therefore relentlessly toxic) culture, a culture of denial, a culture of death, and to ask how one might posit against it (and in the hope of being in some small way an agent of healing) a culture of life and affirmation. The better nature, the truer affections that sometimes hold sway among God's children are, as Berrigan sees it, under perennial assault by . . . what? The prince of the power of the air? A spirit of accusation the ancients call Satan? Something in our DNA?

Rooting out the idols and ideologies to which we sacrifice our own lives and the lives of others was at the core of that longer, slower, deeper work to which

Berrigan would devote his life as a prophet of the wide-angle lens among us. In that classroom, this perfectly respectable poet-priest was still a couple of decades away from undertaking any word or action that could easily brand him "political" or "radical." But there remained the question of how to be a witness to—how to somehow even embody in word, deed, and idea—a life-giving alternative culture amid the reigning catechesis of a taxpayer-funded dream of an eye for an eye and then some. How does one begin to counter the powers of proselytization—the never-ending calls to worship—of the military-industrial-incarceration-entertainment complex?

SOME OF THESE DAYS

One human exchange at a time. Keep in your mind an imagery of infinite possibility. Beloved Community invites us to turn our clichés into lived realities, to revalue devalued people, and to think harder about our own thinking, thus representing the better, coming world in our tired and troubled one.

"Some of these days" is an especially effective phrase to characterize the extreme makeover, the reversal of fortunes that is the reign of God in which the different way of doing things is more fully inaugurated (Jer. 31:31–34), a grand rejuvenation occurs (Ezek. 34:25–31), God's righteousness occupies all of creation (Isa. 66:18–24), and the Spirit of the Lord is poured out on all flesh (Joel 2:28). It envisions a future hope that colors our thinking and doing in the present. And the Lord's Prayer invites a robust living out of this new order as a prayer for the wit and invigoration to respond to God's abounding grace in the here and now. Those days get to make their dwelling among these days. Now is the new later.

If we reduce this hope to a future dispensation mostly divorced from the present or imagine that the way of life Jesus introduced isn't to be bothered with until sometime after "the Rapture" (a suitable theology, incidentally, for a fully privatized faith), the possibility of earthbound, incarnate witness is tragically vitiated. In a spirit contrary to our pantheon of elders, a derisive and haughty attitude toward creation develops among self-described Christians who seem to think their faith is primarily a matter of what happens to their spirits when they die. Here again we often witness the move whereby skipping straight to the title of "Christ" reduces the witness of Jesus to a symbol that demands nothing of us. No loving of enemy, no sharing of resources, no prophetic or ethical heft. "Christ" becomes a fully sentimentalized ghost friend who blesses our violence as God's will.

But the reign of God changes everything now. The here and now is being sanctified already, and all authority in heaven and on earth is the Lord's. There is a coming day, a new order, some of these days, but if we aren't especially invigorated by it now, if it doesn't inform our imagination now, what are we expecting then? Do we want it in the meantime? Does the love of God infect our view of other people?

In N. T. Wright's *The Resurrection of the Son of God*, the final section ("Easter and History") opens with an amusing excerpt from Oscar Wilde's *Salome*. Herod has received word that there is a man who's been raising other men from the dead. Herod doesn't like this: "I do not wish him to do that. I forbid Him to do that. I allow no man to raise the dead. This man must be found and told that I forbid Him to raise the dead. Where is this man at present?"

"He is in every place, my lord," the witness explains, "but it is hard to find Him."[3]

In its portrayal of a confused ruler who's just been confronted by an elusive yet ubiquitous peasant defying the well-established rules of the game, this exchange rather brilliantly introduces the political significance of Easter. Herod is terribly displeased by all this, because resurrection is bad news for anyone whose power depends on lethal force. He doesn't want dead people coming back. That ruins the whole point of his illustrious career. It means that history isn't written only by winners, and that might perhaps does not make right. The "silenced" aren't ultimately silenced. They might come back with a word, and an especially authoritative "once upon a time . . ." The once-sure thing of ruling by the sword is being delegitimated. Victory over death deprives power of its primary means of persuasion. There are, it turns out, no closed books.

When Beloved Community is taken seriously, "What can we do about it now?" is no longer a conversation stopper. History isn't simply the memory of states. And pondering over how many died, and why, and how necessary it was is no longer a luxury a "realist" can't afford, because reality isn't quite what we thought it was. Blood cries out from the ground. What really happened takes on a disturbing new relevance.

It wasn't a compliment and his concerns were never pursued, but during war with Mexico a young Illinois congressman was nicknamed "Spotty Lincoln" for pushing President James K. Polk to admit that the spot where blood was first shed in the conflict was not on US soil. These were Abraham Lincoln's "Spot Resolutions." The truth matters, Lincoln insisted, because right makes might. The living concern with what really happened (and not simply with whether or not the living can be persuaded to be pleased later on) will occasionally distinguish a culture. It's a sense of rightness that enlarges perceived self-interests. And divine judgment resides over it, calling us to larger considerations than whatever we think we might get away with. If the reign of a God who will repair, restore, and remember everything we degrade, destroy, and *dis*member is really at hand, coming on earth as it is in heaven, what do we do with our liturgies of torture and remote death?

"Elimination of potential rivals," "collateral damage," and "antipersonnel weapons" take on a different aura when resurrection is brought into play. And "worthy is the Lamb who was slain," as an announcement of Jesus' kind of lordship and the kind of honor, power, glory, and praise that characterize the cosmos, marks a politics of resurrection. Hitler once insisted that success is the only earthly judge of right and wrong. But Easter overturns whatever inhumanity might manage to proclaim a success, sanctifying the human form for all history. A radical humanism is born.

When Martin Luther King Jr. insists that when it comes to human beings, the image of God is never totally lost, he's operating within this continuum. Humans will require the utmost reverence from now on. They can't not matter. Necessity that suggests otherwise is forever delegitimized. Lenny Bruce was especially troubled by standards that claim to maintain all that's right and true while playing fast and loose with human life: "My concept? You can't do anything with anybody's body to make it dirty to me. Six people, eight people, one person—you can do only one thing to make it dirty: kill it. Hiroshima was dirty."[4]

COME ON, PILGRIM

Any consideration of the significance of a risen Jesus requires a long look at why a world would find him distasteful. Woody Guthrie's "Jesus Christ" is a robustly helpful song in its insistence that American culture (like all others) would not have him, and while this is probably an uncontroversial point for anyone willing to voice the traditional prayers of confession, we're often in danger of assuming, without much thought, that we're not the kind of people who would put Jesus to death. We sometimes presume we're in general agreement with what Jesus has to say, as if all "decent, God-fearing people" are. But a consideration of our pantheon of elders and a casual glance at the Sermon on the Mount might have us wondering if we haven't created for ourselves a domesticated Jesus. Does the witness of Jesus and the prophets have a following in America? Is there a continuum?

I believe that there is. But we're often guilty of assuming continuity with unthinking presumption, speaking of Jesus as if he is easily incorporated into our lifestyles while viewing too radical an apprenticeship to his way as too extreme. We put him on a pedestal that sometimes serves to place the question of real discipleship out of consideration. In this sense, I often think that people who at least take Jesus seriously as a teacher, as the wisest individual who ever lived, are entering into the kingdom in ways that those who only want to have their sins removed for the afterlife aren't. If our interest in Jesus as an atoning sacrifice cancels out our attentiveness to the things he did and said, something has gone horribly wrong. Do we want the benefit of God's blessing minus the specifics of Jesus' commands? Do we think there's a difference?

When we think of his life as our pantheon of elders would have us do, we see him as a real-world individual whom American society can hardly tolerate.

It was this sort of realization that W. H. Auden cited as the reason for his conversion. While Muhammad and Buddha and Confucius struck Auden as reasonable figures not too difficult to agree with, he experienced Jesus as a stumbling block, a man whose visions elicited from Auden's heart the words "Crucify him."[5] In Auden's view, it isn't the case that, if there were no Jesus, we'd probably invent him, because Jesus' summons to a different order, a kingdom coming, subverts all our favorite, sanctified orders and mythic realities, exposing and undoing our unacknowledged groupthink.

It's important to remember the proposed civilization of Beloved Community doesn't come to us easily. If we forget, we mistake our good intentions for God's purposes and become a Babylon impenetrable to prophetic witness. If Jesus' gospel, the announcement and description of God's kingdom, is the standard by which all human orderings will be judged (our politics measured by his), how are we doing? What will it mean for America when the cosmos is liberated from its Egypt? Are we on the Lord's side in this process? Will we know how to call it good news? Do we know now? There are no foregone conclusions in these discussions, and according to the promises of Scripture, all manner of things will somehow be made well. But what do we think this means? Will we know the smell of victory? Is it what we're looking for?

In the spirit of Kurt Vonnegut and a little dash of Walker Percy's *Lost in the Cosmos*, I'd like to offer a fanciful scenario in the interest of sparking a thought. A "What if?" for our radioactive days, submitted in the hope that readers might begin to make up their own. This is only a poor sketch to serve as a friendly provocation. Dig, if you're willing, a picture, or a thought experiment. It's a day like any other day. It's morning again in America. And word eventually comes to you that the president is going to be on television to make a special announcement, so you tune in. The president appears with an odd look, not nervous exactly, but somehow unwound and no longer sporting the obligatory assertiveness Americans expect in a president. And there seems to be a look of genuine surprise and perhaps, truth be told, an aura of relief. The speech begins:

My fellow Americans. I bring you good tidings. Something tremendous has come up. Something wonderful. To be frank, many of us have given lip service to this event over hundreds of years, but we were all alike in ignorance. We did not know that of which we spoke. It was Thomas Jefferson who once remarked, "I tremble for my country when I reflect that God is just." As I speak to you now, I am intensely aware of the inadequacy of my speech, and I am pleased to know, as I never dreamt I'd be, that I will not stand before you in this capacity again.

My fellow Americans, the Lord is among us. The messiah appeared at the East Jerusalem YMCA today in conversation with people who happened to be near at hand. And we're still unsure as to what this means, but we do know this: God's rule, from here on out, goes. This will involve many adjustments. And while much is still unforeseeable, we can be assured that it is good news. The steadfast love of the Lord will never cease.

In our nation's history, we often swore our oaths with our hands pressed on a collection of documents that forbade oaths, and we often believed we were handing out or denying sovereignty to nations even as we read that God alone is sovereign. We raged with a sense of sovereignty, we plotted and schemed, and we often believed we were just. We were rebellious and we did not know what we were doing. But now, the way of the Lord is on. No good thing will go unrestored. God's way of living life and giving and loving is the way things are and were and will be. The Lord is here.

It is possible that we are approaching the days when none of our flags are still there, but the star-spangled universe was never dependent on them. The nations will now continue to prove the glories of God's righteousness. Truth is marching on and making us free. God's mercies never come to an end. It is good. Good morning. Blessed be the name of the Lord. . . . (static)

What would something like this mean? What do we imagine would follow the end of the transmission? When we imagine God reigning forever and ever, do we give much thought to what that forever would look like? Does it include the kinds of things Jesus said in the Sermon on the Mount? If we think of God's kingdom, as we're taught to pray, as a new order on earth as it is in heaven, what does it change about our today? What does it mean to "repent, because the kingdom of God is at hand"? It is good news, but is it what we have in mind when we say "gospel"? Is our gospel good news for everybody? Have we drawn lines in the sand that the Lord doesn't recognize?

I suspect we have. And I believe we do well to entertain all kinds of thought experiments when we contemplate the meaning of the prayers we pray, prayer as a determined experiment in trying to see the truth about ourselves: the tragic, the comic, the precious, the ridiculous, the out of control, and the angry. The Lord's Prayer has an amazing way of relativizing our have-tos, calming our nerves, and recontextualizing many a needful thing. The prayer invites us to reorient our hopes in the direction of resurrection and rejuvenation, reconciliation and redemption, not just for our kind of people, but for all of anxious creation, all nations, and the whole beloved, not-American world.

WATCH AND PRAY

Americans are possessed by a wide variety of stories about who matters, who no longer matters, who's the most despicable pain in the neck, and who out there will "get what they deserve" when they're finally put down or thrown out of office, and stories whose only conceivable end is terror for someone else. These stories, in some form, have always been with us, but according to the gospel, they inevitably hide the reality of things. The apocalypse of God's righteous rule doesn't offer itself as one story among many or a "Wouldn't it be nice?" for the "spirituality" section of our psyche. The apocalypse resides over all matter and history.

If we believe that Jesus' good news describes the real world, our lesser stories will be subordinated. Our understanding of what's absolutely necessary (for personal happiness and homeland security) will be transformed by it. But it could be that this process is most immediately obstructed by our inability to stop talking or in any way quiet down our chattering minds. We have to become aware of our own confirmation bias, our own unwillingness to be objective, and our own rage at a challenging word to our groupthink. We can refuse knee-jerk defensiveness and opt for silence. And if we're going to perceive Beloved Community making its way into our busy chattering every day, we have to. We can pray and occasionally keep silence. We can watch and pray. We might begin to feel our ignorance and be sobered as we see that not only do we not know where we're going, but we don't know exactly where we are right now. We're neck-deep in mystery. We might learn to keep silence as we constantly remind ourselves of the limits of our always fallible visions.

Silence might sober us long enough that we'll repent of the ways our tough talk presumes omniscience. We might begin to see the ways a sense of Beloved Community can infuse our processing of the news of the day and the ways the word of the Lord will make us see and speak differently. We won't have to know all the details of salvation, righteousness, and the end of history, but we will know that Beloved Community is never a separate issue. A radical remembrance belongs to these people, because they bear witness to the reign of God. Any authority that tries to reduce this community to a "spiritual" role is speaking with a false objectivity, because the kingdom to which this community tries to bear witness encompasses reality. And "repentance" is the word for the speech and action that acknowledges the distance between our proud little kingdoms and God's larger order, power, and glory, which are forever. It cannot be controlled, bought off, or ultimately silenced. And within it, our spectacles, our power plays, and our perceived successes are righteously relativized. God remembers everything violence forgets.

Notes

Introduction

1. James Baldwin in "I Am Not Your Negro," directed by Raoul Peck, *Independent Lens*, PBS, January 15, 2018.
2. James Baldwin, *Notes of a Native Son* (Boston: Beacon Press, 1955), 24.
3. Vince Staples, interview by Tyler, the Creator, OnSmash, February 18, 2016, http://onsmash.com/music/tyler-the-creator-interviews-vince-staples/.
4. June Jordan, introduction to *June Jordan's Poetry for the People: A Revolutionary Blueprint*, ed. Lauren Muller (London: Routledge, 1995), 3.
5. John Lewis, Andrew Aydin, and Nate Powell, *March: Book One* (Marietta, GA: Top Shelf, 2013), 6–7.
6. Ursula K. Le Guin, *The Left Hand of Darkness* (New York: Penguin, 2016), 176.
7. Henry David Thoreau, *Walden and the Famous Essay on "Civil Disobedience"* (New York: Signet, 1942), 12.
8. Dwight D. Eisenhower, "Farewell Radio and Television Address" (January 17, 1961), Dwight D. Eisenhower Presidential Library, https://www.eisenhower.archives.gov/all_about_ike/speeches/farewell_address.pdf.
9. Martin Luther King Jr., "Beyond Vietnam" (speech, New York City, April 4, 1967), The Martin Luther King, Jr. Research and Education Institute, https://kinginstitute.stanford.edu/king-papers/documents/beyond-vietnam.

Chapter 1: The Moral Mercury of Life

1. Layli Long Soldier, *Whereas* (Minneapolis: Graywolf Press, 2017), 72.
2. "Conversation with Layli Long Soldier," by Diana Whitney, *Kenyon Review*, April 17, 2017, https://www.kenyonreview.org/2017/04/conversation-layli-long-soldier/.
3. Tweet by @realDonaldTrump, October 13, 2017, https://twitter.com/realdonaldtrump/status/918885859230875649.
4. "The National Security Strategy of the United States of America," September 2002, https://www.state.gov/documents/organization/63562.pdf.
5. Miranda Blue, "Franklin Graham Claims Trump Gave His Heart to Christ at Billy Graham's 95th Birthday Party," Right Wing Watch, November 8, 2016, http://www.rightwingwatch.org/post/franklin-graham-claims-trump-gave-his-heart-to-christ-at-billy-grahams-95th-birthday-party/.

6. Martin Luther King Jr., "Beyond Vietnam" (speech, New York City, April 4, 1967), The Martin Luther King, Jr. Research and Education Institute, https://kinginstitute.stanford.edu/king-papers/documents/beyond-vietnam.

7. N. T. Wright, *The New Testament and the People of God* (Minneapolis: Fortress Press, 1996), 350.

8. Ibid., 353.

9. Reinhold Niebuhr, *The Irony of American History* (Chicago: University of Chicago Press, 2010), 133.

10. Howard Thurman, *Jesus and the Disinherited* (Boston: Beacon Press, 1996), 65.

11. Fanny Howe, *The Wedding Dress: Meditations on Word and Life* (Berkeley: University of California Press, 2003), xxi.

12. Abraham Lincoln, "Meditation on the Divine Will," September 30, 1862, available online from TeachingAmericanHistory, http://teachingamericanhistory.org/library/document/meditation-on -the-divine-will/.

13. Abraham Lincoln, second inaugural address (March 4, 1865), The American Presidency Project, https://www.presidency.ucsb.edu/documents/inaugural -address-35.

14. Arthur C. Cochrane, "Barmen Declaration," in *The Church's Confession under Hitler* (Philadelphia: Westminster Press, 1962), 237–42.

15. Joan Didion, *Political Fictions* (New York: Knopf, 2001), 7.

16. Episcopal Statement by the Council of Bishops, African Methodist Episcopal Church (January 31, 2017), https://www.ame-church.com/wp-content /uploads/2017/01/Episcopal-Statement-Council-of-Bishops-re-Trump -Actions.pdf.

17. George W. Bush, "The President's Address to the Nation" (speech, New York, September 12, 2002), http://usinfo.state.gov/usa/s091102.htm.

18. Maya Jaggi, "Signs of the Times," *Guardian,* October 12, 2002.

19. All movie quotations are taken from my own transcription.

Chapter 2: For Mine Own Good All Causes Shall Give Way

1. James C. Foster, "Fred Friendly," The First Amendment Encyclopedia, https://mtsu.edu/first-amendment/article/1331/fred-friendly.

2. Lou Cannon, "Reagan Acknowledges Arms-for-Hostages Swap," *Washington Post,* March 5, 1987.

3. Robert N. Bellah, Richard Madsen, William M. Sullivan, Ann Swidler, and Steven M. Tipton, *Habits of the Heart: Individualism and Commitment in American Life* (Berkeley: University of California Press, 1985), 221.

4. Ibid., 235.

5. Toni Cade Bambara, *The Salt Eaters* (New York: Vintage, 1992), 13.

6. "Republican Presidential Candidates Debate in Des Moines, Iowa" (December 13, 1999), American Presidency Project, https://www.presidency .ucsb.edu/node/276338.

7. Harold Bloom, *The American Religion: The Emergence of the Post-Christian Nation* (New York: Simon & Shuster, 1992), 15.

8. George W. Bush, interview by Tom Brokaw, *Nightly News,* NBC, April 24, 2003.

9. Bambara, *Salt Eaters,* 92.

10. Nathaniel Hawthorne, *Mosses from an Old Manse* (Manhattan: Collier, 1900), 318.

11. William Shakespeare, *Macbeth,* act 3, scene 4, lines 134–39.
12. Tweet by @realDonaldTrump, October 11, 2016, https://twitter.com /realdonaldtrump/status/785842546878578688.
13. Herman Melville, *Moby-Dick,* A Norton Critical Edition, ed. Hershel Parker and Harrison Hayford (New York: Norton, 2002), 139.
14. All quotations in this paragraph from ibid., 143.
15. Walt Whitman, *Leaves of Grass* (New York: Signet, 1955), 41, 43.
16. Whitman quoted in F. O. Matthiessen, *American Renaissance: Art and Expression in the Age of Emerson and Whitman* (London: Oxford University Press, 1941), 547.
17. Whitman, "Song of Myself," *Collected Poetry and Selected Prose and Letters,* ed. Emory Holloway (London: Nonesuch Press, 1967), 30.
18. Whitman, "Roaming in Thought," Bartleby.com, https://www.bartleby.com /142/270.html.

Chapter 3: Everybody Hurts

1. Jeannette Winterson, *Why Be Happy When You Could Be Normal?* (New York: Grove, 2012), 40.
2. F. O. Matthiessen, *American Renaissance: Art and Expression in the Age of Emerson and Whitman* (London: Oxford University Press, 1941), 5.
3. Ibid., 6.
4. *The Simpsons,* season 15, episode 22, "Fraudcast News," directed by Bob Anderson, aired May 23, 2004, FOX, https://www.amazon.com/dp /B072M62B6Y?ref_=imdbref_tt_wbr_aiv&tag=imdbtag_tt_wbr_aiv-20.
5. Matthiessen, *American Renaissance,* xv.
6. Toni Morrison, *Beloved* (New York: Knopf, 1987), 275.
7. W. E. B. DuBois, "On the Training of Black Men," in *The Souls of Black Folk: Authoritative Text, Contexts, Criticism* (New York: Norton, 1999),74.
8. James McIntosh, *Nathaniel Hawthorne's Tales: Authoritative Texts, Backgrounds, Criticism,* A Norton Critical Edition (New York: Norton, 1987), 55.
9. Ibid., 57.
10. Ibid.
11. Herman Melville, letter to Nathaniel Hawthorne, [April 16?], 1851, *The Life and Works of Herman Melville,* http://www.melville.org/letter2.htm.
12. Matthiessen, *American Renaissance,* 321–22.
13. Herman Melville, *The Confidence Man: His Masquerade,* A Norton Critical Edition (New York: Norton, 1971), 158.
14. Matthiessen, *American Renaissance,* 32.
15. Nathaniel Hawthorne, *The Scarlet Letter,* ed. Seymour Gross (New York: Norton, 1988), 53. Further citations of the book in this section are given as page numbers in the text.
16. Herman Melville, "Hawthorne and His Mosses," in *Moby-Dick,* A Norton Critical Edition, ed. Hershel Parker and Harrison Hayford (New York: Norton, 2002), 527.
17. Ibid., 525.
18. Melville, *Moby-Dick,* 103. Subsequent citations of the book in this section are given as page numbers in the text.
19. Nathaniel Hawthorne, *The House of the Seven Gables: A Romance* (Cutchogue, NY: Buccaneer Books, 1987), 201.

20. Melville, *Moby-Dick*, 21. Subsequent citations of the book in this section are given as page numbers in the text.

21. Melville, *Confidence Man*, xiv.

22. Ibid., 58.

23. Ibid., 59.

24. Ibid.

25. Richard Gray, *The Life of William Faulkner: A Critical Biography* (Oxford: Blackwell, 1994), 272.

26. William Faulkner, *The Sound and the Fury*, ed. David Minter, A Norton Critical Edition (New York: Norton, 1994), 203.

27. William Faulkner, *Go Down, Moses* (New York: Vintage, 1942), 331.

28. William Faulkner, *Absalom, Absalom* (New York: Vintage, 1936), 218.

29. Ibid., 392.

30. William Faulkner, *As I Lay Dying* (New York: Vintage, 1930), 223.

31. William Faulkner, *Light in August* (New York: Modern Library, 1932), 47–48.

32. Faulkner, *As I Lay Dying*, 165.

33. Faulkner, *The Sound and the Fury*, 222. Subsequent citations of the book in this section are given as page numbers in the text.

34. Toni Morrison, "Making America White Again," *New Yorker*, November 21, 2016, https://www.newyorker.com/magazine/2016/11/21/making-america-white-again.

35. Toni Morrison, "Nobel Lecture" (December 7, 1993), https://www.nobelprize.org/prizes/literature/1993/morrison/lecture/.

36. "The Language Must Not Sweat," interview with Toni Morrison by Thomas LeClair, *New Republic*, March 20, 1981, https://newrepublic.com/article/95923/the-language-must-not-sweat.

37. Jasmine Rose-Olesco, "When 'the Talk' Is about Staying Alive," *Riveter*, June 5, 2015, https://www.therivetermagazine.com/when-the-talk-is-about-staying-alive/.

38. Morrison, *Beloved*, 42. Subsequent citations of the book in this section are given as page numbers in the text.

39. Toni Cade Bambara, *The Salt Eaters* (New York: Vintage, 1992), 219.

40. Quoted in David Witzling, *Everybody's America: Thomas Pynchon, Race, and the Cultures of Postmodernism* (London: Routledge, 2012), 159.

41. Thomas Pynchon, *Gravity's Rainbow* (New York: Penguin, 1973), 167.

42. Allen Ginsberg, interview by William F. Buckley Jr., *Firing Line*, PBS, May 7, 1968, https://www.youtube.com/watch?v=vBpoZBhvBa4.

43. Thomas Pynchon, *V.* (Philadelphia: J. B. Lippincott Co., 1963), 366.

44. Thomas Pynchon, *Vineland* (Boston: Little Brown, 1990), 195.

45. Pynchon, *Gravity's Rainbow*, 167.

46. Ibid., 164.

47. Ibid., 262. Subsequent citations of *Gravity's Rainbow* in this section are given as page numbers in the text.

48. Thomas Pynchon, *Mason & Dixon*, (New York: Henry Holt, 1997), 9. Subsequent citations of the book in this section are given as page numbers in the text.

49. Ronan Farrow, "Donald Trump, A Playboy Model, and a System for Concealing Infidelity," *New Yorker*, February 16, 2018, https://www.newyorker.com/news/news-desk/donald-trump-a-playboy-model-and-a-system-for-concealing-infidelity-national-enquirer-karen-mcdougal.

50. "Fraudcast News," aired May 23, 2004.

Chapter 4: The Freeway of Love

1. J. Freedom du Lac, "Aretha Franklin, Music's 'Queen of Soul,' Dies at 76," *Washington Post*, August 16, 2018, https://www.washingtonpost.com/local /obituaries/aretha-franklin-musics-queen-of-soul-dies-at-76/2018/08/16 /c35de4b8-9e9f-11e8-83d2-70203b8d7b44_story.html.
2. Michael D'Antonio, *The Truth about Trump* (New York: Macmillan, 2016), 340.
3. Ella Baker, interview by John Britton for the Civil Rights Documentation Project, June 19, 1968, Civil Rights Movement Veterans, http://www.crmvet .org/nars/baker68.htm.
4. Ibid.
5. Henry David Thoreau, *Walden or, Life in the Woods and On the Duty of Civil Disobedience* (New York: Signet, 1942), 71.
6. Ursula K. Le Guin, *The Dispossessed* (New York: Harper, 1974), 89.
7. Ralph Ellison, *Invisible Man* (New York: Random House, 1952), 581.
8. Whitman, "Song of Myself," in *Collected Poetry and Selected Prose and Letters*, ed. Emory Holloway (London: Nonesuch Press, 1967), 49. Subsequent citations of the book in this section are given as page numbers in the text.
9. Herman Melville, *Moby-Dick*, A Norton Critical Edition, ed. Hershel Parker and Harrison Hayford (New York: Norton, 2002), 103.
10. Ishmael Reed, *Mumbo Jumbo* (New York: Doubleday, 1972), 11.
11. Ibid., 216.
12. Ibid., 6.
13. Theodore Sturgeon, *More than Human* (New York: Farrar, Strauss and Giroux, 1953), 181.
14. William Blake, "Annotations to Bacon's *Essays Moral, Economical and Political*," in *The Complete Poetry and Prose of William Blake*, ed. David V. Erdman (New York: Anchor, 1988), 623.
15. John Gerome, "Country Legend Johnny Cash Dead at 71," *Detroit Free Press*, September 12, 2003.
16. Robert Shelton, *No Direction Home: The Life and Music of Bob Dylan* (New York: Beech Tree Books, 1986), 200.
17. Ibid., 203.
18. Ibid., 211.
19. Bob Dylan, interview by Nora Ephron and Susan Edmiston, August 1965, in *Bob Dylan: The Essential Interviews*, ed. Jonathan Cott (New York: Simon & Schuster, 2017), 53–54.
20. Shelton, *No Direction Home*, 260.
21. Bob Dylan, *Live 1964: Concert at Philharmonic Hall—The Bootleg Series*, vol. 6, Columbia/Legacy.
22. Tony Tanner, *City of Words: American Fiction: 1950–1970* (New York: Harper & Row, 1971), 178.
23. Patti Smith, *M Train* (New York: Knopf, 2015), 104.
24. Mikal Gilmore, "Bob Dylan at 50," *Rolling Stone*, May 30, 1991, https://www.rollingstone.com/music/music-news/bob-dylan-at-fifty-244505/.

Chapter 5: The Signposts Up Ahead

1. Shannon Hale, *The Goose Girl* (New York: Bloomsbury, 2003), 165.
2. Philip K. Dick, "The Android and the Human," in *The Shifting Realities of Philip K. Dick: Selected Literary and Philosophical Writings*, ed. Lawrence Sutin (New York: Vintage, 1995), 187.

3. Ibid., 187–88.

4. Ben Popken and Anna Schecter, "Hidden Camera Shows Cambridge Analytica Pitching Deceptive Tactics," NBC News, March 19, 2018, https://www.nbcnews.com/news/all/hidden-camera-shows-cambridge -analytica-pitching-tricky-tactics-n857936.

5. Kerry Howley, "The World's Biggest Terrorist Has a Pikachu Bedspread," *New York*, December 25, 2017, http://nymag.com/daily/intelligencer/2017/12 /who-is-reality-winner.html; Etgar Lefkovits, "Jerusalem Court Hears Vanunu Appeal," *Jerusalem Post*, July 8, 2008, https://www.jpost.com/Israel /Jerusalem-court-hears-Vanunu-appeal.

6. Philip K. Dick, "My Definition of Science Fiction," in *Shifting Realities of Philip K. Dick*, 100.

7. Philip K. Dick, *The Man in the High Castle* (New York: Vintage, 1962), 41–42. Further citations of the book in this section are given as page numbers in the text.

8. Ursula K. Le Guin, *The Left Hand of Darkness* (New York: Penguin, 2016), 34.

9. Ibid., 39.

10. Kurt Vonnegut Jr., *Slaughterhouse-Five; or, The Children's Crusade: A Duty-Dance with Death* (New York: Dell, 1968), 3.

11. Octavia E. Butler, *Kindred* (Beacon: Boston, 1979), 17. Further citations of the book in this section are given as page numbers in the text.

12. Octavia Butler, *The Parable of the Sower* (New York: Grand Central Publishing, 2000), 7.

Chapter 6: True Garbage

1. Tim Cahill, "The *Rolling Stone* Interview: Stanley Kubrick," in *Stanley Kubrick: Interviews*, ed. Gene D. Phillips (Jackson: University of Mississippi Press, 2001), 198.

2. Gene Siskel, "Candidly Kubrick," in Phillips, *Stanley Kubrick*, 187.

3. Philip K. Dick, *The Transmigration of Timothy Archer* (New York: Simon & Schuster, 1982), 55.

4. Kelly Reichardt: "My Films Are about People Who Don't Have a Safety Net," March 15, 2017, https://www.youtube.com/watch?v=Q9A0M6S0nbE.

5. Eric Nordern, "*Playboy* Interview: Stanley Kubrick," in Phillips, *Stanley Kubrick*, 68.

6. Martha Duffy and Richard Schickel, "Kubrick's Grandest Gamble," in Phillips, *Stanley Kubrick*, 168.

7. "David Lynch Lists His Favorite Films and Directors, Including Fellini, Wilder, Tati and Hitchcock," video, Open Culture, September 18, 2013, http://www.openculture.com/2013/09/david-lynch-on-his-favorite-directors -including-fellini-wilder-tati-and-hitchcock.html

8. David Lynch, *Catching the Big Fish: Meditation, Consciousness, and Creativity* (New York: Penguin, 2006), 17.

9. "David Lynch Explains Ideas and *Mulholland Drive*," YouTube video posted June 12, 2007, https://www.youtube.com/watch?v=gkIQy0iblQE#t=80.

10. Lynch, *Catching the Big Fish*, 109.

11. Ibid., 129.

12. James Joyce, *Ulysses* (New York: Vintage, 1961), 142.

13. James Baldwin, "As Much Truth as One Can Bear" in *New York Times Book Review* (January 14, 1962).

Chapter 7: An Imagery of Infinite Possibility

1. *Publick Occurrences Both Forreign and Domestick,* September 25, 1690, available from the National Humanities Center, http://www.nationalhumanitiescenter.org/pds/amerbegin/power/text5/PublickOccurrences.pdf.
2. Jessica Hopper, *The First Collection of Criticism by a Living Female Rock Critic* (Chicago: featherproof books, 2015), 18.
3. Northrop Frye, *The Great Code: The Bible and Literature* (San Diego: Harvest, 1981), 200.
4. Student Nonviolent Coordinating Committee Founding Statement, The Sixties Project, http://lists.village.virginia.edu/sixties/HTML_docs/Resources/Primary/Manifestos/SNCC_founding.html.
5. Jim Forest, "A Biography of Dorothy Day," in *The Encyclopedia of American Catholic History,* ed. Michael Glazier and Thomas J. Shelley (Collegeville, MN: Liturgical Press, 1997). Also available as "Servant of God Dorothy Day" at Catholic Worker Movement, http://www.catholicworker.org/dorothyday/servant-of-god.html.
6. Dorothy Day, *Selected Writings,* ed. Robert Ellsberg (Maryknoll, NY: Orbis Books, 1992), 33.
7. Ibid., xxv.
8. Day, *Selected Writings, 271.*
9. Ibid., 98.
10. Ibid., 111.
11. Ibid., xviii.
12. Ibid., xxxvi.
13. Dorothy Day, *House of Hospitality* (New York: Sheed & Ward, 1939). Also available online at Catholic Worker Movement, http://www.catholicworker.org/dorothyday/articles/442.html.
14. Day, *Selected Writings,* xiii.
15. Bayard Rustin, quoted in Clayborne Carson, et al., comp., *Reporting Civil Rights: American Journalism,* part 1, *1941–1963,* Library of America Classic Journalism Collection (New York: Library of America, 2003), 15–18.
16. Martin Mayer, "The Lone Wolf of Civil Rights," *Saturday Evening Post,* July 11, 1964. Also available online at http://www.reportingcivilrights.org/authors/selections.jsp?authorid=133.
17. Thomas L. Connelly, *Will Campbell and the Soul of the South* (New York: Continuum, 1982), 88.
18. Will D. Campbell, *Brother to a Dragonfly* (New York: Seabury Press, 1977), 218–23.
19. Ibid. 188.
20. Ibid., 243–47.
21. 1Ibid., 187.
22. Daniel Berrigan and Lee Lockwood, *Absurd Convictions, Modest Hopes* (New York: Random House, 1972), 211.
23. Daniel Berrigan, *Consequences: Truth and . . .* (New York: Macmillan, 1967), 56.
24. Daniel Berrigan, *Prayer for the Morning Headlines: On the Sanctity of Life and Death* (Baltimore: Apprentice House, 2007), front cover.
25. Daniel Berrigan, *Jeremiah: The World, the Wound of God* (Minneapolis: Fortress, 1999), xii.
26. Daniel Berrigan, *Poetry, Drama, Prose,* ed. Michael True (Maryknoll, NY: Orbis, 1988), xi.

27. Daniel Berrigan, *No Bars to Manhood* (Eugene, OR: Wipf & Stock, 2007), 66.
28. Daniel Berrigan, *Night Flight: War Diary with 11 Poems* (New York: Macmillan, 1968), 4.
29. Daniel Berrigan, *Wisdom: The Feminine Face of God* (London: Sheed & Ward, 2002), 61.
30. Sharon Erickson Nepstad, *Religion and War Resistance in the Plowshares Movement* (Cambridge: Cambridge University Press, 2008), 47–48.
31. Spencer C. Tucker, ed., *The Encyclopedia of the Vietnam War: A Political, Social, and Military History* (Oxford: Oxford University Press, 2001), 92.
32. Daniel Cosacchi and Eric Martin, eds., *The Berrigan Letters: Personal Correspondence between Daniel and Philip Berrigan* (Maryknoll, NY: Orbis, 2016), 43.
33. Quoted in Walter B. Kalaidjian, *Languages of Liberation: The Social Text in Contemporary American Poetry* (New York: Columbia University Press, 1989), 164.
34. Daniel Berrigan, *To Dwell in Peace: An Autobiography* (San Francisco: Harper & Row, 1987), 201–2.
35. Daniel Berrigan, *The Trial of the Catonsville Nine* (New York: Fordham University Press, 2004), 127.
36. Berrigan, *To Dwell in Peace.*, 201.
37. Rose Hackman, "Sister Megan Rice: The 85-Year-Old Nun with a Criminal Record Remains Defiant," *Guardian*, July 16, 2015, https://www.theguardian.com/world/2015/jul/16/sister-megan-rice-nun-prison-nuclear-weapons-protest.
38. Berrigan, *Poetry, Drama, Prose,* 267.
39. Thomas Merton, *Raids on the Unspeakable* (New York: New Directions, 1966), 9.
40. Wendell Berry, "Two Economies," *Review & Expositor* 81, no. 2 (May 1984): 209–23.
41. As recounted in David Halberstam, *The Children* (New York: Random House, 1998), 137.

Chapter 8: God Remembers Everything Violence Forgets

1. Wendell Berry, "Heaven in Henry County," interview by Rose Marie Berger, *Sojourners*, July 2004.
2. Daniel Berrigan, *To Dwell in Peace: An Autobiography* (San Francisco: Harper & Row, 1987), 108–9.
3. N. T. Wright, *The Resurrection of the Son of God* (Minneapolis: Fortress, 2003), 684.
4. Ronald K. L. Collins and David M. Skover, *The Trials of Lenny Bruce: The Fall and Rise of an American Icon* (Naperville, IL: Sourcebooks, 2002), 3.
5. W. H. Auden, "Purely Subjective," in *The Complete Works of W. H. Auden: Prose*, ed. Edward Mendelson, vol. 2, *1939–1948* (Princeton, NJ: Princeton University Press, 2002), 184-97.

CPSIA information can be obtained
at www.ICGtesting.com
Printed in the USA
FFHW010624050419
51526270-56969FF